Th Pathway Back

A unique plea for justice from seven betrayed heroes

Dave Kelly

www.kelfoxhouse.co.uk

The Pathway Back

First printed as an E-book February 2012

Revised, updated and republished in United Kingdom and internationally in E-book and Paperback, September 2012 by

Kelfox House Publications

Norwich, Norfolk, NR6 6UF
Tel: 01603 423827
www.kelfoxhouse.co.uk
Email: info@kelfoxhouse.co.uk

© Copyright by Dave and Pauline Kelly 2012

The right of Dave Kelly to be identified as the author of this work has been asserted by them in accordance with the Copyright, Designs and Patents Act 1988.

All rights reserved. No part of this publication may be reproduced, stored in a retrieval system or transmitted in any form or by any means, electronic, mechanical, recording or otherwise, without the prior written permission of the author and copyright holders.

ISBN: 978-0-9574144-0-2

Edited by: Jayne Thomas

Cover Design & Artwork by: Esther Lemmens
www.zestydesign.co.uk

Landscape Cover Image ©Mike Page Aerial Photography
www.mike-page.co.uk

Printed by Witley Press Ltd, Hunstanton, Norfolk
E-book design by Witley Press Ltd, Hunstanton, Norfolk

This book is dedicated to all those brave Americans who gave their lives to the cause of freedom.

A very special bunch of men and women that gave the ultimate gift – the gift of life to live on in all of us, no matter what creed or country.

God Bless.

*For what we once took for granted
can easily be taken away.*

Michael Shelly Hall, Jr

CONTENTS
Page

***PROLOGUE** by Dave Kelly*   *1*

PART ONE – THE SEVEN YOUNG AMERICANS

Chapter One	How it all began	7
Chapter Two	First call to action	11
Chapter Three	Settling into camp life	18
Chapter Four	The first sortie	20
Chapter Five	Combat life	23
Chapter Six	Time out	26
Chapter Seven	Off to the seaside to bomb V weapon sites	28
Chapter Eight	More missions	31
Chapter Nine	Buck's story	33
Chapter Ten	Sacrifice and recognition (an observer)	35
Chapter Eleven	Relationships borne out of war	39
Chapter Twelve	Michael's thoughts	41
Chapter Thirteen	Michael trains with the British	46

Interlude 1 *by Dave Kelly*   49

PART TWO – WE ARE IN THIS TOGETHER

Chapter Fourteen	Steve James and Operation Blue Wheel	55
Chapter Fifteen	A secret mission to rescue a forces personality	61
Chapter Sixteen	Buck Quinlan	72
Chapter Seventeen	Steve Lursquom – Seething 1943	74
Chapter Eighteen	Rupert Kovloski	81
Chapter Nineteen	Bernie Jameson	84
Chapter Twenty	Al Permando	92
Chapter Twenty-One	Mike Preston	95
Chapter Twenty-Two	Glenn Miller	100

Interlude 2 *by Dave Kelly*   105

PART THREE – THE FINAL PREPARATIONS

Chapter Twenty-Three	Mike Hall and unusual happenings in Thetford Forest	111
Chapter Twenty-Four	The time approaches	118
Chapter Twenty-Five	Steve Lursquom, Sniper 1	126
Chapter Twenty-Six	Steve Miller	146
Chapter Twenty-Seven	Michael Hall, B-17 gunner	174
Chapter Twenty-Eight	Montgomery – War Cabinet – January 1944	183

Interlude 3 *by Dave Kelly*   191

PART FOUR – THE TOP SECRET MISSION

Chapter Twenty-Nine	The preacher – a player in the game	199
Chapter Thirty	My name is of no consequence, my nationality is British	207
Chapter Thirty-One	Members of the American Elite Forces	218
Chapter Thirty-Two	Michael Hall – Mission Flight 10 February 1944	222
Chapter Thirty-Three	Al Permando – Mission Flight 10 February 1944	224
Chapter Thirty-Four	Buck Quinlan – Mission Flight 10 February 1944	230
Chapter Thirty-Five	Michael Hall – Mission Flight 10 February 1944	235
Chapter Thirty-Six	Rupert Kovloski – Mission Flight 10 February 1944	239
Chapter Thirty-Seven	Steve Lursquom – Mission Flight 10 February 1944	243
Chapter Thirty-Eight	Buck Quinlan – Mission Flight 10 February 1944	248
Chapter Thirty-Nine	Mike Preston – Mission Flight 10 February 1944	252
Chapter Forty	Michael Hall, rear gunner – Mission Flight 10 February 1944	256

EPILOGUE – Our death is not the end *by Dave Kelly*	269
Postscript	278
After Thoughts	288
Additional channelled session – 8th May 2012 talking to Charles 'Buck' Quinlan – Pilot	292
Another channelled session with Dave, Steve Lursquom, Mike Preston and Buck Quinlan	298
Another channelled session with Dave talking to Michael Hall	302
ACKNOWLEDGEMENTS	305

PROLOGUE
by Dave Kelly

When all this began I didn't realise it was going to be a book. It started early in the year 2001 and to those who have not had the experiences that I had over the following five or six years it is possibly difficult to understand exactly how such a thing can have happened. So I will do my best to explain as simply as I can without holding up the reader too much at this point.

The real importance of this book is the story told by the seven young American airmen who went through it and I don't wish to detract in any way from that or hold up any further the process of reading it. But I also know readers are going to want some kind of rational explanation from me about how the book came into being and why they should believe it is based on facts and the truth.

So I will simply say here that all the writings that follow in this book have flowed through my pen onto paper at my home in Norwich, usually in the evenings or at weekends. All the names of those involved, famous men and so far unknown men, the places, settings, everything, all arrived first and foremost by what can very generally be termed 'psychic' means. But it does not just stop there. With my wife Pauline I very quickly began to do some factual research and make checks to see if the information stood up to rational scrutiny. At this point before I go any further, I would like to add that without Pauline's help and support overall throughout this whole project, I would not have been able to do any of this.

We went first to the Norwich Library now in the splendid new Forum building, which has a special comprehensive local section on the United States Army Air Force (USAAF) because of the large presence of that branch of the American forces in Norfolk during World War II and ever since. We quickly found some corroboration of the background to our story and we have gone on doing research of this kind on and off ever since.

We have several times visited the former USAAF Station 146 at Seething, eight miles outside Norwich on the Bungay road from where the Top Secret Mission was abortively launched, and also been frequently to another USAAF base that figures prominently in the story at Thorpe Abbotts near Diss, a few miles further away in the direction of Ipswich. Some of the original World War II buildings still exist at both airfields for the purpose of holding archives and museum materials. They are opened to the public at certain times and periodic visits are still made to these bases by former American airmen and their families, serving American airmen and interested British people. We found fascinating and intriguing confirmation and corroboration of our story in each place, both of the reality of the story and the fact it has been officially covered up or hushed up.

We also several times visited the special USAAF cemetery at Madingley near Cambridge to check records of flights and deaths from the Second World War to the present that are meticulously archived there. I will fully describe the results of these visits at appropriate moments in Interludes in the story as we proceed. We were even able to give surprised American officials at Madingley, information that was clearly missing and deliberately omitted from their records about Michael Hall and all seven of the men in this story. When they asked how we had come by such information and we told them 'by psychic means' their expressions were an interesting mixture of careful, official guardedness and personal amazement.

All of this may at first sound weird and strange. Over the years of writing for me, Pauline, and a few close friends who knew about it, the story became very obviously real and true. But it has not been a continuous or obsessive process. It has never for example been a matter of 'hearing' it in my head but when it is arriving it is very powerful, almost overpowering, and I simply have to put pen to paper.

This whole experience has been a new journey for me and the book has had a big effect on my life. How it all started for me was little more than a thought. A name came into my head for no reason, a name I did not know and I did not take that seriously at first. It was a name that kept repeating itself, it was so strong at this point that I had to put pen to paper. One name, two names, places, dates – all unknown to me – came through.

Why for one thing should all this information come through me I asked myself? At that time I had no idea what it was. The first thing that came to mind was that maybe it was some kind of communication from 'Spirit' – that, I now know, is the term used by mediums and other practitioners working with the paranormal. I thought maybe it was a communication from someone who had died looking to find their family, that is all. I did not feel at the time that I was sufficiently 'aware' to receive communication from any great level – that was for experienced mediums and suchlike not me, I did not know enough to do anything about it. But that was all to change in the coming months – I was on a crusade for this. It was to my advantage that my wife Pauline was spiritually developed to a great degree and was able to help me because sure enough if I had been on my own I have no idea what might have become of this information. But thankfully with the help of Pauline and a dear friend Jacque, and their confidence in me right from the beginning, I managed. Without them this book would not be in print.

I am not responsible for the words, only for writing them down. Sometimes it came in at a rate of up to twenty-five pages at a time, at other times in ten page stints. And sometimes there were long gaps when nothing arrived for a while. I will say more about that and other fascinating experiences in the Interludes that follow, but for now it is most important that Michael Hall and his fellow crew members begin to tell their own story, in their own way. Here in Chapter One that follows are the opening words of their story, exactly as they began coming through to me at the outset, one evening round about the 10th February in the year 2001 – the 57th anniversary it seems of the fateful crash!

PART ONE

THE SEVEN YOUNG AMERICANS

Chapter One
How it all began

It was December 7th 1941 and Charlie Quinlan a fast-talking, hard looking 19 year old was going about his normal day, hustling at the local pool halls of Brooklyn, New York. You had to be a guy from a special kind of mould to get on in an environment like this place and Charlie (or Buck, as his closest friends and family knew him) was that kind of person. By all accounts it was his main aim in life to make a fast buck, so why not call him by it?

The usual crowd was in, no big deal. No sign of any punters – too early yet. The guys had a radio on in the corner of the hall, not taking any notice of the sudden change from music to a serious sounding voice coming from this little box. Suddenly all hell broke loose – people going crazy, old men crying in the corner, guys throwing bottles around. Buck ran up to the bar and shouted, 'What's going on?'

'The Japs have bombed Pearl Harbour!'

* * * * * * *

December 7th 1941 and Mike Preston was going about his business in Mundo, California as usual messing about with cars. On this day he was tinkering with the engine of his father's car, wanting to drive it because he couldn't afford one of his own. The music that was being played from the window at the back of the house suddenly stopped and a slow melodic voice took over. Then came a shriek from his mother, the banging of doors and his father shouting at him to come inside.

'Listen son,' he said, 'those bastards have blown up our boys in Pearl Harbour.'

* * * * * * *

December 7th 1941. Bernie Jameson really wanted to follow in his father's footsteps and be a doctor – it was what he'd always wanted to do. But now at the age of 21 he wanted to do other things that his family were not so keen on – like gambling and just enjoying life. Bernie liked playing poker and was good at it, that and young ladies were Bernie's forte. But on this particular day he was at the local barber's in Horn, Oregon – a small town where everyone knew everybody else. They were having a laugh and a joke as usual when the music on the radio was rudely interrupted by a slow, melodic voice coming from way inside that wooden box.

'It is with regret that at approximately…at this hour, our forces in Pearl Harbour were bombed by Imperial Japanese war planes.'

Then, silence from the wooden box and from everyone sitting in the seats of the local barbershop. Not a word – just total silence.

* * * * * * *

December 7th 1941. Rob Lursquom really looked forward to the days when his father was on leave from the army and they had some special time together. His father Steve had brought Rob up to give respect to the gun and he was good at firearms, he knew the ins and the outs of the smallest to the largest and was a very good shot for the age of nearly 18. His treat when his father came home was a drive out to the desert from Carson City, LA, where in the remoteness of the shrubland they would try out the latest firearms.

On the way there his father turned on the radio as usual, the pair of them talking away, oblivious to the music in the background. Suddenly a man's voice broke the joyful sounds with its slow, melodic tone, 'It is with regret that today Pearl Harbour was attacked and we have many casualties and heavy losses.' Rob looked at his dad – not a sound – just tears flowing down his face, one by one.

* * * * * * *

December 7th 1941. Al Permando was happily going about his work at his father's restaurant in Long Island, New York. His father had put him in charge of looking after the guests as they arrived – it was a start. His parents were very strict – a big family needs to stick together and look after their own; they had allowed Al to be himself but now at the age of 21 it was time to go into the family business.

This particular day was busy and going just fine when one of their chefs ran into the foyer, screaming at the top of his voice, 'We're at war with Japan, they've bombed Pearl Harbour!'

'No... it must be a mistake!'

'No, no mistake.'

* * * * * * *

December 7th 1941. Rupert Kovloski was a quiet guy from the relatively small town of Rhode Island, New York City – the farming world of good old USA. On his father's farm he was king, but in and around the town where he was born he was a loner. He was a very good shot which seemed to go hand in hand with living in America – you had to be a good shot.

This day it was Rupert's turn to go into town to get some supplies at the local stores. He'd wanted to join up in the Navy last year when he was 18 but his mum had put a stop to that – he longed to be his own person and to see what lay over the horizon. This day he did a little bit of business in town, got his father's supplies and dutifully came home to his mother and father's farm.

Driving to the bottom of the steps leading to the house, he had got out of the truck and begun to bring the supplies in, when his mother ran through the door nearly taking it off its hinges. Grabbing Rupert and giving him a bear hug, her voice chattering, she was sobbing and would not let go of her son. Rupert looked bewildered at his father, now coming out of the family home. His mother, not even giving him an inch, hugged him even more.

'What's happened?' Rupert shouted.

'Pearl Harbour is no more son.'

* * * * * * *

December 7th 1941. Wanting to fly since you were old enough to walk sounds a bit outlandish to say the least but that is what Mike Hall's ambition was. To be a flyer in whatever capacity and to be a pilot, well, that would be something special. Already in competition with his brothers on the large farmstead of 'Cedar Rapids' in the beautiful surroundings of Cleveland, Russell County, Virginia, at 19 Mike wanted desperately to be at the controls of the crop sprayers in his father and brothers' business.

This one day however, would overshadow this special family and they would need all the strength in the world after it. At the lunchtime family gathering, the laughter and joking was suddenly interrupted by a knock on the door. Mike's father Shelly opened it slowly to find a close friend from the town, his face tearful and tired. Mike's father, deep in conversation with this man, finally shut the door and sat down, his face low, not looking up.

'What's the matter?' his wife asked, her hand on his shoulder, she was looking decidedly concerned now.

He looked up, 'We're at war with Japan now – they've bombed Pearl Harbour.'

* * * * * * *

These seven guys going about their everyday business would now take a new pathway, one that would eventually bring them together in a way they would never have thought possible.

Chapter Two
First call to action

The next few months were a series of events at home and worldwide. The prospect of going to war against such a formidable foe as Japan and the thought of why they should want to go to war in the first place conjures up the brief idea of a greater power at work. The sheer size of America and the resources at hand were staggering. For a power such as Japan is as a nation, it makes you think what possible gain they may achieve in all of this apart from bloodshed so vast and loss of life running into thousands, maybe millions at the end of it all, both innocent as well as perpetrators – the doers in one corner, the military and the politicians in the other, and the innocent in the middle.

All these things were going through Mike Hall's mind as he went about his normal day-to-day work but what seemed run of the mill, tedious and boring now took on new meaning through the course of an action against his fellow countrymen in what was ultimately a matter of just a couple of hours. The day-to-day routines of fellow Americans going about their business – families, children, mothers; going to school, looking forward to the weekend. All these little things you take for granted but in the space of 120 minutes (no time at all is it?) all this had gone.

Those that survived now had a new perspective in mind, body and spirit. Revenge and retribution in the name of freedom and the way of life we hold most precious. This one act would catapult the day-to-day mundane life we knew and put a whole new perspective on a new world order for the next few years. Heavy thoughts maybe but nevertheless they were there. Life would never be the same again for the whole of Earth's people as we went into a new age.

America now had its tail bitten and the recoil of this animal, its thoughts and anger at the source of this, was swift. It is a fact that people will group together and bond as one against a new foe but without one we squabble with each other. Funny that.

Reading the papers was a necessity now. Every day brought more news and suddenly we were confronted with a new fighter entering the ring, two against one – or was it? The new fighter flexed his muscles and stood by the side of Japan in the bravado of entering the ring, bringing the hand of friendship to one whilst holding up a clenched fist at the other in the corner, and all this in the blinding light of exposure. We were still upholding the Stars and Stripes no matter what, and then from the shadows a light came forward to stand by our side. This flag was already in conflict with the new fighter and had shed blood from both cuts. This flag was as ours, in union – the State of our Union, and the Union Jack.

This was now turning into a new fight – the Stars and Stripes and the Union Jack against the Rising Sun and the Swastika sounds more like the Clash of the Titans. The winds of time now took a dramatic change – we had our hands full with Japan but Germany coming to their side blew it out of the water.

The recruiting drive now got underway. Whether we liked it or not we were going to be swept along on a tidal wave of emotion. Who would lose or who would win? These questions needed answering, but not at this point in the game. They would be answered at some time but this was the birth of a new age, the conception of which was who knows? Little things had triggered a greater concept and suddenly we were confronted by a tyranny that we could not ignore: good against evil. Would the good conquer this time? Who was good and who was evil at this early stage of the game? The true players were yet to emerge and only then would we see who is good and who is bad. But the rules of the game had been set and time must now run its course. The winners of this would be those who were strong of heart and knew that they were truly the good – whoever they were.

* * * * * * *

The next few months went really quick for Buck. From being a loose cannon on the streets of Brooklyn he was catapulted into the mass hysteria which was war. He had childhood visions of wanting to fly and now his chance was there; enlisting was first priority, his second was to enlist into the USAAF. This is what he wanted to do – fly in combat, the training was now over and his chance to put it into practice was here. Now aboard the Queen Mary leaving harbour on its route across the Atlantic to England, Buck had never been out of Brooklyn in his life but without fear he looked out at the Statue of Liberty, as the ship that would be his home for the next few days strolled past her great presence.

* * * * * * *

On the same ship that day was another pilot – Mike Preston, a long way from Mundo, California. These last few months had been eye-opening even for Mike. He didn't have any choice about signing up for Uncle Sam but he did have a choice of what he wanted to do. His father wanted him to go on ground crew as he was always tinkering around with engines but Mike had other ideas – the image of a pilot weighed heavily against that of a mechanic.

Standing on the deck of the Queen Mary, as Mike looked upon the Statue of Liberty he thought, 'That's what we are fighting for – to live in freedom.' As the land slowly went out of view, the lump in his throat was becoming too much. What lay in store now?

* * * * * * *

Bernie Jameson's last few months had been a roller coaster ride of ups and downs of such magnitude that not even he could keep up with it. This had been a good excuse to earn a lot of money and lay a few good ladies in the process. The glamour of the Bomber Group was way above that of being cannon fodder in the infantry, and throughout his childhood and teenage years Bernie was good, very good, with guns. His aim was dead centre and the army wanted him for Special Services – being a sniper was their target for him. So he signed up for the USAAF primarily as a gunner but was put in as a bomb aimer.

The thought of going over to England maybe or Africa maybe...but the thought of England...the opportunities there were endless. Again, the Queen Mary was now home for this guy for a couple of weeks, and the game of poker would be played at its best in the next few days.

* * * * * * *

Rupert Kovloski's mother was now very worried that her precious son would enlist no matter what her feelings were. He would do it his way. It was right and she knew this deep in her heart, but she flinched at the thought of her only son being swept up in this tidal wave of hate and knew there would be casualties. They are part and parcel of wartime, and she knew that her beloved son would not be coming back up the driveway to greet her and give her a kiss on the cheek as he always did. Once he left for a foreign soil her little boy would not be coming back, but she knew she had to let him go, this is what he wanted.

Rupert's ancestors came from the old country of Poland originally; it was this and the fact of Japan now being in bed as it were with Germany which had invaded Poland, that put a double stamp on it for Rupert. He dearly wanted to go to England and do his bit. His family who had distant relatives still in Poland, were aware of the part Polish fighters had played in the Battle of Britain and this overwhelmed Rupert. He joined the USAAF as a gunner, he was also a good shot, taught by his father. This is what he wanted to do.

His training over, it was time to leave and take the long-haul down to New York to catch the Queen Mary. He was all kitted out and ready to go, his mother holding tight, not wanting to let go, but eventually forced to give him one last hug before he jumped on the waiting train that would take him to New York. His father shook his hand and nodded to him. Not one for showing his feelings was his father, but a tear rolled down his cheek onto his collar – he knew also this would be the last time they would see Rupert alive. Now they hugged each other and asked the Lord to keep a look out for their special son.

Another passenger for the Queen Mary, Rupert was now on his way, the waiting was over. This is what he had always wanted and it was his turn now to show what he was made of – for his country and his ancestors.

* * * * * * *

The old bottles sat on the roof of a burnt-out car in the desert just outside LA, the rifles ringing in tune and in time with the breaking glass. This guy was special, his father knew it, he had a talent and that talent was shooting. Right up to the start of America's involvement in the war that was to engulf everybody on the planet, Rob Lursquom had his sights set on working for the FBI. He loved the prospect of that kind of life – a little bit better than the normal cop.

But now everything had changed and Rob wanted to get involved straight away, without hesitation his sights were set on a new adventure. His father wanted him to go into the Army but Rob felt that he wanted to be something else; some voice in his head said no, that's not for you, your place is in the air. He told his father this and was laughed out of the living room never mind the dinner table, even his mother looked at him in surprise.

It was no secret now, the advance on Japan and also Germany had taken on a new perspective and a friend needed support – an ally that had kept the wolf at bay for a good while but now needed the help of the all-seeing eagle. Rob knew his destiny inside and knew in his heart he wanted to fly. Bringing in his skill of shooting obviously put him in the prospect of a gunner or something to do with ammunitions.

His call-up papers had taken the decision of staying or going away for him. He was to report to the local military establishment in his area, he was off to England or Africa. The USAAF was being formed and he was part of that. His time had come.

* * * * * * *

Al Permando's life was in turmoil now. His mother and father were upset and his family were grieving for the thought of what may become of them and also their family in the old country. It was something that was in the thoughts of everyone all over the whole of the country – how they would cope with war conditions. Everybody was flooding to the military bases wanting to sign up for Uncle Sam, many of those around New York had signed up for the Army as foot soldiers. Al wanted something else.

His mother wanted him to be in the family ice-cream business and that was it, but no, a greater force pulled Al towards a new beginning. In everybody's thinking, life would never be the same again. He had made his mind up; he was off to another country, a place the other side of the world to Al – another place the other side of the universe to his mother.

* * * * * * *

As for myself, Michael Hall that is, I've made many friends on this journey back to the 'Old World' as my family call it. They originate from England so it is a homecoming for me in a way. I look forward to being based somewhere that hopefully reminds me of home – farmland, green fields and the corn fields of Virginia.

We dock at Southampton. There are a lot of us all going in different trucks; not knowing where you are going is frustrating. My brothers have been stationed in England for eighteen months now. From reading their letters when they finally reached the farm it sounded exciting yet dangerous and you felt you were there. I hope to be a pilot like my brothers who were all taught by my father to do crop spraying and enjoy flying. They've grasped with both hands the opportunity to go to another land and defend the righteous.

We are all church-going people and believe in standing up against an evil tyranny that would wreck our constitution and way of life. My brothers are reckless individuals and have no fear as long as they're flying a plane, especially a B-17 Flying Fortress – that's something else; for the chance to fly this son of a bitch, well, what can you say?

It's a long journey. We leave Southampton at nightfall and travel in lorries to our destination, catching up on our sleep along the way. A bump in the road wakes me up and stirs a lot of the other guys as well – surely we must be close to where we're going, this island isn't that big is it? Well, we're here, I don't know where we are but there's a lot of activity. From being in absolute darkness suddenly there are lights everywhere – this must be a big base with such a lot going on.

The lorry stops. A guy says, 'All out, get your gear and follow me,' and leads us into this large hut, full of tables and chairs, 'sit yourselves down.' By all accounts there has just been an Air Raid – as we were coming in through the camp the All Clear was being sounded. The British go by night and we go by day, it would scare the hell out of me to fly at night; I can't imagine it – not natural.

Chapter Three
Settling into camp life

'Welcome to the 100th boys and to Thorpe Abbotts.' Well I know where I am now and my brothers may be stationed here or at other bases in the area. It's just a matter of finding them.

All I wish to do now is get some sleep but we are taken to another tent and given new uniforms and gear, then taken by jeep to another part of the base and come across an old building or billet – it's in a right state. As we all pile in to find a decent bed I find mine and throw my stuff on it, glad to finally be here as a voice breaks through my thoughts.

'Make the most of it kid!'

'What do you mean?' I ask, as this flash bloke – obviously from the big city – throws his kit on the bunk above mine.

He just laughs. 'The name's Buck, get some shut eye – you'll need it.'

Morning breaks with the sound of engines going at full blast it seems in my head – not outside – there's a lot of noise. Buck jumps down from his bunk. 'Come on we'd better get some breakfast.' Getting out of this billet is a relief – fresh air. With breakfast out of the way it's straight on to briefing in the main tent.

I don't know who I am assigned to. I am obviously looking for my brothers – they must be around somewhere. Silence comes over the tent and then the sound of this officer's voice. 'Gentlemen, thank you for your attention on this sunny morning. Today we target Bremen. We will meet up with other bomb groups and target this area.' He shows us our target on a large map – everyone is writing furiously.

My task for today is to be a side gunner with the crew of a B-17 – *Torchy Three* is her name and I hope she takes us there and brings us home safe and sound. With the briefing done we are taken to the planes by open-back trucks and jeeps, all the crews together. The ground crew must have worked all night to get the planes ready.

Chapter Four
The first sortie

At this moment in time I have my heart in my mouth: the experience – things that I have to do. You are so wrapped up in what you're doing you have no time to reflect on the big picture as I call it. Staring at this majestic plane, towering above me, built with care and love to be sent to another country to do its work, I realise that for fours hours a day this is our lifeline. We will have death facing us every day.

And this is what I'm thinking, on my very first day here – to do my work properly and focus. The lives of us all are interwoven – we've become instantly bonded with each other. Though you may not get on with the people socially you must be a team, here and now. With a sudden jerk as this whale of the sky starts her engines, looking out of the side door I see others waiting in line – all these Flying Fortresses look like well-trained dogs waiting for their master's voice to go for a walk.

As we head out to taxi to the main runway we gather speed and it's time to sit down and switch on, all checks done. As we lift off above the trees and farmhouses I close my eyes and feel like I'm at home. The warm sun on my face, the wind rustling through the corn, I hear my oldest brother Jack shouting at me, 'Come on Mike, let's take the old girl up for a spin.' Our neighbouring farmers employ my brother to fly his Gypsy Moth plane over their corn. He sprays their crops with stuff to make it grow better or something – I don't know what it is but it stings your eyes if the wind catches it and you get it full in the face. Jack loves flying, he wants to join the Army Air Corps – it's all he goes on about. We jump in his plane and we're away, flying over the fields that seem to have no end.

Suddenly I am back in the Flying Fortress. I don't know whether I was just daydreaming there or was I asleep – the sudden cold and a smack on my shoulder from a fellow gunner, another Mike, has probably brought me out of my dream. 'Put your mask on Mike, the air up here is a bit thin and very cold.' The heavy jacket they gave us at briefing was bloody uncomfortable then but it's a godsend now. Looking out of the doors on either side we are now in formation, following the trails of smoke from the planes in front of us. So many planes, it's so unreal – as if time could stand still up here. We're moving but it seems as if we're not.

The guys are hyped up – there's a lot of shouting from the men up front. These pilots are a breed above all others and I want to be a pilot someday maybe. All eyes are on the sky now, looking like hawks at anything moving that's not one of us, hands shaking in anticipation of what might be ahead, who can say? Looking above and below I can see we're a massive force; it looks as if we are joined together by some invisible cord.

Without warning we are now hitting shrapnel as ack-ack bombs go off all around us, seen in the distance like puffs of smoke that are suddenly there without warning. There's a lot of shouting – we must be focused on what needs to be done. The navigator, Al, is frantic in the corner with his maps and rules. As he heads towards the bomb bays it is close now – again without warning we hear a sudden explosion to our left as a Fortress is hit in the belly. Lurching to the left, she drops as if all the life has gone out of her and we look around to see if the crew have jumped. I count three and wait, then she explodes with such force you feel the wind rush on your face – the hit in the belly must have ignited her bombs and up she went.

Target is ahead – two minutes, be steady. That two minutes seems a very long time then bombs away – the plane lifts as we leave our presents behind. Our work done we bank to the left, gather height, and look below us as the next wave of attacks are coming in. We look around at each other in silence, knowing it's not all over yet – we have to get back home. 'Keep an eye out you guys on the side and back – give Steve a tap on the glass.' Steve is the ball turret gunner. What a job he has. I would definitely not volunteer for that post.

We cross the channel now, on our way to our new home. I'm looking forward to getting into the other bases around Thorpe Abbotts to see if I can find my brothers, all four of them, all pilots – jammy buggers.

As our landing gear comes forward, the landing strip is in sight and our first mission is over and out of the way – what a relief. We're all eager to let off steam. The plane touches down and I say a little prayer for the crew and myself. In the briefing room a lot of smiling faces and sad ones also – we've lost a few today. I don't know how many but you have this feeling inside that hurts and never get used to it.

'Lets go into Norwich and have a few drinks, what you say Mike?'

I'm startled out of my daydream. 'Sure, why not let off some steam before the next sortie.'

'These English girls sure are pretty!' comes a voice from the back of the room as we leave the barracks and go off into the night air.

Chapter Five
Combat life

The cold hits you like a brick in the face at these heights, it can be very numbing – you tend to drift off into the silence then the flashing red light and crying-banshee sound coming from the cockpit bring you back into the stunning reality of the moment. On hearing the yell they give before going into battle, I'm sure these guys have some rebel blood in their families going back to the Civil War. It's time to switch on now; your life hangs on a thread – in a split second it could be yours or a fellow crewman's that's over. You bond together very quickly in this theatre of war. You may hate your pilot, navigator or fellow gunner for some reason – he's pinched your girlfriend or you've had a fight the previous night or whatever, but it all goes away here for at this moment we are one until we reach home. Looking down from my gun emplacement I see all of us like a formation of birds going into battle as one.

When one of our planes falls out of the sky it's as if part of you has left your body and an emptiness is left, a dark void. You pray it's not you next time. Our boys in the P-51s cover our rear until we get close to the drop zone then for a short time we're sitting ducks for the Krauts. We are going into the lion's den on this raid, right into the heart of Germany. We are part of a much greater force and I try not to look at the big picture too much. It's coming from a small community – we keep our values close, that's our way. If everybody in this war looked on it that way perhaps I wouldn't be in this hunk of metal dropping bombs on mostly civilians and innocent people, but I am and I have a job to do whatever my inner consciousness tells me.

The B-17 to our right has smoke billowing from two of the engines on its right wing. We can see the parachutes start to drop – 1-2-3-4-5 – in quick succession. The plane is well on fire now all down the right side, and the pilot is struggling with the controls trying not to crash into any of the other planes. We are all shouting for them to get out now – 7-8-9 – one more guy to come. The nose is well down and the plane is dropping, then number 10 is out and his parachute is fluttering into life, thank God. We give our thanks to the *Yankee Flyer* for her protection. 20 missions in her lifetime God bless her, and God bless us to get home.

A jet black spot to my left is coming around firing from its wings, the smoke belching as if snorting like a dragon. My sights are on its mainframe, I let my finger press down on the trigger; it's like a magnet – I can't let go – firing what seems like thousands of smoky white pellets at the black mass well in my sights swinging around and above us, and I hope some of the guys above get him before he gets one of us. The white of the swastika hits you as this buzzy little firing thing does its tricks in the sky – an explosion to our left and he's bought it but there are plenty more coming towards us now.

It's very cold, but the adrenaline kicks in and you're warm then cold as ice. 'One minute boys to drop, then let's get the hell out of here.' Lots going on now – be focused, another 23 missions and I can go home.

Shit! We open the bomb doors…a split second and away…and suddenly the old girl lifts up and goes to one side – our mission is now done – then up and to the right. 'Let's make our way home boys – a pint of beer and I don't care if it's warm!'

The Krauts are not letting us go that easy – we've stung them in the tail in this one mission. Lots of our guys are buying it now and they're picking us off like flies. Three or four of them zero in on just one Flying Fortress and then go on to the next – the crews of the Mustangs can only do so much. At this point we pray that we make it safe. Below us the beach comes into view then the water – we're on our way home now.

We touch down and come to a halt. I can't stop shaking inwardly – I have this day faced death and in order for me to survive I have to do this another 23 times. We are debriefed and then go back to barracks. Get some sleep – must sleep. The dreams that I have are really mixed up but I'm sure they have their own little message, they can be frightening sometimes like being in a crash and surviving. How I've actually survived is a bit blurry and fuzzy but never mind.

Chapter Six
Time out

This morning is bright and sunny and I'm going into Norwich today to meet up with Trish – I'm looking forward to spending some time with her. The time I have is very precious to me and on reflection it gives me the strength for when I may be standing in death's doorway. As my father told me, 'Live for the day for tomorrow is another life.'

I manage to get a lift into Norwich having arranged for a message to be passed on to Trish via another girl at the camp. I hope she'll get it as time away is very short. Coming into Norwich once before to pick up supplies did not give me a sense of where I really was, so I say in my note to meet outside the Cathedral gates at 2.15pm.

It's 1.45pm and the guy driving me knows even less about the area than I do. Finally he drops me at the gates, 'You have exactly two hours my friend – I'll meet you here at 4.15pm.' Luckily for me I have a 24-hour furlough – two missions in succession and they give me a pass for a day. I know it may not sound like a big deal, but from where I'm standing it looks bloody good.

Will she show up? There's a lady selling flowers outside this little café – very convenient I think. 'Hey sweet lady, pick a bunch of flowers for me?' She smiles and thanks me, and asks for two shillings. I haven't a clue about this English money so I give her a pile of change.

'I don't want all that sir, here you go, I'll just take these two coins thank you sir.'

I walk towards the gates and Trish is there looking the other way, so I tap her on the shoulder and she jumps a bit. 'Hi, these are for you.' She smiles sweetly and kisses me on the cheek, it's worth coming all this way just for that. We make our way back to the little café and as it is such a nice day for the end of January we sit outside and talk, mostly about our families – hers and mine. Talking about my hometown, my family and things we used to get up to – it all seems a lifetime away.

We take a walk past the Cathedral and down to the river. As we stroll along I notice other couples doing exactly the same thing – funny how a war brings people together to become more focused on what they're doing. As we pass a headstone and memorial in the Cathedral grounds Trish points out the name of Edith Cavell, a nurse in the First World War who was put to death by the Germans. We stand for a while reflecting on what's said in the inscription:

"Edith Cavell, who gave her life for England. October 12th 1915"

Strange – I feel a warmth around me at that moment with a slight chill at the same time as if someone or something has moved around and through me. I shrug it off and suggest that as time is short we make a move, and we find a pub. 'Come on I'll buy you a drink.' We sit outside The Red Lion on a stone wall by a bridge, oblivious of time, just talking about everything and nothing. I take a coin out of my pocket and give it to Trish saying 'Make a wish and throw it into the river.' She closes her eyes and makes her wish but there are tears in her eyes when she opens them again and looks up at me.

Andy has said he'll pick me up where he dropped me – for a station commander he's all right. I don't know where he goes when he's on the supply run and I don't ask questions of such senior ranks; I just do as I'm told, up to a point. I say my goodbyes to Trish and deep down hope this will not be our only one, telling her quickly not to worry. She rushes off to catch a waiting bus, I'm already five minutes late and Andy's not there but then I see him, coming round the corner with a screech of brakes, a cigar in his mouth and a big grin. He calls out 'Hey Mike, sorry I'm late! Won a few dollars…or, sorry…pounds, off this local bobby in a poker game. He gave me this watch as a marker for the rest of the cash – looks as if it's worth a bit! Have you been waiting long?' He's so full of himself I don't tell him I'm also late. As we start our journey back to base its dark and just starting to rain.

Chapter Seven
Off to the seaside to bomb V weapon sites

The date is 14th January 1944, and the journey back to base has been slightly hair-raising – God knows what it's like with him in control of a B-17! There's a bit of a panic on when we arrive; Andy has a word with the guy on the gate as we go in and throws his cigar on the ground. His face is stern and focused now as he drops me off at the shed. I have just enough time to go inside and get my gear, Buck is on his way out, 'Come on Mike, here we go again!' As we run to the briefing room looking over to my left I see small lights, the pink of the afternoon sky, and rows and rows of sleeping giants waiting to awaken to aid us in our quest. Every one of these giants has a name given to them with love and so they live. Whether they be metal, wire and glass, as long as we give them their identity and love they will serve us until we need them no more.

The room is full now as we all gather together, the smell of tobacco, cigar smoke and sweat is a combination that will wake you up, believe me. A silent hush goes around the room as the CO appears – a serious looking guy, his face pencil thin, followed in by Andy the station commander, now focused totally on the mission.

'Good afternoon gentlemen. Our mission today is…' as the curtains are opened they reveal a map, completely dotted out with pins of different colours. He continues, 'Today you lucky bastards get a trip to the seaside. Don't forget to take your bucket and spade! We're off to Pas de Calais, it's a hop across the pond you guys. We have other crews coming along with the 100th – the 91st, 92nd, 303rd, 306th, 351st, 379th, 384th, 401st, 44th, 93rd, 389th, 392nd, 445th, 446th, 448th, 385th, 388th, 390th, 447th, and the 94th, 95th and 96th. You will have escorts all the way gents, from P-38s and P-47s.'

'These sites and the 21 others are the V weapon sites. We wish these to be no more guys – they have done a lot of damage to London and Coventry and other areas of importance. Let's make this a good one guys.'

Commanding officer Patrick Kelly certainly has a presence about him – he leads from the front. His crew feel as if he is a shield against all that is thrown at them and his command of this Bomb Group displays a certain bit of respect for that statement.

And so to work. The former hush of the briefing room becomes a tidal wave of noise as we go out. The two doors open wide and for me everything slows down to slow motion, as if I am looking at a movie in a cinema. I sometimes have these moments – it is as if time stands still for a short while. As we walk out I look over to the other doors and another crew comes in and sits down. I look at each of them, all very serious looking, all new guys – I have not seen them before. Our CO has left with us, I don't know who these guys are or what they're doing. There are rumours going around about secret missions at night but these have been firmly quashed by the CO – we've been given the excuse of leaflet drops in France and the Low Countries. Maybe these guys are from another base, who knows?

'Hey! Snap out of it Mike,' says Mick, our number 2, 'where have you been?'

'He's been thinking about that girl he was with today, isn't that right Mike?' says Andy.

'Oh yeah.' I say.

I have only known the likes of Mick, Buck, Andy and all the other guys on the base for a short time. You get the odd few who are assholes but you have to have the good and the bad in everything. I get my gear together along with Al, the right gunner; the belts of ammunition stacked to one side as we clean our guns in preparation. I love this old war horse, it's as if she welcomes us into herself and smothers us like a mother, making us secure once more. I am ready to enter the gate and walk with God as this old girl shudders, spits and comes alive once more; say her name and she smiles.

We trundle along on this concrete pad feeling all the bumps and then she stops – only for a few seconds which seems a lot longer then it's as if a rush of wind envelops her wings and we're away. Sitting by my trusty guns, looking out of the door at the green fields rushing away from me, I say a silent prayer that I shall see these sights once more.

The mission is a success in the eyes of the ruling hierarchy, but I have seen these Flying Fortresses drop from the sky with my fellow countrymen in them and it's not a pretty sight. You're watching and waiting for everyone to get out of that war bird, one by one you count. Knowing that there is a guy on another plane doing the exact same thing fills you with pride to be an American, serving this great nation for the good, but we must look after each and every one of us – that is the key.

Chapter Eight
More missions

We go quickly to the briefing room. We have mixed feelings about some short missions code-named *No Ball* – mission attacks on weapon sites. We feel that though the missions are very short in comparison with long haul ones into deepest Germany, there is more chance of you being hit by heavy flak. The weather does not help also as it can change very rapidly. Believe me, in these machines any kind of turbulence can be felt.

We feel lucky today however – thankfully we did not lose any of our group coming back. We're waiting for one more to come in – we wait in anticipation for their arrival. I pinned two ME-109s today but we were on the tail of the group and I know from what I saw and the noise over the radio that the guys in the middle group got a bit of stick. I finish my briefing – very short. As I leave the building looking forward to some sleep I see a Flying Fortress land on the runway to my left obviously in a bit of a state, her engines crying out as if in pain just getting down on the ground and thankfully she does. They're safe that's the main thing.

Oh well must get some sleep, off to the not-so-lovely Quonset Hut we call home (Quonset Huts are what you call Nissen Huts). I feel like shit. I want some sleep badly and it doesn't matter to me if the place is freezing, I just want to get my head down and get in from the cold. Thankfully one of the guys has lit a fire in the stove so it's not so bad. Standing over its flames your mind sometimes reflects on what you see from the turret of a plane as you fly over the fires far below, it's as if from above a giant marionette is controlling your feeble-looking plane and all of the destruction going on below you.

As I lie on my bed my eyes close and I lapse into what I call a dream world which seems to calm me. I'm surrounded by an extreme amount of electric blue in these dreams, I'm aware of what's going on around me and everything seems normal but certain things happen, certain aspects within the dream that are surreal. I'm with family but feel very weird – that's all I can say. My brothers are in my dreams. They're very close to me – the very thought of something happening to any of them fills me with dread. But the overriding feeling in these dreams is about seeing planes crashing and guys staggering away from wreckage and then I suddenly awake with a start. These dreams began when I came to this base – I never had dreams like this before – perhaps it's to do with what's going on around me? I must admit I have never encountered feelings or experiences like I've had over the last few months.

At the Christmas party for all the local kids in the village we have a good laugh. The excitement and joy on their faces seems as if it's acknowledging we're their protectors, against the darkness that is not that far away.

Chapter Nine
Buck's story

Since coming over to England, Buck in his own way had to come to terms with his emotions over how his family reacted to his own little offshoot. After the events of '41 he was going through a lot of turmoil and his mother and father were not very happy at the prospect of their youngest son being married to a Japanese girl – they had only been married for two months when all hell let loose. She was a lovely girl and had taken a shine to Buck from their very first meeting.

Buck's life in the Brooklyn area was fast and you had to learn to look after yourself. Day-to-day life is somewhat forgotten in the unfolding pages of history but when you look at events that change history the people who live in those times are put into a large melting pot and left there; the struggles of individuals are sometimes overshadowed by the mass explosion of chaotic events. But through all the history-turning, gut-wrenching things that might change your life, for the last eighteen months Buck's was relatively peaceful.

He was now a pilot. The very thought of that two years previous would have made this hard but fair guy laugh all night and put him off his shot at pool. He was respected now, and I expect revered by Goering's Luftwaffe. The one thing he did love about all this misery was the quietness of this country; having been thrown from the depths of Brooklyn to the shady trees and green fields of Norfolk he could not now get enough of being based in Thorpe Abbotts.

He had made some good friends here while getting on with the day-to-day routine, and could sometimes go off into the fields that surrounded the camp to give thanks and send a thought to his family back home. Blood and carnage seen on a daily basis changes your opinions on the human race, that is if you have an opinion in the first place. The fact is that what we do to one another in any form brings a hatred forward and then in some way you retaliate and it escalates until you have everybody feeling the same way. Certainly with events now happening Buck had probably become more like his real self – what he really was, a leader; and this was his time to lead other guys into battle.

Chapter Ten
Sacrifice and recognition (an observer)

The next few months were a telling time for the Allied Force as a whole. In the day-to-day trudge of events the loss of life was at a scale the authorities were not willing to accept, but in the same breath, the end justified the means. The powers-that-be all wrapped up in their nice, cosy little buildings, safe for the time being, making strategic manoeuvres that would ultimately catapult somebody into a life or death struggle in a very personal fight.

The powers-that-be were open to suggestions right from the start of the war against Germany. There were rumours of an elite unit being trained by the Americans and British to go in and capture Hitler or Goering or one of his lieutenants (his 'disciples of war' as one dignitary called them), or even an assassination. This was a very bold if not suicide mission for a very elite group who would be giving their lives in a no-win situation for them, but if successful it would change the whole spectrum of looking at the balance of power within Germany. If Hitler were to be taken out who then would be given Fuhrer status, and would Germany change its motivation for dominant world power at any cost?

All these ideas were brought forward – the secret part of the Allied advance into squashing an evil tyranny. But there are many wolves in sheep's clothing as well as wolves and sheep in their own clothes, as it were. The rights of the individual are taken away in matters such as war and you are labelled to do a set task, to fulfil that task you must be strong of heart and brave to vanquish the evil foe. Who is good? Who is bad? The powers-that-be make the rules that we live by; if those rules are not obeyed we are punished. It is when the context of how a negative force is that perceives itself to be ultimately evil, or that the force is that positive it deems itself angelic, that the powers-that-be manipulate this context into the reality of war.

Each force deems itself to be righteous and therefore positive. It is up to the individual person taking part in this theatre of conflict to make his mind up. So everything escalates a hundredfold. There are sacrifices on both sides of a conflict but it is how these sacrifices manifest themselves against the weak and hungry and those that cannot fend for themselves – these are the sacrificial lambs to the slaughter. In a conflict on a magnitude of this level, the end justifies the means – how far are the-powers-that-be prepared to go to get a just result so we have a positive way of life? Ending just one person's life will make a difference in this case because his positive force is the exact opposite to the Allied Power base.

The German government with Adolf Hitler at the helm devise a plot to capture Winston Churchill – the secret war going on. What schemes are developing? A special task force set up from the elite storm troopers, Panzer and Wolf units i.e. the infantry, tank, and submarine forces. A combination of all these to be trained to go in behind enemy lines and take out one of the Allied commanders would be a very bold move, but what a force! So how successful would they be? Perhaps they did try already in certain areas – we will never know, but what if the Allied Forces were also that bold and got together a highly gifted team of guys to take on this task of taking out the wolf in his lair with all the might of the pack around him?

When ordinary guys get involved in the super secret part of high government policies and situations, the powers-that-be manipulate lives and use the ordinary guy as cannon fodder. It goes very deep if the individual realises that they have been used in such a way – to give their life for a cause is one thing, but to be taken for granted and not given their rightful respect means the voice of that individual should be heard. When that sacrifice is manifested in many losing their lives and they are not given their rightful respect, then heads will turn and the dog will bite his master!

We draw together the talents of these individuals, seven guys brought together in the make-up of this war to be used by political and military forces (some might say cannon fodder for suicide missions) to assassinate the Chancellor of the Third Reich. A very bold idea as this would take out the one main focal point of Germany's driving force and may end the war very quickly. Psychologically and mentally the German war machine would come to a massive halt on the one hand, whilst on the other we would only be sacrificing seven guys. What price do you pay? When on this scale does personal human sacrifice come into it?

When looking back at war or any conflict there has to be casualties – it is a fact of life. When walking around the military graveyards looking at all those names and where they come from and who they were, you become overwhelmed by the sheer mass of it all. But take a step nearer and you will see the individual person – their day-to-day life, coming together with others to overthrow a tyranny and giving their life for the right of freedom to carry on.

That is all life, be it yours or the enemy's. Now take a step closer – just imagine that person. You are looking at his or her name on a gravestone, imagine you are living his or her life and the sacrifice you would be making is your life. To many in this world in their thinking, you are only here once so give it your best shot. You as an individual have a right not to sign your life away for nothing – what is more precious than life itself? To experience life – to wake up in the morning, to go about the routines of life we take for granted, you would not let that be taken away from you without a fight so the individuals who make up a fighting force have a right too.

They know the dangers of warfare and take that chance but there comes a point when life is discarded and the individuals are used as mere machinery to see the final bell ring. When it is finished what is left is personal grief on a scale we cannot comprehend, and letters are sent to their loved ones for they must pick up the pieces and get on with life. These men and women who have given the ultimate sacrifice are not forgotten by their loved ones but they are forgotten by the very people who ordered their deaths.

For just one moment of your life imagine in your mind's eye that you were one of these people. You would be thoroughly pissed off if you gave your life for nothing, to be swept under the carpet and not recognised by your very own people. So this story of these seven men is even more precious and should be looked at, but not with sadness – they knew the dangers.

For we are they and they are us; and we are all the same, each and every one of us.

Chapter Eleven
Relationships borne out of war

The day-to-day process of the war carries on. We go about our business getting the job done – sorties in the early morning and some at night. Looking at this war from my own perspective as Michael Hall, it has been a harrowing experience since leaving the States. I miss my family very much and wish sometimes I was back home doing my everyday things that I took for granted.

There are, I must admit, exciting things happening on a daily basis here. There have been many friends come and go since being in this situation. I cannot describe to you what it is like – you must use your own imagination for that – but day-to-day life is different in so many ways, sometimes mind-blowing, sometimes bloody boring. You have so many different characters around the place they all have their own irritating little habits – you get to know people working and living as closely as we do. We become a family although you do not realise it at the time, but it is a giant family. We cry, we laugh, we eat, we drink, and we all live in one big house – and that house is our base. When one of us is sick we all nurse together, and if one is taken from us we grieve like a family, brother, sister, mother, father – we are all these and when we live in this way, this place becomes a focal point for everybody.

Sure there's a lot of grief with war but in the day-to-day life we lead you must have friends and love. We drink together, we laugh together, as well as going over the Channel and doing the business – whatever our government tells us to do. We love our country and our people and must maintain our way of life as we see it, those we are at war with look upon it in exactly the same way. They live their lives, individual lives that are brought together for one purpose, at one moment in time; they will be remembered by their loved ones and forgotten by the very people who put them there to fight. I myself am very patriotic; I love America and what it stands for. It fills me with pride to be a part of a fighting force to uphold the very essence of our being.

The day-to-day life we take for granted is very precious to us all. My aspirations in this life go very deep although I am but a mere gunner. There are guys here that could fly these birds like taking a bike down the local pub, they are aces in their own right. Every one of them living life as if it was their last day, for some it is, but others skip and hop over the grim reaper as he sits and waits for us to fall out of the sky one by one into his hand, to be whisked away into the next life.

These guys I am sure were put here for a purpose. Before the war they were just run-of-the-mill blokes, probably going about tedious, mundane existences, drinking and doing other things to excess and just thinking that's it, this is my life, accept it. Then this war happens and their very core of living changes, their world is blown away – it doesn't exist any more. You are brought into a situation where, as an individual human being, do you honestly matter? The collective matters, not the man in the street playing pool and having a beer every Saturday with his buddies – no, that doesn't matter any more. What matters is that the very substance of going out every Saturday with your buddies is suddenly going to be taken away from you, and you my friend are going to have to go many miles away to fight for the very fact of your life as you see it.

So these guys taken from their cots and cradles, their loving mothers and fathers, their families, brothers and sisters, daughters and sons – they all have personal skills to bring them to the front. Pick the pilots, the navigators, and the ground crew, and pick me as the gunner.

We all gel together as one unit, so we live together and we die together, and that's the way it is. These guys and women that make up my base replace my real family and the bond grows more and more as we work together – that will never die. We will be together beyond all the grieving and the bloodshed and tears, we will be together – that I know in my heart, and that is what keeps us going day-to-day, night after night, the love we have for our country and our way of life.

Chapter Twelve
Michael's thoughts

Look deep into my eyes – what do you see? Pain? Hurt? Guilt? Sorrow? What do you want to see? We have to go through some sacrifice some time in our life; it is the life we live at a certain time. Pain comes with the living, it is part of it, or is it the whole? That is the mystery of it. The time I am living in now is painful because of what I feel and see. The five senses come together for you to experience a time of joy and pain. It matters not what level that joy and pain it is your journey, your personal journey, and it is up to you on a physical level what must endure as physical pain and pleasure.

When I was born of this life I was thrust into joy, the joy of love from my family – they surrounded me with love and I had love for them, there are others that are starved of this and are confronted with pain. So straight away from that small beginning we have one and the opposite – light and dark. Manifest that by ten and you have the love of one and the hate of one, small at first but slowly building and building, bringing together others that are of like mind – one love, one hate. Then muddle them all up, multiply by a thousand fold and you have a nucleus for confrontation – a war.

You as an individual may not have love or hate for what you are in this war but you are being manipulated by greater forces to compete in this theatre. For that is what it is – a theatre, a play, a film to be acted out again and again not necessarily by you or me, but by the human race, individuals that come together to bring forward an energy and that energy is either for good or bad, light or dark.

For that is what we are told from birth – are you for us or against us? You need a tribe. Whether we think we are true individuals and look after ourselves and family and that is it, is just hearsay. You and me belong to a tribe, a family if you will, and it doesn't matter which country or religion you are born into, what matters is what flag you are born under. This brings you unity where there was none before, that flag can represent a country – a bigger family – that unites together kindred folk that will uphold anything to bring the energy of what that flag represents.

That flag can represent anything and if that flag or sign brings forward a common good overall then that will have a seal of approval from the masses – the collective. Perhaps in time we will be united under one flag, perhaps we will not. It is what the one wants that will win the day because the will of the one is the will of all if that will is true. There are those that walk the path of darkness because that is their light – that does not mean they are bad. There are those that are drawn to the light and those that are drawn to the dark – we must as individuals, as one, make up our own mind. I was born under the Stars and Stripes and for me it is the light, for others it is the darkness. Am I fighting for the good, or the bad? It is how we perceive it to be. We are confronted with how human beings treat each other.

We all have a right to live but when one wants to take from another on a small-scale – the child that takes another child's toy – we see that happen, we tell them off and get them to give the toy back to its rightful owner. But what if we did not see that happening, what would then unfold – an unseen growing force taking everything because it could? That is what we think is bad but the child growing up doesn't know that. He hasn't been given any guidelines as to what constitutes good or bad so he goes on taking not giving, and as he brings others into his way of thinking where does it end? It has no end. There has to be a good and a bad, a black and a white – it all depends how far in the black or white you wish to stand and feel good with yourself.

I fight for my country but I feel for those brought into this conflict like me. One little dot on a giant piece of paper alongside a lot of other dots of one colour and dots of other colours. How I will survive as a person will depend upon how many dots I can wipe clean from this piece of paper. It is sometimes hate that spurs you on or one's love, it is drawn together in one's self this conflict goes on; that is an inner war within yourself and eventually there can be only one victor, your true self and no other for that is the common good.

When we know in our hearts that the conflict and fear is worth it then we must unite to overthrow that which is wrong. It is an inner feeling and when you have that in a person and persons you will achieve great things, and that covers everything, not just war. We are a small group of guys that have been brought together for a purpose – to overthrow an energy that manipulates the weak. We are prepared to give our lives – some say with raised eyebrows, some say from the heart, at this moment we are not ready to give our lives so lightly. There are many suffering in this war, ordinary people who just want to live their lives but because of the flag they are born under they are confronted with all kinds of brutality inflicted upon them. That is wrong.

If this were on the small-scale of say one child taking from another or someone being bullied by another in our own backyard, we could administer local justice there and then to right the wrong on the spot or bring in local justice to administer it. But when it is to this extent then something obviously has to be done on a bigger scale. There are those who will be sacrificed for doing no wrong and those who will get away with their crime in this material world but not in the next. All these things we tend to forget or are told it doesn't matter what people are experiencing individually.

We are told to not think of what is happening when we unload our bombs. From this height we only hear the drone of the engines and then the release of the bombs, what happens 10-15 minutes later we have to blot out. Ok, yes, we have a job to do, but we are ultimately taking someone's life in a terrible way, what has that individual person done him or herself to warrant the kind of cruelty we have inflicted upon them? And we are doing this in the name of peace so there has to be casualties.

You have to live with a moral dilemma. I fight to survive for a purpose, my way of life justifies me winning for I am of the light. The man that stands opposite me thinks exactly the same, but he is of the dark.

In this present time and place my thoughts and feelings have no place. They are not recognised because we keep them to ourselves, if we manifested them in actions we would be put to the sword. But ultimately it is what we think emotionally now that has a greater if not infinite impact in times to come. If I survive this war, when I am old, sitting in a chair on a porch looking at the sun going down, then my thoughts matter for I have to live with what goes on in this time and place. And if I do not survive this war as I think I shall not – for I have a feeling deep inside that my days on this Earth are numbered – if there is an Afterlife where all we have done is accountable, then yes, it does matter.

I love this life, even now what is going on all around us. The death and destruction will not go on, there will be a time when all this will stop. We are not the first to be at war and I do not suppose we will be the last. We have a job to do and will do it to the best of our abilities, that I am sure of. The day-to-day struggle of life is of no matter. I say 'struggle', but recognise life as if the next day is your last and you would have a different aspect on life then my friend. You would not see it as a chore you would see it as an adventure, waiting to be played out like a play in a theatre – when the sun rises again you play your role once more with open eyes, looking on as if opened for the first time.

My friends and I are here for a purpose. That purpose is to rid this time and place of an energy so profound and pure that if it was for the good and not bad, then it would be an everlasting light for us to be guided to. But alas that is not the case for we are dealing with a cloud of energy that grows and grows and gets blacker and blacker until it rains hard on the insecure and frail innocent. This energy manifests itself in one person that radiates the force of dark light upon those that are willing to do his duties, and then beyond that, the weak will do the duties of the disciples.

My friends and I have been brought together to rid this time and place of one energy that manifests itself as Adolf Hitler. How can you say that the six crews being trained can get at the one person that can bring an end to this bloodbath we are going through at this time? We have been brought together because of our talents, our expertise in firearms and military hardware. We do as we are told – we strike at the enemy in a day-to-day uniformed pattern, but behind the scenes of normal warfare there are the hidden corridors of secrecy that if revealed in public circles to the masses – the population as a whole – the structure of self belief would be threatened here in the physical. So when confronted by these all-powerful agents giving us orders we go along with it for you have to. You may not like it but you know deep down inside that it has to be like this, and you as an individual will not come into the equation in this instance for it matters not that you will die for the cause – the cause being the right to live with peace and harmony and not be dictated to by one who inflicts physical harm on others, as in this case, at such a magnitude as to take up the whole world to eat in its gaping mouth.

I am telling you this story from my perspective – a simple guy from Cleveland, Russell County, Virginia, USA. My crew are from all over the Americas and I can tell you their individual stories leading up to this one moment in time and place but I am not going to do that – what matters is this time and place. We as individuals cease from this moment in time. We have to be as one breath together, as one entity, for if we are to succeed in this mission then we must be at our best – second rate is not good enough. We have our talents and they must be brought to the surface to bring forward our abilities to overthrow what is going to be a very strong adversary. For we must not underestimate them – for us to get into the fox's lair we must first overcome those that do the fox's bidding.

Chapter Thirteen
Michael trains with the British

Torchy Three – a great name for a sturdy horse of the sky, I have been put with a good bunch of guys, a couple of English blokes in the crew. After all it is their Lancaster bomber – they have the right to call her what they like. We as a group with the talents have been split up for a while to develop and see other crews. The flying of different planes is a must for we have to be aware not only of our own aircraft but other instrument workings also in case of emergency. We have to fly at night and we must get that into our awareness in the eventuality of conflict.

For protocol reasons I have been given the name of rear gunner in the photograph and listing of personnel. There always has to be a roll call and for reasons I will not go into we have to be listed and given a name. So for the record officially I am Michael Shelly Hall of 8 Squadron, Thorpe Abbotts, rear gunner, requisitioned to RAF Bomber Command but really I'm gunner unofficial Mike Shelly Hall of 8 Squadron, Thorpe Abbotts, under the codename *fox lair pilot sniper*.

So you see what is official and what you may see on the outside is not always the truth deep inside. My crew have been divided for a purpose, that purpose is for their self preservation, if we are to survive this mission then we must be at our best. I am enjoying my time with the crew of *Torchy Three* – they are very good. They like myself have their thoughts as to why the Americans and British have been brought together to fly and learn all aspects of flying. There are British guys in with American crews for just the same reason as I am with these guys.

Perhaps not for the same reason as I am at this particular time but they have their own thing going on with their own hierarchy, the people who ultimately pull the strings. Flying at night is an eye-opener for me. To see the ground in all its glory during the day is one thing but to see it at night – the lights, the constant flames from all corners – you are given an insight into the darkest realms of the word hell, for at any moment you feel as if you might just disappear into its depths.

Being away from my friends is getting to me a bit I must say. I am at an RAF base in Lincolnshire – RAF Waddington. I am living on the base with a few other guys from the States. They thought it was wise that we didn't come into contact with the British guys as there may be fights or different aspects might come into the fore. Being over here and having different opinions, the English girls like us more than their own guys, so we are not to be given the same rights as at our own base. We have the freedom of the base but we are virtually prisoners here. Some of the guys resent this and they feel we are all in it together.

I haven't a problem with it but some of the brash guys from New York are not impressed. They want a good time no matter where they are, if we were prisoners-of-war in Germany they would still want a good time with the locals. We have our enemies within our own force as it were, we do not all think the same. Unfortunately the British public think that at any given time we are going to take advantage of their womenfolk – I could be more explicit than that but I shall not.

There are certainly some characters here – one is Steve James from Connecticut, a flash guy, always looks immaculate. The one thing that makes you sick is this guy is brilliant – he is used to having the authorities eating out of his hand. I am sure he is here because of his particular talents – he is a scrounger and will get anything that you want. Put him in a situation where you need supplies and he will get you those supplies no matter what. He uses people. The big chiefs, the high ups who call the shots think they can manipulate this man to their own ends but believe you me, they do not know the full potential of this guy – he is phenomenal.

We put it to the test. We are not allowed out of the camp for security reasons. We are told that there are spies everywhere. At this time in the war what would the significance be of a group of Americans in a pub having a good time and where is the closest American base of operations? A long way off, and they are there with pointed ears, waiting for any news of anything substantial. So we do not go out but we give Steve a task. He has to get a Flight Lieutenant's uniform, a sports car, get out of the camp, and get a girl, preferably a blonde – we give him the option on that but she has to be good-looking. Now, how are we going to know he's accomplished this? He has to take one of us along. A big task you might ask? We think he might get away with this as two officers might not be looked at in the same way as a bunch of guys on the pull, so we send him to work.

There's a routine schedule – we have to do briefings and everything, but for a guaranteed 24-hour break we are not flying due to weather conditions over the proposed targets and the Channel, so *Operation Blue Wheel* is put into motion. I have no idea who or what the blue wheel stands for – we've just given it a name at this point. I will let Steve carry on – this is his story after all.

Interlude 1
by Dave Kelly

Before Steve takes up his next part of the story, it seems appropriate to break in here just very briefly to give some further background about the checking that was done into the writing as it came through. I have to be honest and say that the detective work I did at the start was minimal. The information was coming through abundantly via thoughts and pictures in meditation and that was then proof enough for me.

I should emphasise that I wasn't dealing with my own thoughts. I was getting names like 'Thorpe Abbotts' and 'Seething' without knowing what or where either of those places were – these were places that then I really had no intention of visiting. I felt at that time it would be better not to show myself in such places as a psychic.

But within a month of getting the first hint of the story I felt moved to go and do some research of some kind. It was early in March 2001 and I was in between building jobs which gave me the time to look into it further. I stayed for many days in the American USAAF Library when it was in temporary premises in Ber Street, Norwich after the main library had burned down. Just sitting there, going through books and trying to find some link to what I was getting from 'Spirit' wasn't particularly rewarding at first. I must admit I nearly gave up many times in the lead up to actually writing the book.

However, what I did find there was detailed information about lots of crash landings – really tragic stories – and the loss of life listed in the archive was overwhelming. This reassured me that there was a very real factual context to what I was receiving at home. To be honest, I didn't really know what I was looking for. By this time I had a name – Michael Hall and a date February 10th 1944 but I wasn't able to confirm that at any time at this stage from the Library records.

Then there was another interesting development of a different kind. A few weeks later after sitting in meditation with my wife Pauline, we felt guided to visit the American Military Cemetery at Madingley on the outskirts of Cambridge. We were starting to get more names and were guided to go to Madingley to place some flowers on unmarked graves there. We were of course looking out for the name of Michael Hall but we didn't see any sign of it.

As soon as we arrived Pauline without hesitation walked into the Information Centre just inside the front gate and asked if they had any record of a crash at Stoke Holy Cross on the night of 10th February 1944. The American official checked his records and then looked at us with some amazement. He appeared dumbstruck in fact and said, 'Gee, there was a crash that night at Stoke Holy Cross except there is no detail of the crew.'

Pauline noticed that there was no identifying tail number for the aircraft either and offered to provide it. We had been given the tail number by Michael at an earlier date. When Pauline gave details of the number the American official looked even more puzzled.

He went off immediately, apparently for his lunch and we spent ten to fifteen minutes looking around outside among the endless rows of white stone crosses and Stars of David. When we saw him again a little bit later he was surprised at our knowledge and asked us how we knew about this. Pauline simply pointed upwards and with a smile she said, 'From up there' meaning from the Spirit World. He didn't make any further comment but still looked very mystified. For us that was a big moment because it put a key part in the jigsaw.

In accordance with Pauline's guidance we had taken a bunch of red carnations to put on various graves and one blue one for Michael Hall which she placed 'under instructions' at the foot of a tree. Pauline said that she had been given specific ideas of which graves to place the red carnations on. They were not necessarily the seven crew members in our story.

The cemetery is beautifully kept up and the crosses stand out on broad sweeps of green immaculately cut lawns. Walking along the rows, looking at the names and dates on them, it is clear that an enormous number of American airmen died in the intensive days of aerial warfare against Germany in 1943-1945. Going there for the first time was a powerful experience, taking us deeper into the story. As my 'writing' continued we would be led back there again for further experiences, but more of that later. Meantime, let us hand back this remarkable story to Steve who as you will see starts Part Two by describing extraordinary escapades in and out of German wartime concentration camps.

PART TWO

WE ARE IN THIS TOGETHER

Chapter Fourteen
Steve James and Operation Blue Wheel

I always have a good laugh over this. The actual event pleases me greatly for it gives me the opportunity to do what I do at its best – the energy flow between two people is such that you can bring in thoughts that would not matter to them and you can take advantage of the situation. I have been transferred to this base for a particular mission – to free POWs in concentration camps. I am airlifted in to secret locations within the French territories, I work with the Free French revolutionaries. I am fluent in all languages, I have no problems getting into concentration camps – if I wish to be captured I let it be.

In order to find certain POWs who are of particular interest to the authorities, I manipulate the governing rule of law within the camp to find personnel who have been captured by the enemy. The enemy do not know who these operatives are – if the Gestapo found out we would be in trouble; my job is to bring a conclusion to their conflict or to get the most out of a bad situation. I am always at the front of escape committees and at the front of the queue, even in POW camps and the hidden camps within the Fuhrer's stronghold – the Gestapo's elite. The camps that are famous are not the important ones, they are for the propaganda machine – like Colditz, a very good propaganda machine this one. Give the freedom of this castle to every officer within the Allied units who has a reputation for escaping and treat them well to the outside world – no matter. There are concentration camps controlled by the inner Gestapo of such magnitude and disgust that the authorities do not wish these to come to the attention of the people. The Allies know, the higher authorities know – there is a war going on within the structure of the outer war that we see.

So, you may ask, how do I know all this? Well, we are trained to do a job and that job consists of many talents and no matter what those talents are the overriding thing is the good of the whole, which is the one. You may look at me and say I'm a talented one-off and in a peace situation I could have anything I wanted – perhaps, but I'm not. I have one talent and that is all, I manipulate on a small-scale and there are those that do the same on a larger scale than I. How do I know what I know? Well, I have a very good memory and I have been put in situations where I see and sense many things. You may ask yourself how I would react in circumstances where I am not in control, I am captured and tortured, and ultimately may die? Well, I have my own personal weapon for that eventuality, I have been trained in many things. I will not let any of the situations and aspects I have seen come to the foreground, they are hidden as they are in the physical world. Not even my dog tag numbers will be given.

So you have an insight of me. I thank Mike for giving me the opportunity to tell you a story that is a laugh but also has a serious side to the equation. We had a twenty-four hour furlough within the camp. Us Americans could not go outside the perimeter of the base so it was time to go forward and make enquiries in the NAAFI. The local girls do get jobs within the confines of the catering establishments – such meaningless work does not come into the thoughts of the establishment's hierarchy. With a little bit of flattery these girls will give you the precise details of their granny's toilet activities given the chance, so we asked for details about the local watering holes, where the locals went, and where were the best places in the big city?

We obviously knew that Lincoln was a major place, so we started with a good map of the area. Next was a uniform, an officer's uniform. It gets you into places you would never think you could get into like the Officers' Mess – a bastion of such magnitude it beggars belief, an Englishman's castle on such a scale that an outsider like myself sees where it comes from. My family are very broad in outlook and it is deeply rooted within me, they would look upon the Officers' Mess as a colonial British thing. Those from New England (that part of America that was so finely attuned to the British way of life and still has a strong bond) would know and be happy with these guys, sitting around, obviously oblivious to what's going on globally, all that matters is their next cup of tea and the next drop of port after lunch.

And so we went to work. You give candy out and no matter what the age they will take, only this time they must give something in return. I had a good supply of Bourbon and between us we had managed to steal a few bottles coming over from one of the supply camps in Yorkshire. We targeted a man at the bar – a new guy sipping on his glass of whisky. Myself and a couple of the guys gave him a bit of stick – 'Go on sling it down in one, my old China'.

He looked at me with disgust. 'What do you Americans know of our best whisky? It is to be savoured, and drunk in a way to glorify its taste, sir.'

'Well, we have our own whisky.' His eyes at this point were jumping out of his face.

'*Your own whisky, sir*? Pray, tell me more.' With this the bait was being sniffed at, and within three good hours and a full bottle of Bourbon the reel was being pulled in, slow but sure.

'I bet that uniform gets you into places my friend?'

'You bet it does. They give us two of these beauties and woe betide me if I lose or mess them up.'

'So you would not be interested in a swap then?' His look was inquisitive and the reel was still being brought in.

'A swap sir? What? A trade you mean? What could you sir, trade for a uniform?'

'Well what about a leather jacket straight from the States, not a mark on it?' (another little trinket from the quartermaster's stores). 'Try it on. You keep the jacket – we only wish to have your uniform for twenty-four hours my friend, that's the trade. What do you say?' Without a word his face was saying 'Yes' to me. Right, that was out of the way.

My twenty-four hours started there – my next exploit or task was to get out of the camp with my friend in tow. I must learn to speak English in a very good accent, a local accent wouldn't do as not many officers who came from the area got stationed locally. So I tried London Cockney – not too 'apples and pears' but enough to convince the locals. My friend (or buddy as we call it) was fellow colleague 'Ralphy' Ralph Peterson from Blue Ridge, Virginia – he was the one with the short straw. The eyes and ears of the group, Ralphy was ground crew so my task of trying to make him into an officer was even more hampered. The uniform was not a problem and thankfully he came across with a good American accent – I knew where he came from in the States but the locals wouldn't have a clue. My only worry was that he's a bit of a joker so I would have to be a little wary of what went on.

We got it together. The uniform fitted a treat, the lingo of the Londoner was not bad, and I had a fair bit of leg-pulling and banter from the guys. We had no problem with American money – we pooled together a kitty. It would not do for an RAF officer and an American officer to walk out of the camp, we needed transport – my case of Bourbon came into the picture once again as a very good bribe for the use of a two-seater Morgan, no questions asked, from one of the guys in the Mess who just happened to have one.

My time was ticking away, I now only had six short hours to get a local girl, preferably good-looking. That was all my task was. Failure did not come into my thoughts, winning is everything – so let us cut to the chase. We drove out of the camp, it was early morning, or early for me – nine o'clock. We drove around, parked up and had a wander about as Ralphy took the opportunity to look at the local talent. We were being looked at as if we were some alien life form whilst getting admiring glances from females of every age. My concern now was to get a stunner, for that we must go to the best places and I guessed this uniform would get us into those places. So we tried the local watering holes – Ralphy was all for this and we had the money.

We frequented a number of pubs and chatted to the local girls some of whom I have to say were stunning but according to Ralphy, his orders were that she must be a stunning blonde with blue eyes – the lot – and he had his orders, laughing like a hyena whilst saying it. My time was ticking away now, I had only four hours. At a large hotel by the river – my oasis in the desert – we made a beeline for the bar and another opportunity for Ralphy to sample the beer. Still laughing, he said 'This is what the guys told me to do!' smiling like a baby with its first toy.

'Ok yeah, if you say so,' I replied, as out of the corner of my eye I saw this girl – no more than 18 or 19 – with lovely blonde hair. Stunning was the word, but she had a friend not so good-looking. Oh dear, should I bring Ralphy into the task? I supposed I had no option, so I went for it.

'Would you ladies like a drink?'

The blonde looked me up and down. 'Only if your American friend sits with us.'

'Come on Ralphy!' I shouted.

'That's a funny name,' she said, 'for an officer.'

'Oh that's his nickname.' I said.

Her friend was all over me, the one I had to target was Ralphy's. Just shows you what a uniform can do – he was a right ugly spud! But there you go, I had no time to worry about that, up to the bar for another drink and I said to Ralphy, 'We've only a few hours left, so my task has been successful even though I haven't got the target, is that right Ralphy?'

'All right then,' he said, 'Mission over.'

'Good – we'll celebrate with a drink. Better still let's take advantage of the situation.'

'What do you mean?' asked Ralphy.

'You take the blonde and I'll take this young lady with me. See you back here in two hours – ok?'

Well, I managed to get back to the camp with a few minutes to spare, and as far as I was concerned, it was 'mission complete'.

* * * * * * *

We last saw Steve at a briefing for a leaflet drop in France. He said his farewells to us and we did not see him again after that. He's still helping somebody somewhere I'm sure, God bless him! (Michael Hall)

Chapter Fifteen
A secret mission to rescue a forces personality

Michael Hall

Our time at Waddington has come to a close and we move on to a local airfield, Scampton, RAF in charge, with annoyance from my ground crew who are Yankees like myself. We are all in this together it seems – crew as in flight crew and ground crew. We must be flexible – be able to turn our hands to any eventuality. These night-time raids I must admit are getting to me – I'm not used to them at all, and the British weather is also taking its toll. I miss the sun – not this continual rain *all* the time! All seems fine within my crew, we are all blending. I sometimes think we really are flying by the seat of our pants.

Sometimes the risks we take seem to go beyond even my comprehension. My brothers would love this as you are a free spirit in the air – the regulations of flying are thrown out of the window. We have respect for the uniform of the RAF but they are sometimes sticks-in-the-mud, a bit fuddy-duddy for my liking. Because we have been given carte blanche – a blank sheet if you will – others of higher rank are a little annoyed. If they only knew what this is leading up to then probably they might understand a little more. At the uppermost it seems we are all putting our lives on the line so there should not be any animosity at all – learn from it and move on.

Our next assignment is a more demanding one: we must land and retrieve agents from the Free French. My memory is of Steve – perhaps he is amongst them or maybe not. Wherever he is we hope he's safe, he's very good at what he does. We must be on our toes for this one, just one hiccup and we are dead. We have been given briefings at Top Secret level from Special Branch and MI5 within the British government, plus a group from our own government, Majestic 12, on how not to give anything away if captured. Mind control techniques and all manner of other things will be used on us if we are captured. We will be interrogated at such a level that we must remain aware of ourselves in giving them what they want. Disinformation is the key – all to do with the mind. Their local police will wire through to a special task force if we are captured and then we will be at the mercy of the inner Gestapo. All this I hope will not happen – I hope we will go in, get what we came for and depart with no problem, but you must be ready for these eventualities as to be aware is to be forewarned.

Departure is at 2100hrs, it is now mid-morning; time for reflection and being optimistic. Certainly, all that's going on around me seems a bit cloak and dagger. I wonder how my good friends are doing while we are here at Scampton. I know a few of the guys are enjoying themselves no matter where they are – getting on with life no matter what, and how bizarre it all seems. .

* * * * * * *

Buck

The Red Cross parcel thrown on the bunk of Charlie Quinlan wakes him with a start as its weight hits his forehead. 'Hey Buck,' says the guy doing the throwing, 'I'm getting better at that don't you think?'

'Go fuck yourself Smitty!' Buck opens one eye and smiles, 'Just because you come from New Jersey doesn't give you cause for lip.'

I'm sad with all this. I miss home very much – I must be more positive in what I'm doing. Let's see what Ma has to say; she even calls me Buck – that's good, the letters and the little mementos of home are a lifeline. The reality of what's going on around you gives you a buzz but when you're given something from home it's a blessing in disguise. I must keep my feet firmly on the ground as far as my mental state goes. I must be positive. The things I've seen, heard and witnessed are in a way it seems a test. You cannot walk away from this without it affecting you. You either let it ride all over you or you hit full on what could happen to you, or what could happen to your friends around you. We are all in this together. No matter which guys you dislike – and there are quite a few – you have to tolerate: to give yourself a boost. Be credible and you will lead. My father always told me go to go the front no matter what, whether in a race or just standing listening to someone, 'Go to the front son, do not let anybody stand in front of you.' And that I suppose is what I have been doing all my life, be it not everything my father proposed at the time he said it. I have been in front in pool halls and bars so I have done right in what he said, up to a point.

What would he make of all this? Sworn to secrecy, not knowing what is around the next corner, separated from the original crew and not being with anybody else as you are supposed to. The crew have all split up – I do not know where they are. We were taken in separately and given our orders and that was it. I must sit down and write to my parents and tell them not to worry; I must overcome my desire to just walk away from all this. I come across to the rest of the guys as a laugh and a leader. I suppose some look up to me in that form, but deep down I feel ashamed at the total disregard for the fighting man in this war. We are used by the establishment as cannon fodder and then we are supposed to take it on the chin, to go and face death on a day-to-day basis like going to the lavatory.

What do they think we are made of? They treat us like robots. Don't they realise the emotions and trauma we go through – not only with ourselves but to see it in others also? Losing one's buddy is very painful, but to see him splattered in all four corners of the cockpit is not a pretty sight. We have ways of dealing with that trauma, we block it out with drink and having a good time. You must have this balance within otherwise you will stew and stew on what is going on around you. The time is now – forget tomorrow, forget yesterday – *now* is the time. Live for the now because in a split second you could be spread over some airfield or aircraft, and that is it.

The feeling I get when I lift these great monsters into the air is like a sword going slowly into my stomach. I know what I am letting myself in for each time we go on a mission, I cannot just walk away – I wish that were the case but I cannot. We have to get on with it. The chance of facing death each and every day just makes my insides explode, I may look and seem calm and collected on the outside but inside, boy it hurts. My drinking is getting a bit excessive at the moment; I am trying to blot out a lot of stuff, trying to come to terms with what's happening. I miss good friends, that is true but I must get on – the camp commander has spoken to me and told me to buckle up and sort my problems out.

I have been assigned a mission. They will only tell me I have been assigned – nothing more. Bringing the talents of a few together to overthrow a regime, that is all I have been told. 'Get on with being a good pilot. You are category 'A'. There are others to take your place if you do not survive.' A bit farfetched you may say, all of this. Sometimes it's hard to swallow myself but that is the way it is. I am only following orders, where those orders originate I do not know. My only wish now is to get this over with and return to my family back in the States – that is my only concern, their well-being is uppermost in my mind. Whatever goes on here is irrelevant – it is an event that will pass in time and be forgotten by a lot of people so what is the point? The point is freedom to live without persecution and free speech – that is all. If that is taken away then we do not live, we survive. I must now carry on until the time of the mission and above all keep myself from harm in any situation.

Scampton is a long way from my base at Thorpe Abbotts in miles and culture. I am used to the guys shouting and the hustle and bustle of Yanks. Here at Scampton is a far cry from there. I am not saying it's quiet but it's different, that's all I can say. On my way to briefing now – not saying much, just silence. Just one crew together in a big room that when full is like an audience at a theatre – packed, some standing, waiting for the curtain to rise. We sit at the front waiting for the base commander to make his mark. He enters the room with other 'no name' guys, in uniform but they have no rank – nothing on their shoulders, strange that. They look at us all the time not looking away. It gives you the creeps.

'Right gentlemen, let's get on with it. We are not targeting anybody tonight. You are in danger from the word go. Tonight my friends, be on your toes. You have no back-up. You will fly with co-ordinates supplied to you when you take-off. Do not, I repeat, *do not* open this document until you are airborne. this is imperative to the success of this mission. There is no room for failure. You will pick up at a rendezvous a very special person that has Top Secret information for the eyes and ears only of the Allied Supreme Command. Thank you gentlemen. This is, I am sure you will know, very important, I cannot emphasise enough the importance of this mission. You have been selected from your various squads. Do not disappoint me. This is a joint venture on behalf of the joint Allied Forces coming together. Thank you. You are to depart gentlemen in one hour – the time now being 2000hrs. Good luck.'

My heart is beating so much it feels as if it will burst out of my chest, my pulse is racing away. What is all this about? I wonder where it is taking me personally – I have never come across such secrecy before, such profound ignorance of personal safety. Why should we risk life and limb to bring somebody back? There must be a better way – a more covert mission by submarine perhaps, surely much safer for everybody concerned? But who am I? A pawn in a more sinister chess game perhaps? That is all it is – a game to be played out. We are used by those in power to execute these charades to better one against the other. I am sure if I expressed my own thoughts about what is going on to my superiors or friends I would certainly find myself on court martial, very severely reprimanded or in the most extreme case, in prison. But I have my opinions and I will keep these to myself for they have no room. As far as I am concerned I have a job to do and I intend to do that job to the best of my ability; I owe it to the guys that surround me with their courage and knowledge not to give credibility to doubt in any way.

* * * * * * *

Michael

It may seem corny to a lot of people but patriotism is strong in me whether or not I come from the USA – it would be just as strong if I came from elsewhere. Before I carry on I must give reference to a loved one. I am to be married in two weeks time to a lovely girl I met here in England – I hope to take her back to America to live our lives together and fulfil all my dreams[1]. Her name is sacred to me and I carry her photograph everywhere. She does not know of my missions to occupied Europe in the covert way we work. Obviously she is aware of the Air Force and its role in the war but I do not discuss it with her, the less she knows the better.

I love her and she loves me – that is all that matters. Love conquers all. You can face the gates of hell itself with love by your side and you can conquer anything. I know. I have faced death many times and I feel at ease with the very thought of it. I am very lucky in a way – there are plenty of guys in the force that have no one and do face and accept death. To go with nobody by your side is a tragedy, believe you me. I am very lucky and I count my blessings indeed. So a thought goes to my fiancée at this time, my heart is with her. I go to do this for my country but they cannot and will not have all of me. That which is most sacred I give to those I love.

Now to work, the last things to be done are more morbid – the letter. Obviously to my fiancée, but as I am not married yet I have to leave a letter for my parents, a last will and testament if you like, it scares me to write it. The very thought of my mother opening the letter: the postman or representative from the government standing on the porch with the obvious look on their faces. It fills me with remorse and convulsion for the sake of my mother whom I love dearly; I would not take her through such pain – I would make sure that this will not happen.

We are all fired up now, we are ready to go. The night air has a certain chill about it. The drone of the engines, the smell of the burning fuel, the uneasy feeling in the pit of your stomach – all these things you feel one after the other as if to torment you to the very end. There are guys that surround me who feed on this kind of adventure, they love it. That is what they are here for, to live this moment. They were living boring lives back in the States, just bumming along some of them – now they have a purpose. A lot will die before experiencing fully the horror of all this but maybe that is what they are here for and myself included – self-sacrifice, a very hard decision to make. It is easy to say but to act it out for real is a very big step indeed and not to be taken lightly, by no stretch of the imagination. These decisions have been taken away from you, you just act it out. If your number is up, if your name is on the bullet, there is no way of dodging it.

The night air gives me the shivers. Can I run away from this? I do not think so. The love of what I do coupled with the love of my country buckles it up together and we get on with it. All suited up now, the short walk to the aeroplane – the monster at night. They are incredible machines to look at in the light of day but to see them at night is awesome. They swallow you up, you feel safe within their shadow and as you go on board you become one with it. For the next few hours we are at one and they are here to protect us. If they fall we all die – the plane as well – but you feel that won't happen, no matter what.

We go through the procedures; I am on tail gun tonight, I don't mind this post, I would prefer to be flying this beast but it is not my time. Let us see what the night brings forward. The secrecy surrounding this mission is something I have not come across in any sortie yet. I am looking forward to this but I am nervous of it also. We taxi to the end of the runway, we sit and wait. These few minutes seem like hours. The lights of the runway ahead, beckoning us to go to each in turn to say goodbye. We cannot wait too long, the chance of the airfield being bombed is heightened even more so by leaving it too long – we must hurry. Slowly the tyres edge forward eating up the lights as we go, then before you know we leave them behind and gone. We're off.

Take-off is always bad for me – it is something I have to live with, even though I love flying I still have this burden. I settle down by myself in the tail. On an ordinary run I would be testing my ammunition by now but as this is a secret mission – and by all accounts a lot is riding on this – we do not want to be recognised in any way. We may even have our own guys shoot us down, we cannot even have a conversation – we have total radio blackout so we just sit tight. It is time to get some sleep, I will wake soon enough if anything happens.

Then it is time to awake – lots of flak around us. Didn't expect this, for one thing the secrecy of this mission would have put us in some form of safety in only being one plane but it seems we have been caught out. With radio silence we do not know if we dare land. This guy we're picking up seems really important – so what do we do? Is the flak gunning for us? It seems as though our mission is so secret that the bomber squadrons are going ahead with nightly raids, so maybe if we change our course and go around from the south instead of the intended north, maybe we can skip a lot of this.

We all get the jitters now. This is so important – one little mistake and we've blown it. We are soon over the proposed target area. We have a set time – the lights of their makeshift runway will only come on for a few seconds at a time until they see our lights. The lights come on now and stay on – this is it. In we go, make it in fast. Slowly we descend – the final bump of the wheels – this field is really bumpy to say the least. Please stop!

We round about and cut our engines. Kevin is closest to the door, he opens it and the night air rushes in. We do not know what to expect, who is this mystery man – or woman for that matter? The pilot rushes forward, 'Let's get this going guys, I want this baby in the air as soon as possible.'

There's a lot of shaking of hands. In the distance this figure comes walking towards us, immaculate white coat, obviously an officer – an American officer. He walks closer. I've seen this guy at Thorpe Abbotts;

he was with one of the crews out of Seething as well. Some big shot from back home. His face I know – some movie actor – what's so special about this guy with all the secret stuff as well? Oh well, we've just risked our necks to save this fly guy.

He gets into the plane – wants to shake everybody's hand. Walks up to me and looks me in the eye, 'You. I know I owe you my life. What's your name soldier?'

'I am not a soldier sir.'

'Never mind, guy, I owe you one – can't say any more my friend, mum's the word on this one. If the Germans had have got me this time I do not know if I could stand it. I would have shot myself instead of their interrogation methods.'

Who is this guy? It's no good I will find out sooner or later. 'Let's get this mother fucker home to bed guys!' says a voice from the bulkhead. I'll second that, back to Blighty for us! She picks up speed and we're away, let's get home. His name I cannot remember, some movie big shot. I will find out more information later, I must find out for myself what was the importance of risking our lives to pick him up?

It seems the real reason for us to go over and pick this guy up is not what it seems. Confusion is the word. I end up talking to this guy on the way back and as for keeping Top Secret material in his head, all he shares with us is that he had a bloody good time at the Gestapo's expense. Brave bastard, he's got some front. This guy jokes all the time, obviously one for the ladies – makes you sick – he comes across as if he's a double agent. You hear of these guys, they have no fear; the ordinary bloke in the street would not stand a chance against guys like these, they are a breed of their own, lone wolves that do the business and then disappear into the night like the scarlet pimpernel or something.

Then it comes to me – got his name! He really is a movie big shot and all round American hero. There was another guy with him dressed virtually the same, but the movie actor had centre stage so the other guy just slipped into the plane as easy as you like. What I feel is strange though is that he disappeared into the cockpit area – no one is allowed in there, that guy must be the real reason for us to be over here. Oh well, just blend into the background now and get on with my job.

The movie actor stares at me and a couple of the other guys – a stare that puts a shiver down your back. He says, 'What's the joint mission for guys? What's wrong with a B-17 or a B-24 taking this mission? Why do the Limeys have to butt in?'

The British guys listening to this start to grumble amongst themselves – one guy gets up, 'We risked our lives to get you out of danger – fuck you asshole. I would drop you back in the drink if it was up to me so just sit down and shut the fuck up!'

He looks over to me and smiles. 'Having a bad day is he, friend?'

'Mike's the name.' I say.

'I know,' he says, 'I know a lot of things. Thanks anyway. Don't want any trouble.'

With that the rest of the journey is uneventful. We cross the Channel and head up the coast, the last thing we want is to be blown away by our own guns.

We land with the sun rising, this has been a long night. I could do with some sleep. We gather our stuff. It's really like heavy now, as we taxi down to the main runway and she shudders to a halt as if stuck in time.

'You guys want to get a soaking or wait?' I just want to get a shower and some shut-eye. The door opens, the transport is there if we want it, I don't bother, the seats are soaking wet. Why bother?

'Hey fella!' I look back, it's the movie actor.

'Just to say thanks again – comrades and all that. The next time you are in New York give us a call, here's my address there. If I am not around just see the housekeeper. She'll let you in, no trouble.'

I say 'Who's the guy that came with you?'

'You don't want to know that. Your life is worth more to the good old USA doing what you know best – killing Germans. Keep it like that. You value your life don't you Mike?'

'Yeah, sure I do.'

'Well, keep quiet. Hey, maybe when I go over to France again I'll ask for you to come over on the plane with us.'

'I'll look forward to that' I say, as he disappears into the Officers' Mess.

Time for a wash and sleep. I do not know when I will be back in the air again, these missions are Top Secret. I wonder how the other guys are doing.

---

[1]Michael Hall and Trish were never actually married due to the various constraints imposed by his superiors and her parents.

Chapter Sixteen
Buck Quinlan

The powers-that-be have really blown me out of the water this time. Whoever pulls the strings of power must hold a really big weight, there's me going through all that training to fly B-17s and here I am flying P-51s! I tell you what, it beats anything I have flown before – you are flying around like a little mosquito compared to the B-17. I did not ask to go on P-51s so why am I here? At the moment I haven't a clue, I am just enjoying the experience. It matters not to me what I fly as long as I finally get home to my wife and child, that's more important to me – let's get this war over so I can get some sanity back into my life.

I am on escort for B-24s at the moment, I have to say I am scared shitless. We have only enough fuel to escort these guys across the Channel and probably to the border of Germany, that's it. Depending on where they bomb it really is a life and death thing. It brings a tear to my eye just seeing them disappearing into the clouds and I cannot go any further, I have seen them dropping out of the air like sacks of shit, me wanting to help them but I cannot – it gets you really deep. I want this fucking war to end! Tears stream down my face. If the guys could see me now – the tough bastard that would go to hell and back crying like a baby!

It all seems to get to me sometimes. The whole thought of us bombing them and them bombing us. My young family back home do not have to run the gauntlet as I do; they do not have to experience the Blitz, the blood and gore that the occupied countries and Great Britain have to suffer. I am thankful for that – knowing they are safe from all this gives me some strength at least. I am not a religious person but I have prayed many times, not only for myself but for my buddies because some of them deserve better – in fact they all do. They give up their lives. We must be thankful for ever for that. To give up your one life – think about it. In situations like this – in war – the true heroes walk forward, their one chance to be alive they give up so readily. Not many do that, I can tell you. I have seen grown men cry in their sleep, I have seen hard bastards crap themselves in this line of work. Death comes with a price.

We all would like to die with some dignity at least – not by having your brains blown out of a cockpit window at 20,000 feet. Not a pretty sight but it would become normal, a sight you would have to endure for a period of time until the landing gear goes down and with the rush of air to your lungs you realise you are back on safe ground. Your buddies shake you by the hand, 'You have brought us back home again Buck. You are special, a very special man. You have been given a gift to handle this monster of a plane like you love it.'

I sit and look at one or two or more of the crew I have spent the last few hours with. Some with their legs blown away, some with their arms shattered – blood everywhere. They do not train you for this but day in, day out you experience it. And then there are the guys that cannot take it anymore – who would rather fall out of their position – bail out and not pull the rip cord. All these things they do not tell you about. You are mere cannon fodder for them. We unite under one flag that is true but we fall divided. You must look after yourself in this war. You bond together much more – you look after each other if you think the same. Believe me, it works – we are all mavericks. I cry for my friends but we are all on our own.

As I was saying, the powers-that-be must either have something really good in store for me or they wish to see me dead.

Chapter Seventeen
Steve Lursquom – Seething 1943

I'm really fucked off with this English weather it's getting me down like hell. I'm missing home really bad now. We had these strange guys come into the camp the other day asking for two of us by name. The camp commander asked for us to be...actually asked is the wrong word, he *told* *us* to be in his office *pronto!* I didn't know what the hell was going on.

'These guys are from Special Branch, some organisation within the British government, all very hush-hush as they call it. Steve it seems you are moving up the road for a short period of time. You are still an American so the British haven't got all the say but this is a joint decision come from the very top – our joint Chief-of-Staffs and the British top brass. They have your file now Steve, you will go with them.'

This all comes as a bloody shock. I am supposed to be over here with USAAF not some super spy outfit. I have no choice in this, I best go along with it. They take me to a camp within Thetford Forest, this camp is guarded very well – you do not even realise it is here. I have flown over this area a lot in the last year and no way could you see it.

We are treated very well I have to say, shower, a decent bed, good grub – I get settled. Obviously there are others in the camp but by the looks of those in charge silence is the order of the day. I am summoned to an office, I knock.

'Come in.' It is dark but for a small light on a table in the middle of the room. A man in a suit stands up, beckons me forward. 'I understand they call you 'Stevie' – is that right?'

'Only my closest buddies know that on the camp.'

'Don't worry, we have your file – everything is known to us. I even know how many craps you have a day son!'

As he laughs, his so-called colleagues give out a roar of laughter also, 'You think he jokes Mr Lursquom?'

I turn around. I am looking at a sterner person now – obviously the boss. 'Sit down please. I suppose you are wondering why you are here?'

'Well the subject did cross my mind.'

'Well, we will keep you in suspense no longer.' This guy is like something out of Shakespeare – he would be well at home in some dungeon.

'Dear boy, you have talent that we are sadly lacking in the British armed forces. It brings me to say that if we had a choice and we had the talent which you have within our own lot, you would not be sitting here. But that is not to be. You, my friend, are an ace shot – is that so?

'Yes I am. Have you that on my file?'

'Yes indeed we have, and much more besides. We are obviously not going to just take it for granted that you can fire a rifle, we have to let you take a few tests. We want you to team up with one of our chaps to spend at least a week deep in Thetford Forest. You have a target. You have a two-man team after you. You will have to keep out of sight for a week my friend. This target is always moving. This, my friend is not a game, the probable, and I say again *probable* end to the war edges on this one little exercise. You shoot to kill my friend – there is no second chance. You act as a team. At this time the team that hunts you are exactly the same. You succeed and you live.

My hands are now very sweaty indeed. I cannot control my anger. 'Do I have a choice?' I croak.

'At this time in the game no, I am afraid not. There is too much riding on this, you know too much now. Once organised and we know who to send, this may be an end to a lot more bloodshed – the overall need of the masses overrides that of the individual. You ask if you have a choice – yes, you do. Return to your duties at your base but I cannot say that you will live very long – you will be constantly looking over your shoulder Steve. You, my friend, are a very lucky man – you have a gift, a gift given by God, and you must use that to obliterate the foe at the door. That will be all gentlemen, thank you for your time. Proceedings will commence in exactly twelve hours from now. Good luck and good hunting.'

Twelve hours doesn't give you a lot of time. What should I do? Sleep? Go for a beer? It could be the last one I have – savour it or be a right bastard and get pissed? Well, none of the above. Let's just see who this target is. I want to see this out. Whatever the chiefs have got cooking it's something hot in the pot and by the looks of things I am not the only recruit – especially not from the American side, there are just as many Brits. The one thing that puzzles me is we are a joint team, one Yank, one Brit in each team and I am assuming there are two teams – it could be more. They are obviously siding their bets.

What would my dad think of all of this? All his training, hoping I would go into law enforcement, if he only knew that I was working for a much higher power it would make him proud I am sure. Oh well, a bit of practice wouldn't go amiss down at the rifle range – a couple of hours' target practice. The shots ring out one after the other – dead in the middle, every time.

A small crowd gathers behind the screens to watch me – I just trigger, watching, my eye never leaving the sight. I sense energy around me, I am focused on the target – I turn around with speed, the gun ready.

'Ok,' says one of the blokes to the side, 'we were just admiring your shots man, no offence.' A trickle of applause is heard, then a thumping of wood in appreciation.

I feel good now – a sense of believing and trust. I give thanks for my father's teaching and must go forward now and get my gear together. I do not know what this Thetford Forest is like. Not concerned – must focus on target. I do not know the name of the other guy, I know he is a

Brit and that is all. I do not know who the other team is – they probably do not know who I am.

It is time to start. The big chief meets us at the gate. 'Hello gentlemen. We await your arrival with the trophy. You have one week gentlemen. Your time starts now.'

We rush into the forest like the wind. We are given maps – that is all – of strategic points within the forest showing clearings and the like. We have also to live off the land, rabbits and hares are our best bet but we cannot use our rifles – that would be too easy. No, we must set up our own traps or starve for a week.

Before very long we begin to feel exactly what they meant when they spoke to us in the huts before this exercise, I am in a serious position here – this means business. I know I am a good shot but this is like nothing I have experienced before and why I am experiencing it now baffles me. Deep down inside I know something big is going on but I have to bite my tongue and get on with it. My partner in this is just as inexperienced as I am; we are thrown in the deep end with this, we are being hunted as well – it keeps you on your toes I can tell you. You keep focused. I still cannot understand this British stiff-upper-lip attitude to life – even in war they are a breed apart. Laughing and joking is not one of their best assets I have to say.

I have to switch on now. We have been searching these forests for two days now, sleeping when possible. No sign of the teams out for us, or of our target. We have come close to troops on manoeuvres but successfully got around that situation by digging in and keeping quiet. We only have two magazines of bullets so we have to be vigilant at all times – to become part of this forest is a must-do thing.

There are markers we come upon now so we must be getting close or the target is on the move – we do not know. Then, suddenly without warning a shot rings out and my partner is lying by the side of the tree where he was resting, a bullet hole between his eyes. My insides suddenly want be free of my physical body. Panic envelops me, I do not know which way to turn. I am on my own now – I do not know if the target is aware of me but I do know the bullet has found its mark.

Whatever the situation I have to remove myself from here; I run as fast as I can, gathering what supplies my friend had and his gun and ammo. Goodbye friend – I didn't know his name. I get out of there fast. The strange thing is only one bullet and that was it, these guys are good snipers. From now on I take this seriously, I must find the target and finish this. Going over to Germany every day in a Flying Fortress is heaven compared to this. I must become a chameleon – a shadow, and disappear into the night.

The night brings cold but I find shelter in the undergrowth. I have enough supplies for a couple of days at least, hopefully enough to survive this. Must get my head down – get some sleep. The morning brings rain – lots of it. I really don't want this on top of everything, what else do you expect in this country but weather you cannot predict?

I could do with a good bath, I feel like shit. Must focus – I gather myself and am aware of everything around me. Being in the forest for three days you become more aware of sounds, the little noises that should not be there are at full volume – a rustling in the trees, vehicles in the distance which sound very close but could be a long way off. Sounds such as these are now vibrating in my inner ear like a warning siren. I go towards them like an arrow out of its master's bow – like the wind rushing through greenery – unaware of nothing but aware of everything. I drop like a stone. There in front of me is a group of Germans! I have to rub my eyes to make sure I haven't been in a dream, or am I hallucinating from drinking the crap water?

No, these are real fucking Germans, two Panzer tanks, all having a nice breakfast around a campfire! I look through my lens. I am still having a hard time believing what the fuck I'm seeing. This is Thetford Forest in England – what the hell are a group of Jerries doing here? The group are laughing and joking; there's a tent in camouflage, light blue in colour, to my right. Its flap opens and an officer walks out clutching a map and shouts to the group around the fire – their immediate response is to salute and run around like headless chickens. The officer goes back to the tent. He just opens the flaps and stands there.

Out of the darkness of the tent comes a smallish figure dressed in bright blue, a cross of iron around this man's neck. Something inside tells me this is the big chief – the big fish. Should I fire and make my mark? Is this for real? Would a soldier give up his life for target practice? I have just witnessed my partner being wiped out for nothing so maybe these are genuine German POWs who have been given a chance to live – to act out a play in the middle of a forest, unaware that any one of these mother fuckers is on the end of a rifle's sights.

Well it's me or them. I am going to be more aware than the norm. I am going to take out as many as I can in one swoop, I have enough ammo. Now I gather myself – get ready. The big fish first. The sweat trickles down the handle as I look at the sight – this has not happened before. Right. My finger closes on the trigger then I feel a slight breeze on my left ear, the barrel of a gun pointing now at my temple.

'Easy son, I know what you're thinking. You want to take out the whole platoon but you're not General Custer and you aren't in the plains of America now boy. Just focus on the little bastard all dressed in blue – go right between the eyes. Make your shot. Do it now.'

What can I do? I have no time for questioning this any more, I let fly. The bullet bites through the air like a crack of a whip. It strikes – the target falls. There is panic all around. They flee like rabbits.

'Well done lad, you have passed. Your buddies were well onto you unfortunately. They had a target as well but you have success written all over you. Please return to camp now with us for a briefing.'

With this I turn around and say, 'Forgive me sir but what the fuck is going on? What did we give up two innocent lives for – an exercise?'

With this statement the guy turns round and smiles. 'All for King and country my lad – those Germans are fucking dead as far as we are concerned and as for your partner he knew the score as you did. We are not pissing around with this. It means the end to this exercise. Please remove yourself back to camp.'

I do not know what I have got into. This is crazy. I have no option but to go along with it, self-will in this predicament is absent to say the least. I wish I was back in camp having a laugh with my buddies.

Chapter Eighteen
Rupert Kovloski

There is one thing that puzzles me with the British. They have to know everything. My name brings forward suspicion – they cannot accept that I am an American and be done with it. Unlike some of the other guys, I volunteered for this. To remove myself from the shit of maybe being blown out of the skies somewhere a long way from my country and not even having the dignity of some part of my anatomy dropping on American soil – it has to be in some part of Europe or the North Sea. Well, they can whistle for that. Let's see what the British have got in store.

As soon as I get here they want me to sign a document, what that is I do not know – you're given no choice. Something to do with the Secrets Act or treason, these are the words I remember on the bit of paper. I know from reading in the history books back home that the English were a bit hot on things like this – executions and all that. They even executed their own king so that tells you a lot.

We are shown into a blacked-out room. No one is allowed to speak, we only listen. 'Good morning gentlemen. You are all supposed to be good marksmen, yes? Well, we shall see. You have one week to accomplish your mission. You have two targets on foot, they are hunting as you are hunting. It is either you or them – a policy of shoot to kill. Is that clear?'

With that statement it's hard to understand the logic. This doesn't sound like the good old British fair play we have come to learn. Well, this is a first.

'Gather your supplies gentlemen. You have exactly two hours to prepare yourself. You are segregated from others in the camp. You are a two-man team.'

I look about in the darkness. I know there are people around me but say nothing. Then a hand hits my shoulder like a hammer, 'You're with me, old boy. Glad to have you on board... a Yank, hey? Good shooting. Jolly good!' And with that he disappears.

I don't know, I'm going for a crap and a bath in that order, and then to get my gear together. Two hours fly by just like that. We meet at the gate to the camp at exactly the time allocated.

'Right, gentlemen! Good hunting, one week!'

With that we run out of the camp as if we are both in a race. We do not talk much in the next few hours, I am slowly coming to terms with exactly what's going on.

'Look old mate, we're in this together. Cheer up – you could be stuck in one of those flying machines you call bombers. Nothing like the good old Lancaster – it would blow the fuck out of yours.'

My lip is slowly getting swollen with me biting on it and wanting to punch the fuck out of this toffee-nosed British bastard. What does he know about self-sacrifice on a day-to-day basis? Let him get on with it. We venture into the forest always on the look out – be aware of sounds that are out of the ordinary. The night is falling rapidly and the thought of spending more time than I have to with this Pratt really pisses me off, but I must get on with it. The next few days go by uneventfully. Whoever these targets are they're good.

On walking out of a clearing I hear the snap of a twig. I fall to the ground – my partner also aware of the sound does the same. I am not waiting for him; I am going forward and seeing what's about. There are two guys not agreeing with each other – one sitting by a tree, the other on lookout. This is my opportunity – a clear shot to the head. I level myself, compose, breathe one...two...and on the third breath release, right between the eyes. He slumps forward and with that I get a barrel in my back.

'Well done son.' I look round and it's my so-called partner! 'You have passed the test.'

'Sorry?' I say.

'You have passed the test. We now return to the camp and await further orders.'

Still a bit bemused, I have no choice. On reflection I am sure I know that other guy who was in my sights – he is an American flyer like myself but that can't be right. What in the hell are we firing at each other like this for?

Chapter Nineteen
Bernie Jameson

As we sit here waiting for the 'big push' as we are told, it seems to me that what is going on around this camp in particular is not all it seems. This out-of-the-way place in the middle of nowhere is suddenly the centre of attention for a lot of the top brass. We hear so many rumours floating around that it's best just to get on with it – forget the trappings and get on with the main meal. But it is getting to the point where a lot of the crews are coming back with stories so bizarre I cannot get to grips with it at all.

They say that on particular missions they are being fired upon coming home by the locals – this takes some getting used to! When I say 'locals' I mean the localised batteries up and down the coast. It has been reported to the authorities but with no response from any of our chiefs or the Allies. The British are not too keen on us being over here I know but we have sacrificed a lot of our guys for this cause and that goes deep within the crews – they matter, not the top brass – they do not go up in the air above occupied Europe and Germany every day sacrificing their lives.

All these things go through your mind when you climb on board one of these winged machines and you think this may be your last time of doing all this. And if it is my time, how will I go? In pain? Will it be swift? Will I be left with no sight or no limbs? Will I live like a vegetable? The actual fact of dying would be pleasing in that situation because to be left with a serious injury would be a living death.

I know I have been earmarked for night ops but I must admit I am not looking forward to that one bit, at least when going up in the light my aiming is good. The night throws it all up in the air for me – I do not feel comfortable with that. Perhaps they will not pick me, I might be lucky and not be listed – you never know.

I am with a good crew at the moment, we look after each other like brothers. We have a good laugh – you have to – it breaks the monotony of all this. I try and win a few bob off the locals down at the pub, but not too much – they get angry and that can cause problems. We take so much then return to base, we know when our company is no longer wanted. I find the locals very suspicious of us – they look on us as very strange people. They are set in their ways, they have had to put up with a lot, we know.

But someday soon this will all be over and then all that has happened will have to be justified – us in what we have done, the British in what they have done but more importantly, what the enemy has done. I know in my heart that we will be the victors in this and God willing, I will be enjoying the laughter and tears of victory also and not lying in some field with my guts all over somebody's corn and hedgerows. I count myself lucky up to now, the endless missions seem like we go up, focus on a job of work, and come home. You have that feeling in the pit of your stomach at each mission briefing that will not go away but you have to put up with it. So with that in mind I now go on my seventh mission from this base at Seething, going into occupied France and hitting an ammo plant that has been detected by Special Forces.

They do not specify who these Special Forces are – that is not our business to know. The little we do know is to our advantage because if we go down and survive we are at risk of being interrogated by 'The Fury' as we call them – the Gestapo. We all fear this. We call them The Fury because one of the guys in a B-17 called *Fist of Fury* was captured by the Gestapo and would not let on about anything. He was the only survivor of that plane – the rest of the other guys got blown away in a ball of fire. He managed to right the plane but with it going out of control and the fire spreading fast, he took his only chance and bailed out. He only had time to pull his ripcord – if he had left it any longer he would have been splattered all over the place. He came down in a forest – got stuck in some trees half-way down and was dangling there.

Unlucky for him there was a group of German soldiers camped in a clearing not so far away; they made a laugh out of it, calling and mocking him as they shot at the trail of parachute above him.

This did not go down too well with Steve – he shouted at them in his best Californian accent to 'Shoot the fuck and get it over with, you square-headed bastards.' As the last shot rang out he fell very quickly, injuring his ankle. He was happy with this, but being prodded with bayonets and told to get up and walk soon changed that.

Obviously this group of Germans were not equipped to deal with an American flyer – they had other things on their minds, they were on the move and quickly by all the shouting and the starting of engines. There was something going on but he didn't know what, Steve was hoping he would perhaps be left at this base, unfortunately this was not meant to be. He didn't know where he was; he was bundled into the back of a truck and knocked out cold on the head.

He awoke in a pit. Pitch black. He couldn't see his hand in front of his face. That it stank of piss and shit he did know, and other smells that he didn't want to know of. His ankle now seemed like a lead weight on his foot. He wished he could close his eyes and open them quickly and be with his buddies again; unfortunately this was not to be the case – he had to grin and bear it. When he had been knocked out he had a deep dream where he felt he was with his buddies, floating along, seeing all the flames engulf the plane and they were still in it, not burning – just floating in the air. Then his buddies were floating outside his cockpit window begging for him to come with them.

Steve awoke with a shock – the pit now became a grave. Time just went on and on. He had to have a piss. If he did this over somebody then their anger would at least break the silence. No such luck – he was just pissing in the stale water and crap around him. Suddenly a light above him as a lid opened out.

'You come, my friend.' Two hands came out of the light, pulling him bodily out of the darkness – the light penetrating his eyes like daggers. He opened one eye then the other to look around and down at where he had been.

The harsh voice came again, 'Come my friend. We have a facility for you to wash and make yourself comfortable. As you are in uniform we must assume you to be a POW. Now, that is what you are? Please come this way.'

With that he beckoned Steve towards a room – hot water, a bath. I must take advantage of this, he thought, I do not know what is in store for me – who knows? He composed himself to focus on the things he loved – to break now would be to put all his friends in danger. The door opened.

'You are well my friend? We will get some attention to your ankle. Do you think it is broken?'

'No I think I have strained or twisted it.'

'Just to make sure my friend, we will have the doctors to come in and give you a look.'

This guy seemed friendly enough but there seemed deep undertones to his voice. Steve felt calm in his manner but he also felt he was being sized up mentally.

'We have all the time in the world my friend. We will see you soon.' With that he glanced up at Steve through his monocle with a look that would put the fear of the devil in you. His black…pure black uniform; the red and white band on his upper arm with the swastika shining out from the white background; his immaculate black boots; his red lapels with the cross of iron upon them, and the cross of iron dangling below his chin as if he was born with it around his neck.

The door closed. I am in deep shit now, how the fuck am I going to get out of this, Steve thought. The door opened and a tray was placed in front of him by what can only be described as a walking robot. He was immaculate, a storm trooper. We heard about these guys before coming out here, we got the low-down on them from briefings back in the States; they look as if they have all been manufactured the same. There was one outside his door all the time. They look like the perfect fighting machine and the stare stops you in your tracks.

The door closed as quickly as it had opened. Steve was left with the tray and silence. Eat it – it may be your last one, he thought. Steve did not know what he was eating but it tasted good – like chicken but he couldn't be certain. The water also had a funny taste.

'Let us begin with your name. Now, let us get on straight away shall we? What is your name?'

Name, rank and number that is all they are getting off me – fuck all else, Steve thought.

'Again – I shall ask no more. What is your name?'

'Steve Riley,' he shouted.

'Good start. What is your rank?'

'Pilot.'

'And your target was?'

Steve shouted '588 63 72.'

'Um. Stubborn hey? Your target! Not your serial number!'

Steve took a deep breath, 'That is all you're getting.'

'Well, we shall see.' The next few hours went like days – interrogation like hell.

'Ok your target. How many in your squadron Steve? Come on, just a few answers and you can have a good sleep.' He was being kept awake – being prodded with needles on his arms. His eyes felt like hell, burning. He couldn't stand any more.

'Let us try one of our own little experiments – a little inducer to hurry things along, I am already late for a dinner appointment. We shall try this.' A white coat came out of the dark and gave him an injection in his forearm. Straight away he went down on his face and they pulled him up again.

'Right Steve let us wait a few seconds and we shall start.'

That is all he remembered. He awoke in the room on his bed. He did not know how long he was out – hours, days – he did not know. He waited now and felt weak. They had managed to bandage his ankle up. The door opened and the guy walked in again.

'Thank you Steve for your cooperation. You will be transported to Colditz Castle with your friends. Thank you.'

With that he was bundled into a truck in the middle of the night. It set off with maybe six or seven other blokes in the truck with him and two guards sitting on the back. Just nods of heads that's all – by the state of some of them they were lucky to be alive. They had been travelling for about two hours when there was an explosion and the truck came to halt, its brakes burning. As they held on to the side panels the two Germans straight away pointed their guns at them and fired into the roof of the truck. Then the flap opened with a shout of 'Get the fuck down!'

With that they hit the deck as machine gun fire lit up the back of the truck, igniting the tarpaulin roof. Fire was now slowly spreading over the top, the two German officers riddled with bullets – not a lot left of their faces.

'You guys ok? Let's get the hell out of here!'

They all jumped out and made off with the noisy rabble ahead of them. The truck was now fully ablaze and ready to blow. They ran into the forest and out of sight with the Free French Resistance being led by an English guy. 'Come on now chaps. It's back to dear old Blighty for you Yanks – you know you love her.'

Steve made his way back to England first by getting to the coast, and then by submarine – fucking lucky or what? I wish all my buddies were so lucky. So, every time you jump in that plane thank your lucky stars you come home every night. After what happened to Steve, he can think himself lucky for meeting up with that English guy leading a pack of French wolves in the night. I thank the Lord every night and every day, and ask Him to look after me. I hope he does on this mission.

As we progress into the depths of this war and all it brings, it strikes me as how we have all been manipulated, and how we must all pay the price of giving up our everyday lives and go and do some faceless person's dirty work. I for one am not too pleased with the thought of that, but in society and under the government that runs that society, we have to conform with the rules that are set out. There are rules in everything. I suppose we have to have them because otherwise there would be no justice and people would get away with lots of things. Not until you are confronted with the mass exodus of one country against another do you realise the magnitude of how hate and greed can manifest itself. Because at the end of the day that is all it is, and through one or two persons' greed and hate they will influence lesser-willed persons, and they in turn will do the same, and before you know where you are it escalates to such a degree of consumption that it is hard to breathe. And so it is – good against evil all the time and in the process there has to be casualties along the way. Self-survival is the key in all this. Work at the survival and look after number one and hopefully we will get through this terrible time.

'Beloved, we are gathered here today to give thanks to this soldier of fortune who gave up his life so his friends could go on.'

It seems ironic that phrase 'Beloved we are gathered here today'. I have heard those few choice words over and over again; countless guys walking to their deaths – for what? There must be a purpose to your life, and we are not some number that can be put away and forgotten or used to be cannon fodder for the powers-that-be. The pain and suffering of people must not go on because simply someone wills it to be.

We love our country and the basis of our lives is sacred, and the families around us mean that much to us. Obviously we have to defend what is ours and our way of life, but at the expense of so many lives? And in this respect the argument may only be between a handful of people who ultimately will not come face-to-face with death over it. It will be left to the lone person going about his business not hurting anyone, who will get a letter through the post stating in a very formal heading that he must report immediately to his nearest station of embarkation to be given further orders – to in fact go and blow somebody's brains out because *we want you to*.

That at the end of the day is what it's all about – the sacrifice of them before us. Who is greater? Who will win the day? I hope very much it is us who will win the day before my death.

Chapter Twenty
Al Permando

Days on the base are very long now. They are very clever, the bosses. They keep you going night and day, looking at you like lab rats in a cage – you will go and bomb this target today and you will have the support of these other groups along the way – then they go and disappear back into their little concrete bunkers, until the next time. I know something big is in the air, after this amount of time stuck with the same people you get to know what has good feelings and what hasn't and there has been a sense of expectancy about this base for a couple of weeks now. Guys have disappeared for a while and when they come back they are not the same. I cannot explain it – it seems as if they have somehow been brainwashed because the personalities of these men are not the same, they are like robots. They go about their business and actually like going over Allied Europe to most probably be captured in enemy territory – they have no fear; those of us who have not had this personality change look upon these people with disgust but who is at fault here? We say anything and what happens? We go on record for insubordination and court martial if we disagree with what's going on.

There definitely is something not right. I intend to find out exactly what's going on, it's in my nature to find things that do not add up. My roots are Italian-American and we do not sit down to be counted and used like everybody else, we ask questions. Why? That is our way. On our last mission we lost our ball turret gunner, he bought it big time. We had to virtually sweep him up and mop up the remains of this poor guy inside his glass coffin. To be a buddy of someone and have to squeeze his blood out of a sponge into a bucket brings it on a different level somehow.

If I survive this war I will not be the same person who left my family three years ago, and if my family do expect me to be the same then they are in for a shock to the system, believe me. That man was a buddy, he saved my life and I owe him a lot. Perhaps someday I will tell him so to his face - perhaps. I have a deep feeling inside that I too will not survive this conflict, it is a knowing that somewhere along the line my name is on a certain bullet and that bullet is waiting for me.

The group of guys that I fly with are a very close unit – to lose one is a blow. The old gal that we go about our business in, *The Pegasus*, or *Flying Pegasus* as we in the crew affectionately call her, keeps us safe. Names are given to our babies and that is what they are, newborn babies when they come to us, so we give them names to carry – like us. We cannot go through life without a name, and they mean the difference between life and death to us, so we give them what is rightfully theirs to keep. There is a certain magic within a name, *Pegasus* – the winged messenger from the gods, a name with power in itself. The fact is that all our contemporaries in the conflicts before, right the way back in time, rode horses into battle; in our case, it's a winged horse.

'Dearly beloved, we gather here today to give this soldier of fortune back to the creator from whence he came. I did not know this man, for as a chaplain of this great army air force I have to perform many of these ceremonies and I cover many bases within this area. But I have spoken to his crew and friends on the base that knew him, and he was loved by many of you, and he touched the funny bone in you even if he didn't know you personally. His sacrifice is our loss and with this I commend him to the Almighty, earth to earth, ashes to ashes. We must carry on in his light from our darkness. Amen.'

Walking away from his grave and hearing all that from the chaplain really brings it home to you. I didn't think it was going to affect me as much as this, losing somebody that close, I hadn't experienced that, not even family loss. A new guy has been brought in to take over his job, some guy from Kentucky – one of these what I call 'robots'. He doesn't hang around with us and supposedly came from another base so I do not know what his background is. He doesn't say much – just gets on with the job. I have noticed one thing though, he looks at the planes going in and out of the base a lot closer than we do – I mean like obsessive. Watches them out and coming in like a hawk – gives you the creeps – and then he sleeps. Doesn't mix with us drinking down the local and all that, he doesn't speak of family or loved ones. Something's not right. I will be glad when Mike and the rest of the guys get back so we can have a laugh again.

Chapter Twenty-One
Mike Preston

Coming back from missions I get very cold streaks in my back. I don't know if they are nerves or what, but they worry me to the extent of going to the doctor back at the base to see what the problem is. Being a navigator you just take the flak from the other guys in the crew and let the main man get on with flying the bucket. I must admit I would like to have a go in the hot seat at some stage in this crazy fucked-up war – who wouldn't? Maybe I'll get a shot at it one day, who knows.

I really miss some of the guys in the base, we have a good crowd. There are a few scattered around now going on other missions from other bases in and around the country. Here we get moved around quite a lot. With casualties and everything you might get a crew stay together for a while but sooner or later one will bite the dust or you'll be split up in some way or, if the whole crew gets blown away, then everything disappears. I don't know how the top brass does it but they just vanish overnight – bed, clothes, private belongings, and pictures if they have any; the lads say it's because they don't want the other crews dwelling on the loss of their friends. All we are to them are numbers – don't we mean anything to these people?

After all, without us it wouldn't work. Still, had we a choice to come out here in the first place? I don't think so. It was all sorted out beforehand. We must carry on – the end justifies the means in their eyes. So much for democracy. I bet one day in the long distant future we will all be forgotten. People will walk their dogs and plough these fields that surround the bases and we will be trampled in with this dirt and be forgotten. In time perhaps, but at this very moment we are the centre of attention.

Off we go to see the doctor. I hope to sort this problem out. The room is full as I approach the nurse who's in charge of this lot, 'Any chance of an appointment with the doctor?'

'Not for about two hours,' she replies, 'is it an emergency?'

'No, it'll wait.'

'I'll put your name down and when it's your turn I'll give you a shout, how's that?'

'Thanks.' I manage to get a chair in the corner – may as well have some shut-eye while I'm here.

'Excuse me.' I awake with a start to a few laughs in the now not so full room, 'Excuse me.'

'Yes?'

'You are next in. Did you have a nice sleep then?'

I must have done. 'How long was I out?'

'Just over an hour'

Wow! That just went like that – it seems like a split second ago I closed my eyes. I look round. The faces I see are distant, not here; these guys have problems – not only physical ones but mental ones as well.

'Flight – you're next,' as a waving arm from the window distracts my attention, 'he will see you now.' As I walk into the room the tingle up my back gets a lot worse – it definitely is nerves.

'Sit down son, won't be a minute. Right then, what's the problem – let me guess? Local ladies – you have a problem? Get my drift?'

I look at him and laugh 'Chance would be a fine thing. I wouldn't call that a problem anyway.'

The doctor interrupts me abruptly. 'Well I beg to differ – I've seen some right sights in that department since being here. Some of them made me want to squint a bit!'

'No it's nothing like that. It's just when I go on missions – up to take-off, for a few minutes into a mission, on the way back and landing, I get cold feelings on my back and neck. I cannot explain it. Is it nerves?'

'It sounds like it to me. What about your seat? Do you feel comfortable in the seat in the cockpit?'

'Yeah. No problem there.'

'I tell you what, I will give you these pills – they should at least calm you down.'

Oh. 'Calm you down' – that's a good one! The stress we are under and he says take a few pills and all your troubles will go away – wishful thinking on his part. What niggles me is I am fine 95% of the time it's just the fear going out and the fear I get coming back in. It's something I cannot explain.

There was this one guy going over on a routine mission – straightforward enough. Got all his gear together, went to his post by the side gun, put all his ammo in, did all the checks. The plane taxied out and took off, no problem, and went into formation. As usual going over the Channel, testing the guns and firing at targets; set out flare guns explode to get your sights right, especially for ball turret gunners. Everything going fine and this guy spins around and begins to pour ammo into the back of the buddy at his side, full on. His buddy lost it – slumped like a blown up tomato, there and then panic came aboard that plane. The navigator went for him but got it straight in the head, in line, all the way down – split him in two, blood everywhere. This was not on at all.

The ball turret gunner was going mental – like a little mouse caught in a trap; he was thinking he's next. This had got to stop – the guys in the other planes in formation could see this going on. The pilot obviously hears gunfire but thinks it's target practice. His co-pilot puts him right and with the arrogant look of a flight officer, turns to him and says, 'Sort it, now!' And with that the co-pilot walks back into the plane, looking ahead like a frightened cat waiting to be kicked in the stomach by its irate owner. As the carnage that is all around comes into view he cannot bring it into his conscious state. It is like a dream – a fucking bad dream, and at any moment someone is going to say in his ear 'Wake up you lazy bastard!' But no, it's silent as he sees a guy on the end of a side gun, ammo at the ready, with the look of a rabid dog – the eyes that will not close, staring right down the barrel of this gun.

He is looking at the co-pilot who just wants to fly this bucket to where it does its business and come home again, that is all, not to put up with this shit. Then from outside, a burst of fire, ammo going like crazy, the red bullets coming in through the door and hitting this guy in the side and back like a meat cleaver, slicing him in two as he falls. The co-pilot runs forward and sees a B-17, so fucking close he can touch it. As the pilot gives a salute from the cockpit, under the window the co-pilot sees its name – *Blue Angel* – very apt. He continues to look along its side to the gunner's position where a man is standing by the smoking gun. With another salute they bank into position.

The tail gunner runs up crying, 'What's going on?'

'Just get into position!' says the co-pilot, and with that he goes back up to the cockpit.

'Everything all right now?'

'Yeah, let's get it on and get home.'

On returning home it is explained away as a direct hit by the enemy, something you can explain away in wartime but not in peacetime. The co-pilot on that mission was me. I'll never forget that guy's salute as they banked away back into formation. I owe that crew my life; without their help I would have been mincemeat. They did not survive by all accounts – blown out of the sky over Germany; I don't know the full details but God bless them, they are true angels on your shoulders.

So, going back to the doc, he says 'Chill out for a while and take a few pills as well.'

Um? Oh well, Glenn Miller is playing at the base tonight. I'll go and have a look and try to forget all this for just a few hours until the morning comes and it all starts again. It's about eight o'clock now as we gather at the base hanger. The lights are full on where the band plays – we shouldn't be having so many lights on, the big chiefs get it in the neck from the Brits. Fuck them – we're over here and doing the business. If we wish to die for the Stars and Stripes while listening to the great man Glenn himself, that's up to us.

There's a good crowd here tonight. A few of the guys have come over from the other bases to have a look. It's good to have someone of the likes of this man to boost morale in the ranks. He is of the old country – a genuine guy who reflects the generosity of the nation in music form and delivers it well. There are few home comforts here and it's a slice of our Ma's apple pie here in Little America. So he starts up his band with the charisma of pure genius and the music fills the air with home for a short while.

Chapter Twenty-Two
Glenn Miller

The nights are the worst for me. As I look around at all these faces in the crowd, all different and all surprisingly happy, it feels good to bring some sunshine into these men's lives even if it is just for a brief few minutes of their time. In twenty-four hours they may be dead and we carry on to the next camp to do the same thing and try to bring some sunshine into those lives. The real reason we are here of course is to go where we like – carte blanche; we go into enemy air space and we get away with it. I sometimes have to pinch myself at the very thought of what goes on in and around the corridors of power – what you can get away with and what you can't. What I have experienced doesn't come into it whatsoever. Nothing surprises me, nothing.

We have had clearance from God knows who to go to occupied France. To fly over the Champs-Élysées with the American ensign in full view, land with the Messerschmitts on the same runway, then be greeted by German officers of high rank and play for them. This is a crazy war and no mistake. If the Germans knew we were taking photographs of them all the time from landing to being in their Mess Halls then the Gestapo would have been on to us for sure. It's like being a double agent; you would dearly love to blow one of them away but those are not our orders. Our orders are simple – we have total clearance to go where we please, I say this without joking. We could fly right into Berlin if we chose to – it's the ensign and number, it covers a multitude.

Does that mean we take full advantage of the situation? Believe me the women of France are in my top ten; believe it, we take a chance in this mixed up shit we call a war and take advantage at every opportunity. Do not take us lightly, we are musicians but we also have very important work to do under the disguise of musicians. Spy is not a word that I like because if caught spying it is to the executioner's block straight away – no messing. This is an art form. To spy is an art, to make it talk is an art form. To paint a picture and to make people look at it and see what they truly want, is an art form. I make this so in what I do. I have direct orders from the President himself to bring as much pain to the German authorities as I can under the disguise of a musician, and a damn good one at that.

The German Third Reich made certain things known; that they would give clearance to certain personnel for the trade of American and British POWs. These agreements were looked at very carefully indeed because the trust between the two was not very amicable, obviously. So on a set date the two gave coded messages that would give an absolute verification as to which, with some to-ing and fro-ing, would agree the sacrifice of the one and the sacrifice of the other. For the Germans it would be the sacrifice of Rudolf Hess the Reich Martial, the second Fuhrer – Mein Fuhrer's shadow. His sacrifice would be the catalyst for the likes of myself and other celebrities to roam around and do what they liked for a price: to play to and amuse the troops; not the men on the ground giving their life for the cause but the generals and officers of the Third Reich.

So bizarre is their thinking you can do this. The whole rational aspect of day-to-day living eludes them. They are not rational-thinking people. The poor bastard at the very front gives his life for his country no matter what. On both sides that is so – it has happened for hundreds of years and will probably go on in time. But these generals who have been in direct contact with the Fuhrer and his close ones are of the same breed. They come away brainwashed into thinking: destroy everything that is good for the good of Germany. And so they go on their rampage, bringing in the officers that with a bit of manipulation they can do what they damn well like. The guy in the street is oblivious to this, he thinks they are here for him and so what does he do? He sacrifices himself on the altar which is the front line. Duty calls even if that means giving the ultimate price – your life.

And so we can go about our business – the celebrities and higher ranking officers can go between front lines. We, the Allies, take advantage of the situation. We are not clouded by greed and insanity – we look at the bigger picture. What is happening in Europe is a mighty blood bath that is for sure but we must be level-headed. Through the Liaison Committee – back home that is a different word for covert forces – and the unseen government's wheel turning, my musicians and myself have been invited to go to the Berchtesgaden in Bavaria to entertain the main man. This I would not do and believe me the authorities, supposedly our side, were very insistent on my being at the centre of the Fuhrer's musical extravaganza in his hilltop retreat.

I was insistent that this was against all my principles – that our guys were laying their lives on the line and I was playing to the very bastards we're fighting against? That is how crazy this war is but it is how you look at it that makes it crazy, or very manipulating. I have upset a few people in high places I know, and this is my belief – the guys winning this war are the ones that matter to me. I use the authorities to get what I want for my men and for the guys in the trenches, boats and planes, they do not know of the things that go on in the higher power games of government seats. The President and the Fuhrer are only puppets manipulated by people with deeper issues that can manipulate the masses by bringing forward propaganda.

At a massive level conspiracy is the legacy – row the boat, don't rock it. Celebrities that use the full ticket that they have do take advantage of the situation – who would not? The corridors of power are very long and you can use and pull a lot of strings just by being who you are. Do not underestimate these people – the hidden ones on both sides – they wield power to those that wait to be told and bring that into fruition and duly done. I am but a small cog in a big wheel; we all strive for the end of this conflict. The enemy has no such desire, they intend to inflict much pain to get what they want and then inflict it again and again until they ultimately end up killing themselves.

I know my time is short. I have to look over my shoulder all the time, I know the risks I take. I enjoy what I do – my heart is with the boys who sacrifice themselves day in day out, I give nothing for my life. I have a feeling, perhaps it is nothing, but just in the pit of my stomach I get a pain every time I go behind enemy lines. We take as many photos as we can for the Allied Forces to analyse and use, the German officers even take pictures of us – all in a group like friends. If these pictures hit the streets back home the American people would start questioning it, but saying that, the manipulation of the hidden ones would come into play. Deception on a massive scale – they would come out with a plan of action so devious to swing it around and probably get the Americans to work more in productivity and so on.

I love my country. I know the risks we take. Just to be on the safe side only two of my staff work with me, the rest think we are just good musicians going around building up the morale of the guys. The trips behind enemy lines you can fob off under the Secrets Act: do not speak of these things – walls have ears.

And so as I leave these shores that I have come to love, I go to France for yet another concert. This time I have not been informed as to who we are performing for, this comes direct from the President. It does seem strange though, nobody is coming with me, not even the usual gang that take flights over, and the other odd thing is we have been conscripted an unusually light plane – I am used to B-24s and the P-24s.

Oh well, farewell Great Britain – I will be back soon. The look I get from the pilot – he nearly breaks ice with his stare! The journey is not long – just over the Channel, not very long; no conversation with this guy at all. It's getting a bit choppy – we're not flying that high, I wonder why the guy is now sweating? Something is definitely wrong here.

I look to my left – a storm in the distance, a flash of lightning and a thought. Every plane I fly in has special markings – this one hasn't...now I really do not like this, I try and think positively. Suddenly the door opens and the guy jumps out – leaving me to fly this machine!

I try to bring it around. I look at the panel – there's hardly any juice in this bucket. The bastards have set me up and what a way to do it – straight in the drink!

I must prepare myself. The sea is coming forward now...must pray.

Interlude 2
by Dave Kelly

Mike Preston describing how the famous Glenn Miller band playing live on the base provided the American airmen with some light relief from the horrors of the war at the end of Chapter Twenty-One led unexpectedly into that harrowing communication in the last chapter that seemingly came from Glenn Miller himself. It is shocking in its content and a complete departure from the main story of this book yet the words of the great bandleader whose disappearance has never been officially explained are almost identical in tone to those of Michael Hall and his crew. A similar bitterness and disapproval of the higher authorities shaping their lives is clearly evident in both their testimonies.

However, before Michael takes up his story again in the next chapter, I thought it might be worthwhile to interject a description of another experience or two that accompanied the continuing arrival of the written story which remember, took over five years to come through completely.

During that time we continued to visit connected places like USAAF Station 146 at Seething, the American Military Cemetery at Madingley and later the USAAF base at Thorpe Abbotts near Diss. In fact I went three or four times to Madingley Cemetery in all and I can remember on cold days in winter just walking around the graves and buildings, only because I felt I had to be there and for no other reason.

Once I remember sitting in my car in the cemetery car park after my arrival and I remained very quiet and still for a time. In my mind's eye I saw a particular place – a building, and many horse-drawn carriages bearing coffins going slowly past it, with men in military uniform and marching bands forming a ceremonial procession. It was very sombre. I suppose I saw all this in meditation – a sudden flash of a picture.

Later, when I took a long walk through the cemetery, I suddenly saw that same particular building which hadn't been visible from the car. I learned some time after that this was the place where the first coffins came in when the Americans took over the land for the cemetery from Cambridge University; I had somehow seen images of some of the early funerals.

The other important location in our story which we visited was the USAAF base at Thorpe Abbotts, close to Dickleburgh in South Norfolk – headquarters of the 100th Bomb Group who called themselves 'the Bloody Hundredth'. We were guided spiritually to visit this location and we went to look around with an open mind to see what we might find. We were armed with clues from our own channelled information received by Pauline and myself but by this time we were starting to receive information from like-minded friends and colleagues with psychic abilities in whom we had confided. Some of them were seeing visual images of planes and airfields which were relevant to the story we were receiving.

At Thorpe Abbots we were greeted by the resident curator who offered to show us around the site. We were taken to the main display area in the old Control Tower where there are many artefacts, photographs and memorabilia of all kinds on display. Pauline remembers 'spiritually' picking up lots of visual and auditory information and with Jacque, a very experienced psychic friend at her side, they went to an upper room of the Tower which had windows all round it where planes would have been watched taking off and landing.

They both 'saw' in the room many people in American Word War II uniforms and we were all later intrigued to find a big collection of photographs pinned on a notice board. They were largely snapshot pictures of aircrew personnel and here I will let Pauline take up the story.

'On looking at the photographs, I noticed one in particular that I knew was of Michael and a group of other people. As I focused on his face I

said out loud suddenly, "That's Michael!" He was very distinctive looking and very handsome. "That's definitely him," I added, firmly.

'The man showing us round asked in surprise, "How do you know this man's name?" and I replied that I had spoken to him only that morning and 'seen' him spiritually during a contact which was connected with our visit to the airfield.

The curator was perplexed and started to look uncomfortable. Then he got curious and showed us the rest of the Control Tower. Later he asked us what we were doing and why and when we explained he became very helpful in finding information from their archives and he even found another picture of Michael for us from a magazine and also obtained for us a copy of the original group photograph in which I had identified Michael.

On other occasions friends and colleagues also 'tuned in' to the same photograph and confirmed Pauline's information. One interesting aspect of the photograph was that it was labelled on the notice board 'Easter 1944' but Pauline said that she had received information directly from Michael himself that morning that in fact the picture had been taken before their fatal crash on 10th February 1944 but the film had remained in somebody's camera for more than two months and had not been developed and printed until Easter 1944! Because they convey the flavour and atmosphere of the time, some of the photographs from that notice board which we saw that day are reproduced in the illustrated section of this book. For the moment, out of respect for any families with relatives in these photographs and others involved, we will not refer directly to the figure Pauline identified as Michael. That however might be appropriate at a later date.

For us, like the first moment during our original visit to the Madingley American Military Cemetery when the amazed official confirmed that there had been a crash at Stoke Holy Cross on the night of 10th February 1944, this sight of the photograph at Thorpe Abbotts was the second vital part of our jigsaw puzzle, to which we felt sure we had been *very deliberately led. The other group photograph that we obtained later which included Michael Hall can also be seen among this book's illustrations and photographs.*

From Thorpe Abbots we also obtained the few printed details shown among the illustrations which indicate that a Michael Hall had died in an Italian POW camp some time before 10th February 1944. It will be remembered that in the narrative of this book it has been made clear that all the men engaged on the Hitler assassination mission were officially declared dead to their families long before that date. So again this piece of information appeared to tally with and confirm that.

On that note it is time to return to Michael's narrative and another chilling description of the dramatic events that were taking place in Norfolk in preparation for the assassination mission. Michael describes how he learns about the 'training' in Thetford Forest which lies about 25 miles from Norwich, on the border with Suffolk.

PART THREE

THE FINAL PREPARATIONS

Chapter Twenty-Three
Mike Hall and unusual happenings in Thetford Forest

It is some time now since I have seen the guys back at the base. I did hear through the grapevine that a few had been moved around but I hoped to eventually return to the old stomping ground which was Thorpe Abbotts. There are loads of little bases dotted about this area so to get around between them is easy either by bike or by jeep if you are lucky to know someone that might take a risk.

Mickey Sturges was that one guy who would take it to the limit. A bit of a fly guy, chatted to the local girls like he was their big brother – that was until he got to know them a bit better then bingo, got his way and went on to the next one. That's how Mickey was. Without that little bit of magic there was no Mickey and once you got to know him he treated you like a little brother. It didn't matter who you were, he would take you under his wing and show you the town and all it had to offer in the way of drinking and womanising. I suppose it was his upbringing made him like that: he came all the way from Chicago, Illinois. He had been left by his parents in a foster home when he was five years old, and from the age of five to fifteen he had just as many foster parents.

That was until he reached the age of fifteen and a half and his whole life took a turn for the better for he fell lucky with a couple from Beverly, Chicago, a district that was part Italian part Irish. This couple were from the Irish part; they were wealthy beyond anything Mickey had ever seen before. He loved the new lifestyle, the clothes, the money and all that went with it, but he still had his humour. That didn't go despite being left and forgotten about on the front doorstep of the local foster home, his laughter was infectious to say the least. He grew up in a hard neighbourhood – being in scraps on a daily basis was bred in him. He knew how to play poker and backgammon and all the other vices that went with gangsters because that is what his foster parents were – gangsters.

He was their only son and he was lavished upon like no other kid in the street believe me, so he knew the high life. His conduct with the Italians was severe. He ruled his mother and father's little area with savagery of a kind that even Al Capone would be envious of, and Al Capone was aware of this young guy on the street and knew of his background. He knew Mickey wasn't Irish and knew of his American roots and tried to talk him into going over to the Italian quarter, but Mickey stayed loyal to his parents and Al gave respect to that saying, 'For that I will leave you alone, but if you change your mind give me a call.' And that was from the man himself. Not Lefty, nor Lieutenant from the Street, it was from *Scarface* himself. That went deep with Mickey and he never forgot it.

That was his little bedtime story every night – that was if you wanted to listen to it. After hearing it thirty or forty times it was getting a bit tedious to say the least but to new crews it was like starting all over again, and if you wanted to listen then Mickey would talk. His nights were legendary in the base – he made sure that new guys coming in would be taken in under his wing at any cost, no matter what. He obviously threw a few dollars to the training establishment back home because he was here as a pilot and supposedly a good one at that, but according to his crew he was a fucking maniac and shouldn't be allowed behind the wheel of a bumper car never mind a Flying Fortress. I can stand on ceremony and say here and now that he couldn't drive a jeep either! How we weren't all killed at some stage by his driving is beyond me.

As far as his plane goes he got the local artist from the other base to come over and paint on the side, much to the annoyance of the CO. It must have been from his days in the pool halls of Chicago and all his dealings, *Eight Ball* as in ==**8**==. Yes, *Eight Ball* on the side of his plane and right proud of it he was. He even got that big shot movie actor who we brought over from France on a secret mission to stand under it and pose for pictures with the rest of the crew – just a few words in the guy's ear and this big shot was giving out autographs at every opportunity.

This guy Mickey had some front. His nights out were with the unofficial permission of the base commander – I say unofficial because the MPs going around the local haunts would check up on you but he always came out with this pass and got away with it. How he got away with that is beyond me. Well, on one particular night he took me to one of the tables in the pub and said, 'Michael this is serious. I am not pissing about now. I have heard from one of the guys off a base in Cambridgeshire – I won't mention his name or his base but I know him and he is genuine. He says he was on driving duty to Thetford Forest, Mildenhall Base; he had to take a load of parts over there. He stopped for something to eat and a smoke on the north side of the forest and thought he was seeing things – a Panzer group – Germans – the whole fucking scamola! About thirty in a group moving into the forest fast, moving like a bat out of hell. What the fuck do you think of that?'

'Are you sure he wasn't drunk or taking anything?'

'Come on, he was driving a truck full of parts for some experiment going on at Mildenhall. You know there have always been rumours about that place and that wasteland they call Lakenheath, there's always something going on there but no one speaks about that – that's hush-hush. So I think he is believable, don't you?'

'I can't believe it, a German Panzer group in Thetford Forest? The next thing you will be telling me is that there is a secret camp in the forest itself!'

'You took the words right out of my mouth.'

'What do you mean?' I said.

'That's the next twist in the tail. Our friend gets nervous now, starts his engine up and suddenly all these guys jump on the wagon – British troops – and at gunpoint actually threatening his life! He has to drive into the forest and eventually into a base that you would not know was there, and to make the story even more strange, he actually saw a couple of our guys with rifles and these were not ordinary rifles – they were long-range mothers. He only saw them for a minute and they were gone. He just knew they were our guys.'

I had to smile – this bloke is winding me up, I thought. I was waiting for the punch line.

'No! I am serious here!' His face changed to one of anger and of being very scared. He was looking around all the time he was talking, hoping what was said would not be overheard. 'Our guy was taken into a room and was interrogated like within an inch of his life, and believe it or not he found himself back at the exact same place. He drove into Mildenhall Base and the guy on the gate asked with a laugh where he had been for the last four hours. But he didn't have an answer, he thought he just had a smoke break on the road and couldn't remember anything else. That is until a couple of weeks later, and it came in nightmares waking him up. He wrote it down bit by bit then gave the information to me.'

'Come on. Am I supposed to believe that?'

'You're right – I didn't believe it. That was until he described one of our guys to the letter – in fact one of your pals.'

'Who's that?'

'Steve Lursquom.'

'Fuck off. What's he doing in the forest?'

'No shit! If he was winding me up would he describe someone he doesn't know but is one of the guys on the base? I don't think so.'

The combination of the Germans and one of our guys on the base sounded a bit far-fetched and the fact that he was carrying a sniper rifle baffled me more and more. I thanked him for his concern. That was the last time I saw Mickey alive. His antics obviously got noticed, he suddenly disappeared. The grapevine said he was on night ops from somewhere in Northampton – a base up there I don't know. His name even disappeared from the roster overnight, this guy who was the joker, the life and soul of the party – just vanished like that.

The information he gave me was mind-blowing and obviously Top Secret. Could this information have something to do with his exit? Did the authorities get wind of him knowing? The sad part about this is his whole crew went with him. They would not leave his side, they obviously went the same way he did – a bloody shame. He was a top bloke and his crew knew it as well. God bless him, wherever he is.

I must admit I miss the likes of Mickey – he was a good guy. Why should these blokes be taken in such a way and just be forgotten? It is not right; after all it is one's life. You have one shot and you must use it to the best of your ability, and to be used in a way that ultimately gives your life for a cause is in my book the greatest sacrifice to give. There are many friends – and when I say friends, it is a privilege to call them that – they are all here to perform a part in this play set in a theatre. One by one we will be replaced by unaware newcomers who after a couple of weeks training will be at the forefront of this conflict. What goes through one's mind when being confronted with the prospect of dying for one's country gives you the goose pimples – the hairs on the back of your neck go up; the very thought of being maimed in a way gives you even more of a shudder. I would prefer death to losing my sight to see, my limbs to touch or my limbs to walk.

These things you put to the back of your mind because what happens around you propels you into another sight. You see, you smell, you touch, you feel; you experience the sensations of war. As a child you read between the pages, in imagination you go through what the soldier or airman in the story might be going through – the excitement, the thrill of the kill – to be a part of it. You think: to be there – I wish! As your mother calls you for your dinner and you race to the table you are catapulted into the here and now; the realisation of your family around you, your brothers and sisters sitting around you. Your father at the end of the table looking at you, the apple of his eye. You know that but he explodes, 'Looking in them books again Mikey? Not doing your chores son?' But you know deep down he doesn't mean it – the hardness of his voice, his cold manner. Deep down you know he's crying in his heart that you do not experience what is in those pages for real, because the harsh reality is that those pages do not give the word 'war' credibility; to give all your five senses the acid test and to see war in its cruellest form, to live the blood and guts of wartime is something that will remain in that soldier of fortune's mind, body, and soul for the rest of eternity. Believe me, I know.

As you read this, I hope in a way you let go of your inner fears and reflect in imagination on what it was like here in the solitude which is war. You are fighting for your own survival – nothing else. They raise a flag above you so that you have a cause, but other more powerful political powers have in fact put you in that position and you feel the pain, you see the pain of others. You smell the stench of rotting flesh around you. You experience this – your fellow buddies, your brothers and sisters being torn apart in front of you. And in retaliation you get angry and bomb the hell out of innocent human beings being manipulated by their powerful and political powers – it escalates in a way that disgusts me.

I read my war books as a child and imagined myself in a plane and being part of a conflict. But in a book you do not see the other side – *who* you are fighting. You imagine them coming at you, but you do not put a face to the enemy. They are like you and me – no different, going about their business until suddenly told they must go and fight for their country at all costs and if they do not they will be fucking shot on the spot. If that is not manipulation at its extreme then what the fuck is? We all fight for a cause, that is true, but the right to live as human beings – for your families to grow in a society where you have no fear? That, my friend, does not exist.

When I eventually get home to Virginia, if I do get home that is, I'll be confronted with the prospect of looking out for myself in the rough towns; being threatened with my life at the flip of a hat. Where does my loyalty lie then? To my country? Will they raise a flag above me then so I can shoot this mother fucker's head off three foot away from me and see his brains float around in the air before they splat on someone's dinner? No, I do not think so, they will lock me up and more than likely throw away the key. But, my friends, they are putting me and many of my fellow countrymen in that position.

Ranging from the age of 18 to 25, they give you a licence to kill or maim another human being '...because we say so, and that is good enough ok? So get the fuck on with it and no back chat otherwise you will see the sword of so-called justice loom into sight and it will chop your head off and that's the end of you. There is always a Charlie to take your place, as easy as that...' Certainly makes you think your cause is greater than theirs! We pray to the same God in churches across the world; my ancestors came from Europe so our beliefs are the same. So what are we doing here? Overthrowing a dictator, as simple as that? I wish it was.

You have to exterminate all those who are under his spell. His manipulation of the masses is to a level surpassing all others in history so why not expel the source? Rid the body of the cancer so it may have a chance to live and breathe as before? Sounds easier than it probably is which brings me back to my present position. I have seen some strange goings on in the play we call war. The backstage goings on, people manipulating other people and so it goes on, but I have yet to experience the most bizarre, explosive situation to be even thought of, yet to be actually put into action. These things will come to pass. I send out my deepest prayers from within myself, for myself and my friends, and there are many.

These prayers are on angel wings to those who will have the fear of dying and pain be put aside and think of their true selves, so they relinquish all known fears and pain.

Chapter Twenty-Four
The time approaches

The key issue in all this is that there are significant rumblings in the smoke signals, jungle drums and rumours that something big is going down in Europe and it's not for the squeamish. That's one thing – if Ike has anything to do with it he will go for the jugular of the enemy's throat that is certain. The rumours circulated are not only from the crews and individual guys getting back from Germany and the occupied Low Countries, but also from the fly guys in the camps talking to ground troops who have been captured and heard through the grapevine that something big is going on. The Germans know there is a big build-up of troops massed in one area and take it that there is going to be an invasion of some kind but its whereabouts is still a mystery. Keeping them guessing and feeding them false information is probably the key, who knows? In all of this what matters to me is my survival. That is probably a cynical way of thinking – I should be worrying about my buddies. In a way I am, but in a more selfish way I best think of self-survival.

Still, back to the serious matter, talking to ex-POWs, and there are a lot believe you me. As soon as they are out of that parachute these airmen try their utmost to get back to base; their main aim is to get back and straight into another plane and do it all over again. To some of them it is an adventure. Their lives before the war were a nine-to-five treadmill of existence and now they fulfil their darkest desires to blast the hell out of another human being and get paid for it. It disgusts me to even be here and to have to go through seeing my buddies and the enemy spilling blood to bring peace, but if that is what it takes then that is the price. Living in these times takes hard living on the nose – you have to live your life.

Perhaps in years to come people will look at us and say we had it all – it certainly looks that way from the press of the day. How the propaganda machine works is a wonder to behold, whoever it was that invented the press and the way it is worded within those pages certainly knows far more than they are letting on. These forms of letting the people of this world know what is going on are subversive; the conspiracy theories they are fed are a load of bollocks.

The truth is put to one side, it is a non-truth. The public are fed little bits and to get the full picture you must stand back from the crowd; the real truth is far, far more in the sky than anybody would believe. The torture and absolute pain of war is something that should not be lived, it is a torment on such a scale it beggars belief.

We are all expendable in the big picture, what will overcome is one power taking over another. We are just the pawns in a fucking game – pure and simple. Cannon fodder to be discarded in such a way as to be used, and used in such a way that if you rebel against it then you are for the chop. The very thought of rebelling against one's country is not even worth thinking about but you must stand up and be counted. We have these thoughts in our heads but you do not let the authorities know of your thoughts or you will go to the executioner's sword. Believe me, the fact that we have to fight or die at the hand of our own kind fills me with hate even more. Don't get me wrong, I will fight and die for and with my brothers, but the fuck will I give up my life for some bastard who doesn't give a rat's ass if I die or not. That is the key. I will lie down with my brothers and sisters who fight with me in battle.

In the old days the big Chieftains – those that wanted freedom and stood for the cause – rode out in battle at the head of their army and showed their courage, and their troops and all those who made up that fighting force would ride and walk to the gates of hell for them. We do the same but under just a flag, day in day out – no compromise, blood and guts on a daily basis. No room for error for if you do then that is your lot – end of story.

This is my story and the story of my crew who will join together to try and accomplish a mission so bizarre it blows you away. It is now early January 1944 and my crew have been apart for some time. We will join together in five weeks' time, for now we have to work separately – they will not let us rejoin one another until then; I do not know why this is. As I said before, there is a build-up of arms we are told, not by the authorities but by the guys coming back from the front.

The blue skies of early January 1944 are so appealing to the eye, especially very early in the morning when the thought of risking your life one more time comes into the conscious mind. The blue sky goes on forever it seems, into the horizon, the white clouds just drift along at a leisurely pace – if only life was like that. But it isn't.

The harsh reality of life in wartime is not a pretty one. You go to the local picture house and there are some colour films, I haven't seen a lot. Black and white films take away the beauty of life, the colour of what goes on around us. We take it all for granted – I do. I have seen blood in colour – not like on a black and white film in a picture house, but oozing red blood coming out of wounds you could put your hand in and the feel of pain on people's faces. As they look upon this person's pain they try to distance themselves from the reality of pain in its ultimate form. What do you go through in your conscious state of mind – do you look at yourself and take the bull by the horns and face the pain of what you might see, or do you vanquish it and not relate to it at all? Turn yourself off from it – a hard thing to do. Somehow, deep inside you know how serious it is – the pain is telling you but you do not want to respond to your true feelings. Your gut instinct tells you it is very serious or you will survive this one.

I have seen this pain in many of my friends and I wish not to have any part of that pain, that point of no return. It will come one day but I will have the say in its final hour, not anybody else. I pray to the Lord Jesus for that, I have seen and heard and smelt the grim reaper walking around us and I do not wish him to take me in that way. I will meet my Maker one day that is certain, but hopefully not for some time yet.

I am looking forward to getting together with some good old friends in the next few days at some parties for the local kids. It's always a time to show off; to let your hair down and forget this war for five minutes, and hope these kids have big sisters or young mothers – it matters not to us. We live for today. Today matters, not tomorrow. Tomorrow I may be a squashed tomato on the bottom of the fuselage in the North Sea, and that would not be good for me or my buddies would it? So we feast upon that in our way, we have a good time.

This reflects on our birds of prey – our girls in the sky, they look after us so we give them names to reflect how we feel – *Hells Angel, Good Time Gal, Hells Belles* – I could go on, there are many with these names. We bless them. They become a part of us, not a chunk of metal but a living, breathing part of us, we have to be like that for us to go and come back in one piece. Sure there are those that will not come back but they know the bird that carries them will die as they will. It is not something you can easily explain; the time and the place reflects the mood you are experiencing and that is all you need to know. You have to have an inner strength to go about your duties in this life that is certain, and to experience this life you need strength of character to overthrow the need to run away, hide under a bush, or be fucking scared out of your life. There has to be a spark to ignite the fire – to get you up in the morning to go about your daily routine. The love you carry in your heart to survive another day, the colour you see with your eyes each day – you take for granted all the little things that matter so much, all these things do matter for they are part of you.

The whole picture of this war is written down as an event that will come into being and then slide into the history books, but to feel, smell, hear and taste all that is going on in the here and now explodes the feelings a hundred percent into the conscious level to be a part of this event. It's something for me to be very proud of, a humble farmer's son, to be a part of such an allied fighting force, to bring the good into focus and repel those that bring darkness into the clear blue skies gives you strength in character. So those that I fight with and stand alongside should be given respect. That is all we ask – no more, no less.

To give one's life is not to be given lightly. In free will it goes a long way to have the thought of one's maybe only life on this planet given up for a cause written down by a person we have not met in our lives. One person or persons in authority or government make the decision to go to war against a tyranny or evil force that holds the people of this land to ransom. We walk forward to take up that flag of honour and truth and walk with pride as our fathers did in the First World War, and our grandfathers who took up the Stars and Stripes against our own kind back home. We hold the flag that brought that nation together and there are many of us who stand under that banner and will give their lives for its cause – what it stands for. Do not underestimate the power of one, for when joined within it gains power for the good it stands by.

There are many of my brothers scattered in every corner of the lands of this earth. They have given the ultimate sacrifice – their one life at this time. They will be heard, that I know. They cry out for justice beyond their physical bodies to be answered. This cause which we fight and know to be true – is it true? And in the hearts of those that wield the sword of power, do they know the price of self-sacrifice? The ultimate price we pay for a life to be given up in a way will not be left unheard, it will cry in the night until someone turns the light on. These things do not go away to be forgotten and used in such a way.

A simple name on a grave and a nice little plot in a nice setting is not good enough. These guys should be given respect and ultimately not – and I repeat, *not* forgotten. Count each grave one by one and each time you count, think of that one and the thoughts and life he led, the tears, the laughter. As you go through the names one by one you realise the hurt which has been given and the life that has been given. Deep stuff is this – it is meant to be. We are all human beings going about our lives as best we can and to be told to go to war and be given no choice in the matter whether we like it or not gives a right to say what we like. For our brains to be splattered across our buddies in the hell that is war gives us a right to choose how we spend our time – fast and furious.

It is time for us all to get back together again within the confines of the camp to begin this exercise we have been training for. All separated, doing the right thing and not being observed by those who may oppose the objective so far out there that it defies logic. Someone's idea of a joke maybe until somebody in a place of authority takes it seriously enough to try to put it into practice at a stage in the war where there might be a crack or seam in the armour of the Third Reich.

Baker Team
Comprising myself, Michael Hall, rear gunner
Charles 'Buck' Quinlan, pilot
Rupert Kovloski, sniper 2
Rob 'Steve' Lursquom, sniper 1
Mike Preston, navigator
Al Permando, side gunner
Bernie Jameson, co-pilot

Juniper Team
Steve Jackson, pilot
Bernie Levringsett, co-pilot
Ray Thomas, navigator
Ritchie Blamos, sniper 1
Blue Stevano, sniper 2
Jimmy Casanno, ammunitions, bomb aimer
Robert Harris, rear gunner.

Magenta Team
This team we have no knowledge of. A very Top Secret team that comprises personnel that have no names as far as outside the confines of their own kind goes. They are a Special Forces team that in the event of us failing they will deploy to do the task of wiping the slate clean. There will be no record of these men so don't even bother looking – outside, to the world around us they do not exist, but believe me they do. I think their own families have long thought that every one of them has died so to the outside world they are dead anyway. So what the hell.

I suppose in a way we are the scapegoats, do not worry about looking for us either in the records, we will disappear never to return. We will be split up on some formal charge sheet, put into crews that have been blown out of the sky, and in time, who the hell cares? Some name to be typed up and put into a library to be looked at for reference maybe or just lost in the system for good, that justifies your life on this planet to individuals that manipulate your total being. It may be alright for those special team operatives but it's not alright for me. I will fight for my country and my friends will also do this, but if the cause is right and justice is done. We are not just rubbish to be thrown away and we object to that very strongly. The country we fight for we feel just and true and in the next few weeks we will hopefully be trained and good enough to take this task on.

Our team, Baker Team, will be going into Germany as far as is possibly good enough to drop our team in, two snipers to object, Target One – the Fuhrer.

Magenta Team will go into the Channel Islands. We have good information that Target Two – Fuhrer Two, will be overlooking the U-boats stationed there at that time.

Juniper team will go in with us. They are a second team into Germany. If we do not succeed then they will be on the hunt for us, it sounds crazy I know but that is the situation. This is a one-off. If we hit flak, if we go down, then we are in danger ourselves. This is a no-win situation for us. If we succeed in this it is the end of the war. Someone has come along with this idea and it's stuck – we have to follow orders. We have the best shots in the whole bomber group. I will give you as much information as I can leading up to this exercise. I do not know if there is a beyond point in this. Perhaps we will carry on after this exercise – I doubt it. I think the powers-that-be have already thought of an escape plan for themselves in higher government, but if they do pull it off, the morale in the German war machine will come to a halt or maybe German propaganda will not allow the German forces to become aware of that information. We will see.

We have much to do landing and getting our right of passage into Germany not to be messed about with. We cannot use our own B-17s. They are in the RAF livery for reasons I do not yet understand – all blacked out, B-17s in RAF livery. The codes on the side are even different and this is because we fly at night but we Americans are not known to fly at night. This is a Top Secret mission make no mistake. I still think Magenta Team have got the best deal; the Channel Islands are a little closer than the south bank of the Rhine.

Chapter Twenty-Five
Steve Lursquom, Sniper 1

Although my name is Robert, my nickname is 'Stevie' (pronounced Steve) to my friends in the forces; it has been a part of my family since way back and so has the rifle. It so happens that even without training my eye was for shooting from a very young age, my family can be traced right back to the Revolutionary days of Jim Bowie and Davy Crockett – my great-grandfather and his brother, my great-uncle, were part of the team that were alongside these great figures at the Alamo. My great-grandfather survived the Alamo but died from his wounds a year after the battle, my great-uncle was pronounced dead at the scene – he suffered a fatal blow to the side of his skull from a fragment of shot from a musket. He was comforted by his wife, she was loading his musket at the time. He would not leave Jim Bowie's side all through the battle. His wife was also devoted to the cause, and Jim and David were the pillars that all would stand on. She would be devastated by my great-uncle's passing and would not recover totally in her mind; she looked after my great-grandfather until his passing, living in less than good surroundings.

It has to be said that divisions in the country were a lot more widespread in those days. The Union had not yet been formed and the USA we know of today did not exist. The state of Texas was being formed and my family with the Bowie and Crockett families, grew together along with other settlers and became strong. The Alamo was the beginning and the end of many years of conflict, it brought together the seeds of the Union – the brotherhood that makes a country and hopefully new beginnings which can be launched into a stronghold on which to build.

And so through time my family moved on and I was born in Los Angeles – City of Angels – and was brought up mostly by my father who I love dearly. His teachings in the art of firepower and the rifle enabled me to go forward into what I wanted to achieve and that was to work in government for my country. We are a very patriotic family and we are very loyal. My father wished that I work for the FBI or the internal borough like the Untouchables that were formed because of The Prohibition – the drink laws of America in the early days. But with the introduction of America into the war effort everything changed and so that is why I chose the Army Air Force. I could have been on the ground – a foot soldier – but my father said, 'No, you go into the air force. There is more of a chance you will survive than on foot and besides, if you are involved in any frontal attack on the ground, your training will come in handy.'

I wish he knew what was going on here today. The whole thought-pattern of this is truly mind-blowing. The powers-that-be must have known of my background in firearms and the training – how else would I be picked for this duty? I am sworn to secrecy about what is going on in and around the camp, but to have this amount of secrecy, to be threatened with one's own life is just not on. The fact that my patriotic viewpoint is under deepest scrutiny is not to my liking and this vibrates among other crews as well. This particular mission is big – will I survive? I have a feeling deep down in my stomach that I shall not, all I know is the hit on Target Two is viable; the Target One option is not open to me and has not been discussed.

There are a few teams working around us. We could be put to one side and into our normal pattern of work and forgotten about – I am not the only sniper in the force there are some other very good ones. The guy that picked my partner off is first-class, I do not know who he is. The secrecy is top, top level – I am sure that if something is said in the wrong place then that person will disappear. Believe me, you do not mess about with these kinds of people, you are nothing to them, they wish to occupy a strategic gain in this situation and that is it. What tools they use is irrespective of the end justifying the means and so it is best to just sit tight, lie low and get on with it. If they pick you it's a ticket home early that is in the deal, they have to give some incentive in the air combat situation. There is only one contender so far – the *Memphis Belle* and its crew of ten might be going home; they are almost there at this time but out of all those air crew only one might be going home – it makes you think how you are treated. And so this might be my meal ticket home to the States, who knows? I cross my fingers and hope I shall see my family again – who knows?

The waiting is over. I am not on Magenta Team that will be Target Two – that has gone to somebody else. I am Target Number One and have to go back to Thetford for a few days. I am with my crew at the moment, sworn to secrecy; they think I've been assigned to another group in Cambridge – that is so as far as they are concerned. I do not know who Target One is yet – someone very high up in the Reichstadt German government; we have our thoughts on who it might be but dare not say as it would be fucking scary to me as well as the other guys. The crew of *Blue Angel* have no idea of this, we carry on from our local camp and just tick over. Who knows what tomorrow will bring? A new day and probably a day nearer to seeing my family back home.

It's back at base camp in Thetford for me now, before when I was here I was nervous but now I am kacking myself really bad. We are sworn to secrecy about all that is going on now. I know I have a target to go for but who knows what that target is? We have been here for two days, just left here to get on with it no interference from outside influences. This is a British camp but there are Americans well in abundance here since the last time in a teaching role. I think something was said to the authorities about the attitude of some of the British officers towards the American men – that's what we hear anyway. I have a briefing in the morning, there are not so many guys around as last time so maybe we have been whittled down somewhat. I know I am not the only sniper here there are a few, not only for one specific job either; there are many potential targets so it makes sense to have as many options open to you as possible. My main thought at this time is to get a good night's sleep, get up refreshed and have a good day.

The night brings many dreams. Some I can handle others I just want to forget about, some so nightmarish that it defies thinking about. Death is their main focus, to die for one's country is a great honour where I come from so that doesn't affect me, it's being forgotten by one's country and countrymen that scares me. What would it all be for if it wasn't for the freedom of yourself and your family? What is worth fighting for if not your way of life and so your country, which maintains that stronghold of dignity that so many people strive for? To live as you wish – that is all. That in itself is worth fighting for.

The morning approaches. I cannot get out of the habit of waking up at 3 o'clock ready for briefing to go wherever to drop a ton of bombs some place. We are roll-called at 6.30. Here I can lay and try to sleep but it is hard to do that, the mind does not rest. I am there with my buddies in the air; we are as one up there in the sky, thrown together by the turmoil of what's going on two miles below us but up there in the air we are at peace with ourselves. We bond together as brothers for a cause that is out of our hands; we are only instruments playing in an orchestra – if we miss a note some other instrument will play our tune as we disappear. That is the way it is unfortunately – we have to face the prospect of death each day and that in itself changes you from being a normal guy in the street to a hard-thinking guy who only lives for one day at a time. Some guys in the force are more adept at flying than others, you have those that bring their inner personalities out, those that were quiet back home and hardly drank or womanised do it to the extreme in circumstances over here. Some get away with murder and are very lucky they do not get found out for their only outlook is to last the next twenty-four hours, that is all. You have twenty-five missions to complete before you are sent home. To fly your plane with pride and gather war bonds for the cause of freedom or, on the other hand, to go home with the Stars and Stripes draped over your own personal body bag.

We gather for the briefing. We are in pairs as before – only three pairs this time. 'Thank you gentlemen, we have one or two of you back from our first little adventure. Now that was a walk in the park compared to this. You are in groups of two – three teams – one team now is the only one that wins. You say to yourself – well so what, I mean to live another day.'

'You will be given a target, gentlemen. This target must be laid to rest – that is, my good friends, eliminated at all costs, there is no compromise in this situation. Once your target is laid to rest you must return to this base at once under your own steam, as quietly and resourcefully as possible. No markings on the floor of the forest – not even your shit, gentlemen, will you discard; you must not leave any of your bodily fluids behind you. Once you have set your target you must leave your set position and return with everything, this is imperative at all costs. So please gentlemen, your target this day is – the Fuhrer.'

Some joker at the back of the room shouts out – 'So you have the Fuhrer in Thetford Forest then? So the fucking war is over if we shoot him?'

'No sonny boy. Your target for today is the Fuhrer, but you my friend have to find him within his own wolf's lair and believe me sonny Jim, that is one helluva job. You are in for a nasty surprise if you succeed. Now gentlemen, please, to the gates where you will have your standard rifles given to you along with three days' rations. This, my friends, is no joke.'

'Your intentions must be admirable. This country and those of the civilised world are investing their last hope in your expertise. You are the mustard. You are the best snipers we have and we expect you to do your duty. This is only a training exercise but the kill is real. You will find your target and you will kill – that is the aim. Which one of you makes a good job of that kill and the retreat from the wolf's lair is the most important. We have operatives within the lair and they are counting on you to deliver the goods gentlemen. Good luck and good hunting.'

I am really kacking myself now. One target, three teams? This sounds crazy; we can't all get the same target! Oh well. My partner is very quiet, won't even speak; so, it's his journey, I'm not bothered. He is a Native American Sioux Indian; his mother was Sioux and his father a local guy in one of the small towns. He was brought up as a white boy up to the age of ten and so badly treated by the whites in the community that he and his father decided he should go to his grandfather, Running Bear, on the Reservation.

He was brought up in the ways of the Sioux. His grandfather was the Shaman for the tribe and so he passed on to Red Eagle all his knowledge. When war broke out and he got his call-up papers he was reluctant to come over here but in the end had no option. He is a master at the rifle, he was taught to shoot by his father like me but with a different focus and great skill. He uses the rifle as an extension of himself and I feel privileged to be his partner, however he does not speak very much so I have to speak first to start a conversation.

He looks at you and speaks with his eyes. I do not know what he is thinking but he seems to understand so many things. He is an excellent tracker and I feel confident we will succeed in this mission. This forest is very big and who knows where our target is. We have three days to make it back here to camp with the full objective in sight.

The mission begins. It feels as though my life depends on this one moment in time. The heartbeat in my chest is nearly exploding – I would not wish this on anyone. I am glad that I am paired with Red Eagle; I would rather use his native power medicine name than his formal name given to him by the white man.

For reasons I do not even want to know we are first out of the track. We have three days to find Target One. It will not be easy, by no means. We have teams behind us who are a threat to us – it is also a case of kill or be killed. This matters for national security. We are being monitored at every step; believe me, the technology is way beyond anything I have seen – with every step we feel we're being looked at. We are given co-ordinates on grid maps that will determine our objective. We must not leave any stone unturned and must not make any venture outside the objective.

We follow the map grading, under cover all the time. There are hand-overs going on, the British forces camping in sites around the forest unaware that they are being looked at not only by us but lots of other people. We move on, we wish not to engage in any crossfire or make targets of ourselves. This is easy for Red Eagle as he seems to sense the smell of where we are headed. Nightfall comes. We can move very quickly in the dark – only the animals are in our way but we must rest and sleep, we are no good to ourselves without rest. We have been given rations and we must keep to these rations, no lighting of fires obviously. We become the forest. Red Eagle becomes part of the night – he is at one with it. We rest, I need sleep. It is two to three in the morning, we rest. Red Eagle says he will see me in the morning, I say, 'Ok,' look round and he has gone. Must rest, go to sleep.

The sleep brings forward its nightmares on a grand scale. What would my parents think of all this? My nightmares take hold of me as they did when I was a child, the thought of being in a secluded place with only the sound of rustling and animals in the distance, with only your heartbeat and your breath for company. These nightmares then go out of control – I am being dragged into the forest by some unknown force and the thought of being devoured by some animal or something fills me with dread. I wake up in a cold sweat and feel more tired than ever. I control myself and look at the rising sun of the morning only to be scared shitless by Red Eagle tapping me on the shoulder and saying we must move.

'We are being watched by two snipers. They have us in their sights. I have seen them. One of them you know.'

'What do you mean?'

'He knows you.'

'How do you know that?'

'I have spoken to him.'

'How can you do that?'

'You do not understand. I have spoken to his self not his personality, his true self – his spirit. He wishes you no harm but he has his orders. There must only be one team to hit the target and he aims to be a part of that team.'

'So he has had orders to eliminate any before them?'

'Yes.'

'So why weren't you and I told of this?'

'Because we were the first out we have the objective in the target. All others that follow must try to eliminate those before them.'

'This is fucking crazy again!'

'This happened last time with Target Two.'

'Oh well, fuck it. Here we go.'

We have less than twenty-four hours now to find Target One, eliminate it and return to base. We come across an opening where there has been a lot of machinery being moved – the ground has been torn to shreds. We hear more clanking of wheels in the distance, we go for cover and follow the noise. After a few minutes we come across a large building all camouflaged in grey with German names on the building's sides. A large tank now looms across my line of sight. As I lower myself to the ground under the shrubs and grass to disappear once more, I say to Red Eagle, 'What the fuck is this again? German names in the middle of an English forest?'

'We are to look for Target One and eliminate. Do not ask questions about who is Target One.'

We have obviously found the point of target but who is the target? The dossier given to us at the base is now to be opened – a picture of the

Fuhrer. Bloody hell! This is fucking Top Secret! *'Eliminate, certain kill and disappear. Make way to neutral country, destroy all known contact with Allied source and if you can, find your way back home. All is well, but you must disappear.'*

So look for target. Well he's not going to come out of his lair and stand by the shed and have a smoke – not that easy. We must find some way of getting closer or actually inside but that's suicide man! I know – we are on a suicide mission anyway so go for it. Hang on a minute, didn't the guy back at the base say to be careful we have known operatives in the area and not to bring them harm? Do you think at a set time these operatives will actually bring out the Fuhrer or get him to move from here completely – worth waiting for hey?

We wait – only one way in and one way out; we have not got much time to get back to base and complete the mission in the allotted time. We wait. Time goes by. I'm busting for a piss – I have to relieve myself, it's no good, the sound of water or in this case urine, hitting the floor at an alarming rate sounds like thunder in the forest, after that I can run a mile in one minute – I feel that light. I do not know where the rest of the teams are, there is no sign of anything. We wait, the door opens – we see four figures emerge into the light.

Figure One, a general of some kind – a big fat guy. Figure Two, a tall figure of a man – he too looks like a general. The third is a smaller man dressed all in black from head to toe, a swastika proudly across the top of his right arm; he trots along like a peacock. He turns to us, his face now shows his true likeness – the moustache, the eye piece...we shoot. Two clear shots.

But we are not the only ones that hit the target – he is blown away completely by at least ten shots from different angles. We are not the only ones that have been waiting. With the shots now silenced the noise of gunfire and shouting erupts – it's time to leave, back to base.

My heart is rushing; it's pounding and jumping around inside me like a jack hammer about to explode out of my chest. I have just experienced a sight that even I am questioning, I saw it with my own eyes yet it seems unreal in some ways. This is an exercise to train for the real thing yet it seems fucking real, I and at least three other squad units have just blown away the leader of the Third Reich – the top man – Hitler himself, yet it can't have been him! It must have been some damn good look-a-like – I thought it was the real thing as I looked through the lens. Whoever this guy was he's in a right state now, hardly anything left of him; those .22 calibre bullets find the mark – all head shots as well.

As soon as one shot was heard it was the signal to deploy all other weapons. Now it's the first back to the base. Whoever the other guys were that were lying in wait they were really good, and I mean *good* – fucking mustard. More like they were not there – just silence when we finished. Myself and Red Eagle are no slouches believe me, but for a few minutes or even seconds after the shootings it was as if nothing had happened – not even a bird singing, not a twitch or sound from anywhere.

There was plenty of panic from inside and around the camp – the Germans or their look-a-likes were running around like headless chickens. Plenty of gunfire, I suppose trying to make it as realistic as possible. They certainly did that – I nearly crapped myself. Red Eagle was not that impressed in my way of lacking confidence; he feels that I should thank the Spirit for keeping me safe. We shall see about that. We have to make our way back to camp double quick, retrace our steps, it's the only way. We manage it, only to be met by a severe looking officer at the gate.

'Gentlemen, your weapons...thank you. Your briefing is in that building there if you would, gentlemen.'

Time is not on our side. We acknowledge his orders and make our way to the building he points to. On opening the door I have this feeling that only bad things are on the other side of it.

'Ahhh...' A voice from the semi darkness interrupts the silence. 'A-Group, come in, we have been waiting.'

'Hang on – we? The other groups?'

'For secrecy matters I hope you don't mind being in the not so light rooms we provide here on this camp for just this purpose?'

Now we don't hang about. So we are the last ones in – who the fuck are these guys? For the point of secrecy we have to forget who they are and forget who the hell we are as well. Mind games are not one of my best subjects I have to say but it looks like I have no choice now. We are in a blacked-out room, we see the guy talking in a light-filled little oasis at one end.

'Now you guys, this is important. You are the best of the best. You are part of an elite squad of snipers ready to assassinate targets in war situations. Don't worry guys. This has been going on since the American Civil War. Lincoln appointed this in a Legislator to Congress and put in it a very stern remark that after the attempts on his own life he was not going to let anybody in authority, no matter where in the world or at home, get too big for their boots. Elimination is the order of the day. Make no mistake, all and I mean *all* orders from Lincoln are set in stone especially where war situations come into play.'

'In peacetime there is also a group that exists to infiltrate any anti-government organisation. These guys are undercover, that is because of the secrecy. They are normal working people and join up like you guys, but they also work for the government. We have been keeping an eye on you Steve, you slipped through the net. Your father was one of a group and wanted you to join one such group within the FBI but circumstances just turned the corner and you know the rest. The same goes for your partner – a little more complex because of his background and family but nevertheless we got over these things. The secrecy is uppermost, you know too much now – that is why you are in the team. You are last back but you were first with the shot and that, my friends is why we are here.

That one shot can save countless lives on the front line and that is why you and I are here. I have mentioned your name Steve – that was wrong of me. You have now become vulnerable as a target because your name is in the conscious state of our minds now as a group member. But no matter; you must think one step ahead.'

'My friends, you are now members of an elite force. Some of you here are members anyway but there are one or two of you who are not. The sentences I have just spoken will be with you friends but in a situation where you are interrogated by an enemy force you will not reveal anything you have heard or said or seen. That is because gentlemen, at the beginning of your involvement with this war you were subjected to hypnotic tones or said words put into your subconscious mind. These, my friends, are like time bombs. They are just as good as having a grenade stuck to either side of your head. Any attempt to avert this and you will implode. All matter, everything you know, will not exist – you will in fact become walking vegetables. I predict at this time anger from you guys, am I right?'

With this arrogant bastard telling me that I have an in-built time bomb ready to go off I feel like blowing him away right now but I must admit, I should blow him away but suddenly I am calm and passive – just as if he hadn't said anything. I am sitting here, I am aware he just said those things, but I am unable to react...bloody hell, what have they done to us? We are in fact like walking zombies ready to do their will! It frightens the fuck out of me how we have been manipulated in this way. If they are doing this to us what are they doing to the guys on the front line? It brings it home to you, what if we are all manipulated in this way then we act out all this war being manipulated and subjected to almightily different things? We are the controlled but who are the controllers – the governments of each country?

If we know of this it's a sure-fired bet that the opposition knows of this and have their elite forces. Like the storm troopers – they are their elite and you know of them, what about the ones you don't know about? It seems the said powers-that-be know of your situation as you grow up and are monitoring in peace time as well as in times of war – how can they do this? And are we all like this, the problem being we cannot do anything about it – it is in our subconscious state. We cannot speak out in a public way or be interrogated for we will in fact die.

'Thank you, gentlemen, for your time. You will be given orders in the very near future. If you will return to your original squads and await further orders.'

We are shown the door. The light pours in, the small space suddenly overwhelmed by the sunshine. I take a glimpse around the faces, lots of them – some of these guys could have been in that room. I see two guys walking away from a main group, one looks behind and stares straight at me. I know that face. He's a pilot from Thorpe Abbotts. What the fuck is he doing here? I rack my brains. I know him, he's pally with Mike Hall...Steve Miller, *Blue Angel* – I knew I'd seen him about.

Someone shouts at me from the hut. It's Red Eagle, he shakes my hand. 'Listen to your Spirit Steve and he will answer your questions.'

'What do you mean?'

'Just listen, Steve. See ya.'

With that I turn. No Steve Miller, he has gone as well. Oh well, return to Thorpe Abbotts, I must admit to missing the place.

Two typical Thorpe Abbotts B-17 crews of 'Piccadily Lily' (above) and 'Our Gal Sal' (below), the former plane was believed lost over Bremen during a raid.

The Thorpe Abbotts ground crew of a bomber enigmatically named 'Fever Beaver' (above) and the fliers of a similar machine 'Sunny II' (below).

Another Thorpe Abbotts crew posing more informally without their aircraft (above) and a squadron fron the same airbase in flight en route towards their German target (below).

A ground crew posing with an awed local Norfolk schoolboy (above), a drawing of a B-17 gunner (below left) and the Thorpe Abbotts Control Tower before it was recently restored (below right).

Dave Kelly's notebooks, research items and photographs obtained during research into USAAF and other archives in East Anglia

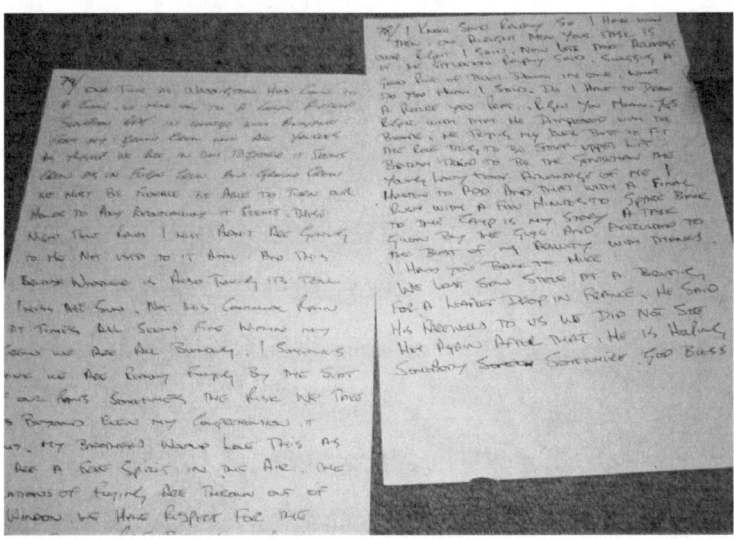

Two Pages from the channelled original which can be seen to have been carefully written in capital letters.

81 Psycotherapy Repression All these things that given if we are captured we will be interogated at such a level that we must be aware of ourselves, in giving them what they want Disinformation is the Key. All to do with the Hind. The Local Route will wire through to a Special Task Force if we are captured and then we are at the mercy of the Inner Gestapo. All this I hope will not happen we will go in get what we came for and depart with no problem. But you must be ready for these eventualitys as to be aware is fore warned.

Our Departure is at 2100hrs. It is now mid morning. Time for reflection and being optimistic certainy all that is going on around me. It seems a bit cloak and dagger. I wonder how my good friends are doing while we are here at Scampton. I know a few of the guys are enjoying themselves no matter where they are ... ... life no matter what

A close up page from the channelled original, numbered in the order it was dictated.

The pile of 700 A4 pages, hand written by author Dave Kelly over a period of six years via channelling and automatic writing.

```
2nd    Lt     Ralph D. Horne, Jr.           P     POW    19/5/44
2nd    Lt     John M. McGrath               CP    POW    19/5/44
2nd    Lt     Douglas L. Hiley              N     POW    19/5/44
2nd    Lt     Jack T. Evans                 B     POW    19/5/44
       S/Sgt  Robert L. Fosdick             E     POW    19/5/44
       S/Sgt  Lawrence C. Willey            R     POW    19/5/44
       Sgt    Carlee G. Hunt                BT    POW    19/5/44
       Sgt    Joseph Perinsky, Jr.          RW    POW    19/5/44
       Sgt    Shelly M. Hall, Jr.           LW    POW    19/5/44
       Sgt    Joseph G. Staron, Jr.         TG    POW    19/5/44

349th Sqdn.  Crew, as above, joined the 100th Group on 9/3/44.
MACR #4948, Microfiche #1768, A/C #42-97607.
```

Michael Shelly Hall was given to Dave Kelly as the name of the apparent main communicator of the channelled text. The above document, found in USAAF archives, confirms his name but states that he joined the 100th Bomb Group in March 1944 (after the mission), and was a prisoner of war in May of 1944.

Chapter Twenty-Six
Steve Miller

My name is Steve Miller. It is no good looking at records of past missions or logs – I am not there. I am a person, that is true, but to the world I am a non-person. It is true I have a life and a good one, but to the collective that is in sole charge of information held at all levels of the community, the government bodies and the military inner governing orders, I as a person do not – and I emphasise the *do not* – exist. You are probably saying to yourself how is this to be? It is a long story. This is my story up to this point in time, but believe me, there are others that have this dilemma or perhaps the burden of having to be a non-person; you give away a lot for the collective at one particular point in time in your life.

It all started for me 22 years ago one February day, the twelfth, 1922, in a little town called Arkansas. My father worked as a farm labourer and my mother worked in a small shop in the town. We did not have a lot as a family. My father's family had the house we were living in for up to four generations so we lived on the fact that we were carrying on a legacy – the house was not that big but it was ours. We had a bit of land but it was somehow tied in with other landowners, and I believe at some point in the family's history there was conflict between two families and the rights to one piece of land were being fought over. My father falling in love and marrying the daughter of the rival family didn't help matters at all.

Well, from the time I was born I was torn between the two families. Having a foot in the two camps as it were and growing up in that kind of atmosphere was not very good – you were in constant turmoil with the fact of growing up and having to deal with who you were loyal to. I used to run away a lot and my Uncle Steve who I was named after, used to come look for me.

I didn't have much in the way of things around me as personal possessions in the early days. We all were taught how to fire guns from an early age – I started when I was four just messing about shooting at targets for amusement more than anything. I had what is described as a kindred spirit with my uncle – he knew me more than my own father. It was as if my father never did recognise me as a person, he was wrapped up in his own little world, didn't express his feelings whatsoever. He and my mother were sweethearts for ages but he didn't actually pluck up enough courage to ask her out and marry her for a long time, consequently I didn't come along until he was thirty-five years of age and she twenty-nine, and that was after two years of marriage. They had been trying to have children but my mother could not carry.

My mother was very spiritual. She told me later on in life, 'Steve, when it is your time to leave your physical self there will be many brothers and sisters waiting for you on the other side.' A very lovely lady who had a rough time; she had not been dealt a good hand in life as well. In some ways my father and mother were well-suited or well-matched. Her spiritual belief was in itself a physical burden to her, my father did not help; he tolerated it to the point of gritting his teeth every time it was mentioned. He loved my mother and she knew he was not that way – enlightened – so she just got on with it. Her family more or less disowned her, calling her 'the devil's daughter' and would not have anything to do with 'that witchcraft'. What I know now of my mother's family is they had a dark side to them that not many living in Arkansas were aware of.

My mother's family, going way back, originated in Oxford, England. They came over to the Americas in 1610 and lived in the town of Naumkeag (later called Salem) for the next one hundred years. They only came to this part of America because of the strong influences of Government. Salem later became the epicentre of spiritual happenings. The witch-hunts and persecution of the community at large were not tolerated by the devout religious leaders who felt that any kind of power struggle within the small townships was unacceptable. The Council of Elders held the power and it was not going anywhere, therefore small families and those who were vulnerable and alone were to be the victims of such cruelty and misdemeanour that it is beyond the belief of common man that a human being should be so brutal towards another. I can understand there being some conflict between males of different families and the like, but for a male to inflict pain and suffering on a female of any age is beyond my comprehension.

My mother's family were in a good position of power. They had land and were respected in the community. The family paid for more of their possessions to come over on the Mayflower in 1620, a flag ship of the English nation. It brought over people that were described as pilgrims who felt they could share their life and faith with others in a new life in the Americas. So the small dwellings grew larger, the land expanded, and the town of Salem was given as a place to prosper and grow, to grow as a community together as one and to have the Puritan values of our forefathers magnified a thousand fold – to expand our true beliefs of who we are and what we are as individuals living in a community spirit.

My mother's family grew in status and wealth in the years of growth in Salem and they produced two girls who were of true beauty in every way, their names were Matilda and Emily. They grew up together and despite being three years of age apart they were as close as twins. At the ages of five and two they were given a brother who would be at one with them, his name would be David – the giver of light. It seemed as if he was their guardian, he would be there for these two little ones and that would be his life. The teen years of their lives were a terrible time indeed. The witch-hunts grew in a panic of such magnitude it would stretch from Europe to England and across the water to America, bringing with it the cancer of hate, malice, greed and possession. The innocent would perish under the flag of the powerful ones – those who acted in the name of the truth, honesty, and light of religion – the underhanded methods of these wolves in sheep's clothing were cruel to the females of the towns and villages surrounding the community. All were affected, but the 'little ones' with the power of David with them went on to do well for themselves, growing up and earning respect in and around the community.

The truth is that these 'little ones' as my mother called them, were in fact white witches. Everything was ok until one night Emily was caught by a so-called do-gooder who said in his statement to the Council of Elders that there was a strange glow of light around her body when walking through the town at dusk. He felt her presence around him and he felt threatened by this so he reported it, feeling it was his duty for the influence of the devil upon his self was against him as a believer in the Almighty, and the thought of this coming into the light of his family was not, he felt, right.

This brought an upsurge of hate towards the family of Emily but the wrath of the family was to no avail. Poor Emily had to go in front of the Council Members and try to explain her misfortunes. Emily knew of her powers along with her sister – they were as one – so as soon as Matilda knew of her sister's plight she stood by her saying, 'If my sister is on trial, so am I.'

With this, David came into the arena and stood not in front of them nor by their side but behind, as if a shield surrounded them. They were grilled in a way not seen before in the witch trials; their beauty was a big factor in all of this, the two girls had grown to be very beautiful women in their own right and there was a power around them. These two factors and living in those times were in itself a strong combination, to go forward and actually live was a bonus. You knew that the Members of the Council were lining their own nests in the name of truth. Because you got the community to give their consent to your voice you were then given power to do as you wish, so these individuals were given the power to exercise any way of punishment or cruelty under the name of the law and not a damn thing could be done about it.

Matilda and Emily knew their fate and accepted it but David would not. He was given the utmost pain – the rack, the thumbscrews, tortured day in, day out to confess to being a witch, or warlock in his case. With Matilda and Emily it was to be the game of death. The thought of these two lovely women going to their deaths without some fun on the way was too much for the Council Members and their small band of hangers on, those that would do the actual deeds of punishment. The Council Members themselves were above all that, to the outside world they were prim and proper but behind the mask of authority they blossomed into hateful voyeurs that manipulated those innocently caught up in this mess. In Matilda's diary it is written: *'No good praying and asking for forgiveness. We pray to the nature spirits and ask them for guidance. The greed of man is within himself and through time he will understand.'*

While all this was going on, the structure of the governing bodies was at a point of breaking under the ruling that these atrocities should end. Luckily for Matilda and Emily they survived this, though God only knows how they did. The trauma of being raped and beaten was etched not only on their physical bodies but their emotional and mental selves had taken a battering too. It was the powerful and true love they had for David that took them through all of this. His fate was not so good – he was the last one in that area to die as a result of brutality against the innocent. He died shouting his innocence that he was not the Devil's child, and giving his loyalty to his sisters in his last breath.

After this the family could not and would not stay in Salem. They moved on. My mother is a direct descendant of Emily, so the powers of the spirit are passed down in the family. Those that can see are but a few – the true seers, my mother is one that it came through in the family and was ostracized because of her talents. And so my family's history is not too hidden in the depths of nothingness.

To carry on with my own progress in this life, I have the thought and the spirit teachings of my mother given to me by genetics, and also her teachings of the white way. When she spoke of David it was as if something within me sparked a light that seemed I was a guardian of some kind. All these thoughts go through your mind growing up. You are only influenced by outside thoughts, those that wish you harm and those that wish to walk the same path as you. I have a strong family around me that gives me strength and the belief of Spirit.

Growing up I have met lots of people that I shall always remember. In the fall of 1932 I was 10 years of age. I was finding my way in life; in my runaway times as I recall them, I was given a path to walk that would change my thinking once again. I had yet another argument with my father who then proceeded to take his belt to my behind and to my back. He made sure that he would not mark my face, hands or legs for even in those times there was no room for excessive cruelty. Everybody knew it went on but only in certain circumstances would the authorities take action; it was left up to the family's inner sanctum to deal with these things.

My mother of course knew nothing of these little outbursts of cruelty. She was under the impression that I was the apple of my father's eye and that was good enough for her. So, for the sake of my mother who I loved dearly, and the father who I hated with a vengeance, I withheld my inner anger and ran away. This was my only solution to a problem that really was not mine but my father's. My father's hatred – for what I do not know – was as though he had to try and force a demon out of himself and I was that demon in physical form.

Anyway, my running away was at its peak at this time and my family accepted it – they knew I would return so maybe a night under the stars would do me some good. Well this particular night I ran and ran, to this day I do not know for how far it was – three miles, five miles, who knows? I came across low ground that was not a chasm or a gorge but a shallow field that had what seemed like a dim light at its far end. It was early evening, just getting dark, not cold but a slight chill. I had a coat and had grabbed hold of a hat so the cold was not my worry, in fact with the hate of my father still flowing through my veins I was quite warm.

I walked, looking at every step towards this light at the end of the field. Like a hawk in the night I watched everything – I was curious. The height of the structures ahead grew ever bigger and to me at that time they were immense in their size and grandeur – they rose so majestically in the night sky I was overwhelmed by them. Then the sound: the sound of many voices, some shouting, some wailing like banshees. The light which I had seen at a distance was now glowing for all to see – the sparks as if shouting to be seen as they sparkled and faded around the ever-glowing form. The sight that captivated my eyes was one that will be with me for the rest of my life and beyond. The colour of the wings and the dance of these people was spellbinding – I could not keep my eyes away from them. My feet were driven not by myself but by the rhythm of the drum, and the singing drew me ever closer to the fire.

It seemed like this went on for a long time. Maybe it was only a matter of minutes or seconds – I do not know. It came to a crashing end when a hand touched my shoulder and I was brought back to the here and now.

'What have we here?' came a voice that bellowed like a siren in the darkness.

'I am sorry, I am lost sir,' was my reply as I looked up.

Looking down from what seemed like a mountain was this man with power in his blue eyes. 'You are lost but now you are found. Sit in the circle little one with my family. Are you hungry?'

With eyes that obviously told him that I was he beckoned over a young girl and he spoke to her in a language I was not familiar with. She smiled and grabbed hold of my hand, dragging me to a table where I was given food in abundance, meat cut straight from the animal itself. I just sat in what now seemed so familiar surroundings – I felt at home here.

It seemed after a short while I was now the centre of attention and the singing and chanting took second place to the attraction of this lost soul. Much giggling and laughing came from the young and the women – a lot of talking, and muttering and nodding of heads from the men. I had obviously stumbled upon a tribe of Native Americans – there had been talk in the town of local Indians but mostly they were in Reservations. I had seen some in the town but they kept themselves at a very great distance from white ways. To stumble upon this was truly to me a wondrous thing, I was now obviously the total infatuation of the entire tribe. There seemed many about me then but looking back there was but a handful of what was the main tribe. They were allowed to do there what white people called their 'rituals' but did not understand them – these were powerful ceremonies.

Another strong hand on my shoulder, 'A man of the tribe you are. Well now, we are only here for one night and we move on. You are from the place they call the two streams, the coming together of two waters that arc together and stream as one?'

'I have not had it explained to me in that way before, but yes.'

'We cross that river where it meets tomorrow on our way to the Reservation in the east. You have crossed a lot of miles to be here. Does your family know of your whereabouts?'

I said, 'That is not a problem.'

It was his concern for his people. Even in this time of 1932 there was a prejudice against the yellow man and in the face of a young white boy going lost and being in the company of such people the gun would rule first unfortunately. In my reply I just said it did not matter, I would not be missed until morning, and with that he walked away, smiling and nodding to a lot of older men that looked at me and just said 'thanks' in their eyes. The young girl that was obviously chaperoning me, grabbed me again by the hand.

'The Shaman wishes to speak with you.'

'The who?' I said.

She laughed, 'Do not worry, the Holy man who you spoke to first. He wishes to have counsel with you. You are privileged. He does not normally give counsel to someone of your younger years. You are nine or ten, yes?'

'Yes...ten.'

'I thought so.'

'What is your name?' I asked.

'Running Lake.'

'An unusual name!' I laughed.

'What are you laughing at?' she said.

'Running Lake – what kind of name is that?'

'It is my medicine name, the name of my true self.'

'Ok.' I said, still not figuring out in my ten-year-old brain what she meant, but never mind.

'Come on – he has given you a name already.'

'Sorry?'

'He has given you a name already.'

'What is it?'

'He must tell you, for you to gain your own power. Now go.'

As I turned, I looked at the now black shape of a gigantic tent – a teepee, its total blackness being shown only by the light of the fire. As I walked towards the flap or door, I wondered, do I knock? I opened it slightly; the pungent smell hit me full in the face – the smell of herbs. A voice from inside said, 'Welcome, come in.'

There was a small fire in the centre of the structure, I looked up; I could see the night sky above me, the smoke making strange shapes in the darkness. Looking back, the opening was small but to me it seemed like the whole night's sky was there in my sight.

'Again, welcome. You are very brave, young one. You are much troubled within yourself. You have much turmoil and hate in yourself. I can see that. You are walking with the Great Spirit. Your mother is one with Spirit, yes?'

'How do you know of this?' I asked.

'You have many Earth Walks. Some are but a stroll, others a marathon, but there are times when you know your own walk and the walk of others. For you my friend, this is your time, you walk with Spirit. It looks after you on this Earth time. You have many friends in the Spirit World.'

'It is true, my mother has the gift of sight and she has taught me many things. The girl – Running Lake – says I have been given a name.'

'That is true my young friend. That has to be earned like everything in life. It is a special gift. It is not given without sacrifice. You have a medicine name but you will come by that name when and only when you have earned that privilege.'

'What is your name sir?' I said in a squeaky little voice.

'I am Black Hawk. That is my medicine name. I also have a name by which the white man gives us identities; they are only there as a mask – not revealing what is our true self. You have to find your true name little friend for in the white man's eyes you are only an identity. You, in their eyes, do not exist.'

'What do you mean?'

'You must find your true self and then you will find the answers to all questions. You have a gift – use it. Use the Spirit inside to give you answers. Look through not white man's eyes. You will venture from these shores and go forth into the darkness. There is much deception around you. There are others you take care of – they look upon you as a guardian. There is one in Spirit that guards all darkness and ill things from you. You have a light around you of great force. Ask for its help.'

I now know of this to be David. He has given me strength in many ways. This Holy Man and Shaman was truly a magnificent power of strength for his people and I of course thanked him for his counsel. I was given shelter for the night. There was much energy around me that night – the dreams of being surrounded by blasts of gunfire and faces give me cold sweats even now.

The light of the day came and with it I felt as if now I had truly been given something special, this was not just circumstance it was meant to be. I was led to these people and given a message, it was now up to me to work for this name of power; I was to go forward in the way of a deliverance.

I walked with these true friends for a while. They came across the arc in the river where I was to walk towards the hustle and bustle of the white man's world. I looked at them going on their way; like ghosts from the past they were waving non-stop, and I ran excited and elated for a while knowing that they were still in sight. I was determined to run up the hill and wave them a final goodbye. As I made it and turned, with a gasp I realized they had gone. But they couldn't have just vanished...into thin air?

The memory of that will always be with me. I am sure they were there for a purpose I did not just stumble upon them. It was a learning curve in my life, it made me see things in a totally different way. As for my medicine name, yes I have a medicine name, a name that was given to me in a dream by a warrior in war paint upon a pinto horse also in war paint. The name of *Blue Angel* was given to me; it gives me strength even by just saying it. It holds many strengths, it lives within me and is sacred to me. What is within a name? Inner power.

My years following this experience bounced along. I gathered as many friends around me as a comfort blanket. My father made less and less impact on my life as I grew older. My mother gathered strength and knew of my gift, she shone when looking at me. All her strength was being given to me looking back, now she has gone to Spirit I know she is with me – no one can take that away. As for my father, he could not live without her. He gave up and took his own life when I was sixteen. The upset of my mother's passing when I was fourteen was terrible, I went through much heartache and blamed everybody – even my father who I knew loved her dearly. My uncle became my guardian – ironic really how the name 'guardian' keeps cropping up in my life.

My uncle knew I was a good shot and introduced me at the age of sixteen to a rifle with telescopic sights. This I took and used with such accuracy it scared even me. Without trying I shot at the targets without one not hitting dead centre. I aim, the cross of the sight meets the intended target and at that moment I release the first finger of the right hand exactly onto the hammer of the ignition. In one fell swoop the deed is done – no mistake. Perhaps this is part of the gift? We are all at some stage in our evolution given a special gift from God – something that sets us a little bit above the rest – something special that gives us an edge. Perhaps this is my edge – we shall see.

The years go by. The volcano that is slowly boiling away in Europe is coming to its final explosion in 1939 with a trickle of news that Germany invades Poland and England declares war on Germany. I have probable roots in England from my mother's side of the family – in the journals she left me there is mention of Oxford.

You grow up fast in this time frame – you do not wait for it to come to you, you go to it. I have a dear friend, her name is Caroline. She has been with me since my mother's passing; she was a friend up until my mother's funeral. What a day to lose your virginity – on the day of your mother's funeral. I was in need of a lot of love that day and Caroline was there – she gave me strength when I was weak. The day was very emotional and come the night we were alone, no one to give orders. We needed each other's company and that's that, nothing to be ashamed of. My mother would give her consent, I knew that, so we carried on.

Caroline is my fiancée now, we plan to marry. The year is 1939, I will be eighteen next year, she will be seventeen – we have our whole life ahead of us. We have heard rumours that the United Kingdom wish us to give them help. The leader of their country, Churchill, has regular meetings with our Teddy but these meetings are of high secrecy and do not open the truth to the public. In my teachings there is no smoke without fire. I sense much heartache in Churchill's voice – when heard on the BBC's World Service you sense he is speaking from the heart but he is also not telling everything. He knows there are spies everywhere and you must be aware of that. I know of the audacity of the German government and its powers – they send their Zeppelins over New York with the crossed emblem of peace but they use it as the swastika. They have no fear and that in itself is a very powerful weapon. Without the firepower of destruction we use today the fear factor rules – you throw away the rule book when dealing with that kind of energy. I feel in my heart at this time that a lot of innocent people are going to die at the mercy of one's personal power trip. What escalates from a mere skirmish will envelop the world in what for some will be the end of the world.

It seems my name has been given to a few government officials at the gun club I go to with my uncle. There are more faces I do not recognize looking in my direction when I am training in the next few days. I need to be at my peak, the annual competition amongst all the different gun clubs and societies comes together in a national event and I have to travel to Chicago for this. These people watching as we train look like the Feds. We know there to be legitimate agencies of law enforcement – the FBI is one of the main bodies, but through the grapevine of different gun club members who have reached a point in their career of shooting a level of "A1 master shooter" within the clubs, we know some have been approached by men in black suits looking for recruits it seems.

I have myself not been approached yet but I know I have been eyeballed. I am captain of a team of four; we represent our club at the national finals to be held at a gun club in Chicago over two days. It's not long. We have a period when if we do not go on to the final we have an option either to stay or come home so it is back to normal until we go to the event. Working for my uncle also gives me time to go to the gun club – he does not mind. Working in construction is hard but rewarding work when it is a family business.

I gather my thoughts for 'the chase' as I call it. Nobody can touch my numbers at the club – my fellow team members are good but not in my class. I have heard there are some good shots and I have to be aware of them. We shall see. I do not have any arrogance or ego in my thoughts when I shoot, I shoot from me within; I am one with the gun. The gun is me and I am the gun and that is how it is and how it shall be.

We gather at the event – a lot of people obviously at this prestigious occasion. No quarter given it seems even in the dress of some of these guys. There are half a dozen guys from Dallas, Texas in their cowboy hats like some Wild West Show; some guys from New York – they look like gangsters; some from New Jersey; some from California, the 49ers State. Some mean business – you can see it on their faces.

I do not have to compete until late afternoon. The primary opening then a few matches and we get stuck in, I am third in the running of my team. We are given targets at different positions and we have to shoot from different angles, standing, laying down, crouched, and one position that is not on the regular list which is given as a competition amongst the elite three. The top three in the whole country go at a head-to-head against a killing house; there are good and bad silhouettes or dummies thrown up at certain points in the killing house as they call it. Only the inner circle of members and officials know of the killing house, we do not mention it in public circles as they would probably take a dim view of it. Although the police do have a similar thing as does the military, we are the only ones outside of these official bodies that do this; I am sure that if you dig even deeper then you would find it is probably funded by an official or unofficial government organization.

I do well. No one else comes close – we are in the top five in the club section. I aim to do well in the individual trophy, my aim is to win at all costs. My team unfortunately lets me down – we come a close second to the boys from Dallas who I must admit are good, their concentration is brilliant. Let's see how the individual event goes. I get through with no difficulty whatsoever – this is my time to excel. I have to get past two main opponents – Tim from Dallas, Texas and a guy from New York whose name I cannot pronounce, he is a good cook so they say. They are one with the gun also; perhaps I will have these as comrades as foretold to me by the Spirit Ones – they shall gather together to do battle as one. But today is my day, I win of course but it is close, very close. Let us see with the killing house, if I come up against these guys again, shall I be the victor again? Let us see. Time for a rest then time for action.

I retire to my room exhausted. Water and a good book but before that sleep to get my head together – must relax and be focused for tomorrow. Already run over one day late as it is, sent a wire to my uncle, have not yet got a reply but never mind, what will be will be. There's a loud knock on the door. Who the fuck is that? I was told I was not to be disturbed.

I open the door to these two guys dressed all in black but for their white shirts. 'Ok what's the joke? Is it the guys from the team's little joke? I've heard of you lot.'

'Yes Mr Miller, we have also heard of you. We have a proposition to your advantage. We want to bring you into the fold as it were. Do you mind us coming in – it's a bit draughty out here.'

'Yeah, sure, I'll hear what you've got to say, why not?' and with that they enter the room. They sit like robots, not even taking off their dark glasses. 'How do you guys look and see in those shades?' I can't stop laughing.

'We have a deal that you can prosper from Steve. There is talk of a conflict in Europe and at some point America is going to be a part of that. You with your talent could bypass a lot of suffering if you agree to work with us.'

'Are you threatening me?'

'No sir, we are not. You have special talents that with the right training could give you the edge amongst those around you. That is all we are allowed to say at this point. Here is a number – dial it and wait for your instructions. The choice is yours. We would prefer you work for us by free will rather than by order if you see what we mean. Oh, by the way, good luck tomorrow in your little competition. We fund it so be lucky. Thank you.'

So much for peace of mind – there is much to learn, these guys sure know how to get to you. They are telling the truth I know that, I can sense these things. A good night's rest is in order, for tomorrow the victor.

Perhaps this day's events will put me on the map as far as shooting goes. This matters to me not only for myself and the honour of my family, but to get at those bastards that have the bare-faced cheek to order me to do anything. What right do they have to threaten an American citizen?

I have rights just as every other citizen of this country has. The powers-that-be are certainly pulling the strings in high places. They and others probably like them all over the world are manipulating and grooming such converts to the cause of justice. You are no better than a hired hand – a bounty hunter for the greater power, a little piece of the melting pot of life. The collective are a lot of energy to be dipped into, just take out those that show promise in whatever field it may be, the active and the counter-active – those that destroy very well or those that heal very well – and just leave the rest to be used as cannon fodder in the physical.

These guys are obviously playing at mind games with me so fuck them, let them go to hell, I shall be the victor. This day in the arena I am up against very good foes. When we enter the killing house we are hooded – we do not know who we are competing against on a one-to-one ratio. We must be patient and wait our turn. I have exactly fifteen minutes to make my mark. As I enter Room One I sense an energy to my left. I look around – no sound, then see a picture to my right, a guy with a gun in a window. He is punished, I shoot without thought. It is as if my actions are a split second earlier then brain kicks in and moves my arm and finger to press the trigger. I go through this routine in 14.25 seconds of automatic firing or not as a bad guy appears or a good guy snaps into view, or the old Granny pops her head around the corner. I feel good. I know I have done well. I hope the judges will see it that way, I hope so.

There is a flutter of news going around the arena and where I have decided to set up camp that there is a new gun in town – an independent entry. I do not know if this is in the rule book; amongst the gun clubs of the country only the top guns from the three top clubs should be put forward. This is a first. I know a statement is being made in the arena – may as well take a look.

Lo and behold, look who it is! In the arena the comedians who had a word with me earlier are now standing either side of an older man of authority. He taps the microphone with his fist as if in anger at the very fact of being here.

'Gentlemen, if we may have some order here!' and with a shrug of the shoulders as if ready to take on a heavyweight boxer in a right brawler of a fight he says, 'Now my friends, we have been entertained here very well by your representatives from the glorified, well-respected clubs up and down the country. Now, as we are...Now as you would say, we are funding this little gathering in the light of world events, we would like a representative from our organization to partake in this little event and to throw our cards on the table as it were.'

There is now a loud ripple of noise, the sound of angry whispers getting louder by the minute. 'Now, now gentlemen – this you must tolerate. After all, this particular event is only for fun at the end of a competition.'

My insides are now getting twisted and taut in a way that even I am getting worried about – this means more to me than just fun and the other competitors are of the same mind. And what about world events, how could they have any bearing on US gun clubs?

'We have two aces gentlemen to throw at you. Their names are not important.'

With that these two guys step forward. They looked focused, I can see that, like robots. I sense energy around them as energy is around all of us but with these two it is as if someone has manipulated their very thought patterns. The weird thing is they look normal and would blend easily into a crowd. They enter the killing zone, one at a time, the next few minutes prove to me that this was more than a mere competition. These guys just blew away my target time by a margin of at least two minutes and with a finesse I have not seen before. If I am not mistaken I believe that these operatives – and that is what they are – have been highly trained and either drugged or had their heads messed about with to bring that kind of focus and determination forward and to be exactly alike. If it was just one guy I would put it down to a gift from God but two brought forward into the same arena means there has had to be some form of skulduggery afoot by somebody.

I must take my leave, I have seen enough. I am intrigued by what I have seen, I must find out what these guys are in town for. What is the end result of our little demonstration here today and my own little meeting and few words with the elusive guys from the fundraisers? I must admit I have never taken much interest in the goings on in the background political avenues of these events, it's a case of just turning up, doing the business and returning to the fold as it were. But with the world in turmoil at the moment all that was classed as normal is now turned on its back. Somewhere, somebody is fucking dying because of greed and lust for power – that is what we are dealt with and it is up to the individual to make a stand.

We are all under one flag or another and we have no choice but to honour that flag. My family came originally from the old country but I am from the bloodstock of this country I call home – America. I will defend this land with my life as my forefathers did, and I will give my life, that is not in question, BUT – and this is the BIG BUT – I will do the business with my own thoughts and what I feel right no matter what enemy is at the gate, whether it be internal affairs or overseas.

I return home to my family and have a good rest. They obviously want to know how I got on but my mind is now on other things. The competition is at an end, I must get on with the rest of my life. Things are moving along at a greater pace than I feared – we will enter a war it seems, but not yet, along with the old country. Our fight for now is with ourselves and the rising sun of Japan.

The hell that now comes upon us as American citizens is truly not comprehensible to human thought. We go about our daily routines – getting up in the morning, going to work, the talk, the banter, the daily ritual of eating at a set time – the things we take for granted; the mundane things like work we may like, we may hate, we may just tolerate – we just do. Even going to the toilet, it is there; and so we just plod along. From this day forward for a lot of us it is not going to be the same as yesterday. Every day from now on is going to be a living hell until at some point we will as individuals meet the demon.

As we step into another arena, one that I and the next person in the street has no control over whatsoever, our lives are now just numbers on one side of a board and we are up against another set of numbers on the other side. How many numbers are on either side does not matter, what matters in the end is who has the guts – at the end. These numbers are individual lives, lives that matter to those that live them nobody else, and to give up one's life is precious in itself. It is a sacrifice, the highest sacrifice any individual makes, and to make that decision takes a lot of guts. These so-called politicians in their ivory towers do not give a rat's ass about human life on a global scale; we are numbers to be brought into the sum – to be used and discarded as they see fit.

I am afraid now though. We need to be standing firm against these people. I speak from my heart. I know I probably will die for this country in the years of trouble ahead and a lot of my fellow countrymen and women will fall with me, but we will go down fighting, fighting not only for liberty but freedom of the will for that in itself matters to each and every one of us on this planet, not just Americans.

This is not just my story. It is the story of many people who have the right to say a small something. What happened to them in a probably very small way builds up a picture, so vivid and clear in its conception that it goes beyond any belief system that any one person might have. This follows a story of a bunch of guys wanting justice for what is called betrayal. Now, betrayal comes in many forms, does it not? A betrayal is not to be taken lightly from so many individuals.

We go on about self-sacrifice – in a way knowing that you are about to die for your country. So those that uphold the said laws and belief systems in the said country is, in its purest form, what you are fighting for – their belief in you; they express power over you as an individual. You look upon them as givers of light.

The structure of life as you see it – the laws that govern this land, its inner sanctum of power, those that step forward and take command of situations whether it be political, military, local government or royal corridors, they are all linked in a very tight way. They govern – we serve, and we look upon them to make the right decisions. We follow – we have no choice, we must take orders up to a point. We may think we live free lives, when you take away the mist and see through freshly wiped glasses at the real light of day, you will see that we do not live as free a lifestyle as we might think, the actual structure of life is more complex. We in one country are governed by circumstances in other states of the Union and beyond in other countries and belief systems. When they clash we must be aware of those rifts in the seabed of political agendas that control the corridors of powerful government bodies that take over at a mere whim.

You live freely in a state of the Union, it may be completely different fifty miles away, or a hundred miles across a border. Those people breathe the same air as you and I, so what is different about that? It's not nature controlling the way we are – we all have to live, breathe, eat, do all those things we have to do in order to survive, and where you are at the point of survival or where you are in the structure of life determines what happens to you in that life. The corridors of power open to anyone who has the insight and knowledge to go forward with their lives. Once in the fold as it were, then the world is your oyster – you can control whoever and whatever you like.

Reading this you may think what does all this mean? It shows that there are powers that govern the man in the street, the woman going about her everyday tasks. We think we are free, we are not. Living in America at this time I live a good life, I have a good family – I love them dearly. But I have a letter in front of me saying I must now go to a point or place fifty miles from here and sign a document that takes me away from my life, my family, all that I treasure; to sign a document that more or less is my death certificate. I cannot say anything about what I might do because somebody – some non-person, sits in a little room and makes up a document to be countersigned by a high-ranking person and then signed by myself. Because of a thing called 'Top Secret, The Official Secrets Act of the United States of America'.

I thought I was a free man to choose the life I live. It seems I am not a free man. Don't get me wrong, I love my country and will fight for what is right, but at this point in time there is nobody giving the right signals as a right or wrong way to go. It is true the Japanese cut first blood, they put down the gauntlet and we now must respond with the killing of innocent individuals who are in essence the same as me. They have no quarrel with me and I have no quarrel with them and in a one-to-one fight we would walk away and forget about it. Not so in the bigger picture. We must now take the lives of each and every person that exists on that continent along with the most innocent of all, the wildlife of that land – they have no argument to settle, no axe to grind, so why should we slaughter those living, breathing individuals? They have a right as do we. Just because we talk we are supposed to be superior in every way, why do we then inflict pain and suffering upon those that are weak and do not communicate in the manner we do? We all have our individual rights and wrongs, the way we govern our own lives makes a difference. Yes, we must look upon these beliefs and live by them for without them life is meaningless; others control you and what you do.

Just because some individual deems it right to encourage less fortunate people who are weak in the physical as well as mentally and structures a course of events to let the weak vanquish the even weaker ones in the surrounding areas. For someone who, it has to say, does not get this power by birthright, and steps up the ladder as it were and manipulates those that have power and feeds off these certain ones that will do anything to get what they want, disregard everybody else. The guy who works to stay alive, who sees the sun rise and fall and survives day-to-day and asks, what is it all about – am I just to see this life go before me and not have any structure in it whatsoever? Just survive until you die and return to the earth?

Now, when someone comes along and boosts your self-esteem through the roof and suddenly makes your life something even though it is as if nothing has happened, it is as if it is mind control. But how can this be? You know what's going on, you are in control of your bodily functions, you believe you are seeing what you are feeling and you know what is right and what is wrong. But do you? Are you being manipulated in a way you cannot fully fathom out?

You go about your duties to survive and you yet feel pulled towards going along with other people of all ages to see a man stand alone and talk sometimes loud, sometimes quiet, and you are spellbound by his words. Why are we here? Does all this make sense? Why should we gather together and in a way, worship this one man? Where has he come from? Does he have the most honest of intentions for us as a nation and us as individuals? Does he give a toss? What are his intentions so far as power? These people around me are convinced he is their Messiah, a very strong word. That one word Messiah, conjures up a box of tricks inside the mind, is he the deliverer of all mankind, the one, the true light?

These souls seem to think so, it seems strange to me, listening to this man in such a large crowd of people. This is not a crowd: it is a mass of heads listening – the call has spoken. You walk towards the call, you do not know why you come, you just do; it is as though he is speaking to *you*. You know it cannot be, this one person cannot have mass hypnosis over all of us – surely not? It seems impossible but this is how it is.

I have been sent by the powers of my country to see and hear what this one individual is doing and the only way to get close enough to see this man is at a rally for the said person. I must point out that at this stage the American government and its peoples have not yet entered the European theatre of war, we are merely observers for our friends in the Allied countries. We have enough on our plates at the moment.

I have been assigned by a non-government agency, officially it does not exist but in truth it does – very much so. Again, I say, we are all just pawns to be used again and again, I do not agree with what I am doing but I must do it or I am no more. There is such a thing as being a traitor to one's country, the fact you are prepared to gives one life. They do not listen to the individual. It does not matter; you are nothing so use it to your advantage. They want something from you. You have a talent. Use it. They will use you – use them. It works. I have been given specific orders not to intervene in anything. I could if I wish end all of this now – if I could get just one shot – that is all I need. I could end probably years of suffering and death by one shot that is as easy as that, but nobody thinks of these things. That is why I say you are being manipulated in every way through subliminal messages sent now in radio wave patterns that go beyond the realms of ordinary thinking.

Try now to switch off all rational thinking and see what you are left with, your own thoughts? Are they though? Are your thoughts put there by an outside force? How can this be? We haven't the technology to obtain this, it goes without thinking – this is 1941. We as a race have not got to a rational explanation for what I am saying, but as I said before, throw away the rule book, fly by the seat of your pants – we are controlled, it is the bottom line, that is it folks. We think we are in control but we are not.

I know I have not been manipulated. Nobody has sat me down and let a pendulum fall from left to right in front of my eyes and put me into another frame of mind. It's far too advanced for that – that is, our world, the world they wish us to see, to live. Me speaking now even invades that pure energy because that is what it is – it is all around us. A lot of the propaganda is of the real truth only filtered in to give a false trail. Walls have ears – how very true – very good propaganda. It is only words to us, but go beyond these words and look at what is said between them. I am talking as a spiritual person now, through my teachings, it makes you look at the reality of life, go beyond what it is you are seeing and feeling. 'Walls have ears' to the lay person is just that – the fact is keep your mouth shut and do not speak to anyone strange or in a public area. Now, see it through the eyes and ears of the spiritually aware, the walls in fact do have ears, and eyes, and feelings – they look and feel and breathe with you. The powers that manipulate how we live and breathe and go about our lives and know what we are doing from the cradle to the grave – in this time it is hard to imagine.

1941. Time was just a few years ago, my father was just learning how to drive this strange-looking machine with a wheel in each corner. The years have gone on from there and technology has advanced at an alarming rate. Even so, it is hard to believe how we can sit here and say we are talking advanced manipulation of the human race on a worldwide scale so advanced only certain areas are aware of it. Those people working for government agencies like myself are used, as simply as that, used and discarded like confetti at a wedding – just swept away. We cannot say anything in the public domain – we are non-persons, we do not exist, it is easy to just disappear. Like a puff of smoke we disappear in this line of work and if this comes to war and my country's involvement as I know in my heart it will, then the ball is solidly driven well out of the ball park. Then, all these powers will be given the green light to express all their desires upon the waking world and we as individuals will have to be sacrificed to get to the point of being one – that is winning, and then control. And it will probably start all over again but with new vigour and status, to go beyond even what it is now and continue.

I for one know that in the bigger picture I do not stand a chance. I have to look out for myself, fuck everybody else. This matters to me. This time I will try and meet others that have broken away from the collective thinking, there are a few but we are branded to be made weirdoes. In the collective, spiritual people are not very well liked among those very religious types and the controlling bodies. Let's not forget going back to before medieval times the Church played a big part in power struggles and a lot of innocent people were put to the sword because of one man's belief system. I know, my family were persecuted in Salem for no reason and those at the head of the lynch mob were supposedly under the banner of the 'Enlightened One', the Cross of Jesus. They were using his name in vain but that's another story – you get my point?

I must focus my objectives in the here and now. I am surrounded by these people, I do not know fully what this man is saying but he certainly has you fixed to the spot, he is obviously of another energy opposed to the normal way of the collective. He has come upon the peoples of this country to bring a message – that of standing up for one's self in the here and now. It is being manipulated, yes, but this is something else. How can one man have so much power? It is after all the collective that thrives on power. It as though he is generating the power and all that look and listen are transfixed – not only through the voice but by the eyes.

I have been given orders to get as close as I can to this person. I have commandeered a uniform from the secret police of this time – the special SS. There are Special Forces amongst this group as well as ourselves – we haven't the blueprint for such small societies or groups that do covert work. This German government and its leader mean business. This is not a walk in the park, by no means. I can get close to this man only because the boss and I do not know who he is. He has made it so the strings of office are interwoven like you would not imagine. Like I said before, throw away the rule book – it does not figure here in the non-world as you, the part of the collective, knows. I may get close to this man but as soon as my real identity is known all hell will let loose and through diplomatic diplomacy I might get through to finally getting home. Me as an individual will cease to exist – only on paper will I emerge to satisfy the public domain and then be forgotten.

I see this man's eyes up close for the first time. I see no hate there, only compassion. For his beloved countrymen and women he is not without fear. He is very strong but he has also his disciples and they can be one thousand times more powerfully destructive than him. He is the engine – he does not drive the car. He in his self is being given the run-around by those that surround him. He is the power from which such are fed; they need to be looked at closely, not him. They have now been given the green light to do what they want to whoever they please. His thoughts are for the good of his people BUT...and it's a BIG BUT...at what price? These poor people do not know what they have given their prayers to. They have unleashed a power so strong that all in its way will be controlled and will not sway from its goal which is pain and suffering on a worldwide scale. Being in control of the masses is one thing, but to try and obliterate all in one's path by death is another.

Who am I to say all this? What I say may be truth and it may not, it is up to you to decide, not me, for that is true free will – to make one's mind up for oneself and not be controlled. I am here to do a job and to use the tools that make that job succeed and then go on to the next assignment. My work is done, I must report to my superior as must others in my team. They have also been at this rally and other meetings, and got close in and observed the Third Reich in all its glory – the men and women that ultimately control the Reich.

'And in a word I must report that all governing bodies within the Pentagon gather all known resources and work with the British Government to be ready for a European and global war.'

This mother fucker means business.

And so this is my life. My name is Steve Miller, I am an American and proud of that fact. My family are true Americans that have shed blood for their country – we go deep within the true culture of this land. But to the authorities and to the American people that have yet to experience this fine land, I am a non-person, I do not exist along with fellow patriots. And that is what we are – we are clandestine, we are of the night, a special task force that to the outside world do not exist. The actual fact of the Americans coming into the (now) theatre of war in Europe and the civilised world, strengthens my very being. I have a name for only a short while for the sole purpose of keeping face – in the Eighth Army Air Corps you cannot be disguised; there is always somebody that recognises you in the hustle and bustle of war.

I have chosen to go in with the Bomb Group. It gives me the chance to go forward in other avenues rather than the cold-blooded world of the lone-sniper working in a non-world of reality. I have kept my real name within the ranks as it were. I'm a pilot having been trained by our group leader. The training we have is not like anything on the conventional ladder, we in a way are programmed to do certain tasks and being a pilot is one of them. We go along with conventional training in the confines of Wright Patterson Air Base flying B-17s and B-24s at long range targets on day missions. This compared to what I have experienced, is a walk in the park. We are still under the watchful eye of the collective thinker – he who watches us at all times. I have no doubt that if I should pay the ultimate price I shall be removed from the collective names that someday will adorn massive pillars, and endless names I know along with other friends that I have in this unit will not remain. In name I shall be forgotten. It hurts me to say this for I love my country and to die for it matters not, but to be recognised by those that wield power gives it credence. I know my loved ones will hold me in their hearts but that alone does not weaken the pain. I need to be loved by my people – those that we fight and die for.

So with good heart I now go forward and go about the duties of a pilot and give my allegiance first and foremost to my crew and to my country. We have much to do. After a Top Secret meeting in the large forest near one of our main bases in England I meet up with old friends. One is Steve Lursquom – I know him from the gun club days and the killing house. He is good and I wonder what the authorities have in store if someone like Steve is on one of the teams (and there are a few more good shots around here that I do not know), what the hell is planned? There is a hit on a big cheese but they must be targeting others as well – we shall see. It's nice to see the guys again, even being in the same camp you miss each other – being in different crews and being stationed around you lose contact with old buddies. If I didn't have my beliefs in the old ways and the true love of my family I do not know what I would do. I ask for the Great Spirit to be with me in these troubled times, the authorities cannot take that away from me. They have taken everything else.

I know there is a mission being organised that is Top Secret and that is it. There are always rumours flying about: on night missions being shot at by what some guys call 'flying bombs' – some planes being blown straight out of the sky and not a bit of shrapnel or crew left, completely blown away. That's the rumours, what is fact remains to be seen. After what I have experienced, who knows what's around the corner?

Chapter Twenty-Seven
Michael Hall, B-17 gunner

In these troubled times it's hard to believe just sitting here in the open fields of Suffolk and Norfolk in England, that wherever you look there's a major disaster going on in war-torn Europe and the major towns and cities of this country. I have to pinch myself to remember that I am in a war; just closing my eyes with the sun on my face I am back home in Virginia with the winds, and the faint smell of my mother's cooking in the distance. She's calling to the family to gather at the dinner table, her warm smile gives a warm glow to my heart.

At that time she was the family. Without her at the wheel of the big ship who knows what would happen – it didn't bear thinking about. She worshipped my brothers and sisters who got the best of love from my mother. Every one of us thought we were her special one but in reality her favourite was my father. He worshipped her and she worshipped him and we were all by-products of their love for each other, the fact that we were all so very close brought us together even more so. The years up to the war had their moments of great joy and laughter as well as moments of great sadness, but with the development of the strikes on our nation's warships in Pearl Harbour, the seed was unfortunately sown in my mother's case – she knew that her beloved sons were going to the defence of their country. She could do nothing to stop it, all she could do was pray.

She was a devout, religious lady, Methodist in her beliefs. It didn't matter what religion you were at this time, you just drew on your faith in whatever form. For me and my brothers it was a time of new adventures – we did not even think that one day we would be in that much danger. It was new to see foreign lands – to go where we would only dream of before. My mother knew what to expect, in her heart she knew and through her deepest sorrow she could not tell us for if she did she knew the reaction would be very stale – we would rebel. She thought the inevitable was going to happen and we would all perish. Not all – not yet.

I am left sitting in this field in Norfolk on the end of a runway in a sleepy little place called Seething. The locals do not have a clue about what's going on in the real world, for that matter what do they care? We risk our lives every day, what do they care? They go about their lives and just look upon us as intruders, the looks sometimes are so angry you just have to wonder what it's all for. If the Germans were now frog-marching up the town high street doing what they do best and devouring everything in their path the locals would have a rare look upon their faces by Lord. But the Germans are not here, we are, so we make the most of it however the locals look at us.

It's different for the women, we get smiles from them. Some are pretty – nothing like our girls back home. True, the folk here have had it bad in the food department. There are those locals who have to pick a fight – it is their way, unfortunately for them they always pick on brawlers from New Jersey or New York or even worse, from Cincinnati. There are some mean bastards from all over but those three areas bring forward the sharks or barracudas, as we call them.

I remember serving with a bunch of those guys at a base in the Cambridge area called Oakington. A moderately large base, we used this for night raids and working with British crews. It was the politicians' idea to integrate the GI with the Brit as often as possible before we joined the war effort in Europe, Spitfire and Hurricane pilots often came over to the States for training and in these times it was obvious that it should carry on, especially with bomber crews.

There was scope for night raids and our policy for daytime raids had left us without night training. We had to go with the British crews at every opportunity and pretty damn frightening it was as well, I've never experienced anything like it. The glow of the lights for miles underneath you, it was as if we were suspended on a great rope and were witnessing some overwhelming force being used below us and around us, yet we were in a little bubble, nothing would harm us in any way. That is what you thought until an almighty explosion guts the fuselage, the wind gusts in, and like a giant hand, grasps you and throws you out into the night air. This is what happened to me.

In this crew was myself and James Jehovah Masterson, or 'JJ' to his buddies. A hard bastard, if he wasn't fighting some British soldier in a bar he was shagging some local girl in a field – he had no morals this guy. I managed to talk to him only once over a pint at the local pub, and he told me in no uncertain terms that inside he had already died and he did not care for anybody's feelings whatsoever. He gave up – not living, but the hope of seeing his family again, the Bronx was a hard place but its family unity was very deep and forever loyal. I knew I was safe working alongside JJ – he had that quality of leadership even though he was a right bastard.

Alongside JJ was a fellow Yank, Jes K Lorenza from Santa Fe. 'The Jester' was his nickname, always joking around never angry – if he was then he hid it well. Another hard bastard to be sure he was part Mexican, part Irish – a good mixture. His father was an Irish immigrant who lived in San Francisco and met his mother in a bar. She had been there with her friends and become smitten with this Irish guy; she had a wild couple of days with the man and Jes was the result. He did not mind speaking of his past – he joked about it a lot, but you knew deep down he was hurting.

So myself on rear gunner, Jes on side gunner, and JJ next to Jes on side gunner, using a blacked out B-17 for night runs; it seems strange – the crew mostly British and us Yanks, and the British flying a Boeing B-17 FF. What the fuck? Next they will have us flying Spitfires and Hurricanes out of Thorpe Abbotts!

The whole structure of what is going on throws me into turmoil. Sometimes these missions at night are clouded in mystery anyway but this particular one was just supposed to be routine ops – just observation, letting a Brit pilot use the controls of a B-17 just across the Channel and back, no big deal. We were there for decoration – if the Brits were using our planes without any Yankee influence then bang goes diplomatic issues down the pokey – it was needed only for the written record, do you see? We were the only B-17 in operation from that base, we were done up like a Brit plane with even the decals and numbers of the Brit Bomber Command.

We did not ask questions. We didn't give a fuck anyway, just do as you are told. We did not even go in for the briefing – the Brit pilots had that sorted, we were just told to sit tight and if there was any action we would be the first to know. So we gathered at the nose of our beloved Flying Fortress, its name obliterated by black paint. That was a bad omen in itself – the fact that we were going up at night and the name of this fine beast was cruelly taken away was in a way a death wish upon her and the crew. We hoped and prayed this was not so, we gathered our wits in our places within the stomach of the winged one.

And so to the skies, we did not know where we were going – still on observation we were told, but no one explained the box in the bomb bay was anything that we should be worried about. We spoke to the navigator and he said, 'Just keep quiet guys and enjoy the ride. That little package there is a little present from all of us in Bomber Command, just a token of our thanks to our captors.'

'What do you mean?'

'Never mind guys. Just enjoy the ride.'

What the fuck was going on? We were in a B-17, being flown by a bunch of Brits who had a box on board and it seems a little present for their captors. I don't know. It could not be far away this drop; we had been up here well on time for a routine flight. I tried to gather my thoughts.

Suddenly there was an almighty explosion in the belly of our ship and the wind rushed in taking me clean into space. Falling like a stone, I was dazed – was I dreaming this? And struggling for my ripcord I nearly pulled the bastard out of its attachment. The cords entangled and the white of the parachute billowed above, thrusting me back up into the night sky. Looking above and to my left, three more parachutes in the sky with flames from the plane shooting all around then another explosion, throwing me to one side. What was in that box – a giant firework?

This had turned into a right fiasco I did not even have a clue where I was or if I were the only survivor. Lucky for me I landed on a brush of trees, only the light of the moon to guide me. I gathered myself, still hanging like a doll on a couple of strings I just needed to get free. I only fell a few feet – nothing to worry about – the last thing I wanted was to have a sprained ankle or worse still a broken limb. I must find the other guys, if they had survived that explosion they had either bailed out or were thrown out pretty late so I hoped they were ok. I ran over to the line of flight – I think I was at this point just guessing, who knows, but anything was better than just standing waiting and being an open target.

My luck was with me. I saw a parachute floating in the field obviously attached to something. I hoped that whoever it was they were still alive. I ran over, shouting in my head although no words were being spoken – what the fuck was wrong with me?

A body lay in front of me not moving. I shouted, 'Are you ok?' Still nothing. Moving forward I turned the body to one side and with that the guy jumped at me and stuck a revolver firmly in my face.

'Mess with me you bastard and I will blow your brains all over that nice white parachute!' I recognised the voice – it was JJ.

'Come on man, it's me, Mike. That's a bit over the top!' and with that he cracked a match with his teeth – his eyes would have made the hardest bastard crap himself.

'Hi Mike. Are you ok?'

'Yeah I'm alright. I wish I knew where we were.'

'You're in England man, no worries.'

'Come again?'

'Don't worry about it, this was a training flight just went a bit wrong that's all. We managed to get out, the Brits are all out.'

'What about Jes?'

'I know he's ok – he followed me. We are best now to gather our gear and find the nearest town – keep low for a couple of days.'

'JJ you knew about this – how come?'

'I overheard the Brits; they obviously knew what was up, we were taken along for the ride. Now if anything had happened – just our luck that it did – and we did not survive, then if there were no Americans found on a B-17 questions would be asked in high places.'

'So what you are saying JJ is that we don't mean dog shit, we were sacrificed. What the fuck for?'

'Well Mike, that little package was for someone but not on this mission. It is full of some liquid that needed to be stabilised in order to stay safe. Any disruption in it and boom – as it did with us, straight out of the blue. They are saving stuff like that for a mass air strike, then it will be deployed with ordinary bombs and see what happens. The Brits are developing carpet bombing where nothing is left. Makes you think, hey?'

'What about the other guys?'

'Never mind them. We are to go back to our bases, report and carry on with our duties. Do not ask any questions, Mike. You know far too much as it is. I know this. Just keep your nose clean and you will be ok. Now let us get out of here before the authorities get wind.'

We walked for what seemed hours and came upon a village – just a few lights, nobody around. We found a barn where we could disappear until light then see where we were. It was early morning so a few hours sleep until daybreak – must rest.

I awoke to the sound of voices not very far away and peered through the hay – a tank on the gravel by the old farmhouse, a soldier drinking what looked like a cup of tea; all dressed in khaki uniform he was laughing with someone to the left near the front door I couldn't see properly. Then this man walked forward and took the cup from the soldier – it was JJ. What was he doing there? Should I jump out and make myself known or what? But my mind was made up for me as I heard my name being shouted.

'Hey Mike, we have a lift. Come on buddy!' and with that I jumped out and rushed forward.

'So you boys got lost on the booze run, did you?'

JJ looked at me intently as I said, 'Yeah. Where are we?'

'Near Rainham in Kent mate. Come on, I'll give you a lift as far as I can. We are on standby for training so we won't be bothered by prying eyes – walls have ears you know. I know we are at war but some of the looks you get driving down these country roads you would think that we were the enemy! Try and make it into London chaps – make the most of it while you can. The Yanks own parts of London, you'll be ok in Kensington – there are clubs just for Yanks. See a few girls, have a good time!'

We were given a lift by these guys. I still didn't know where we were, the countryside was all very much the same. After a few miles and some very bumpy roads the soldier gave the signal to stop.

'Ok chaps, you walk for a couple of miles down that road and you'll hit Gillingham, you can then get a bus into London. Good luck!' With that we scampered off the tank and began to walk. He said a couple of miles, it felt like twenty but we got there.

'I just thought… money… have we got any?'

'Yeah, no problem,' said JJ.

We did have a very good couple of days in London until the time came for us to return to our bases, myself to Thorpe Abbotts and JJ – who knows, he told me but that was probably a load of crap. As for Jes, I don't know if he survived or not. I arrived back at base a bit worse for wear, as soon as I entered the area two MPs came out of nowhere, handcuffed me, threw me in a jeep and took me into Officers' Quarters where I was led to a room, thrown in a chair and left for what seemed like hours.

A voice out of the darkness said, 'Well Mike, you survived our little away trip.' I glanced at this shadow.

'You do realise Mike that now you are our property, as it were – we can officially make you dead now and officially you do not exist so you have to do as we say.'

'Do I have an option?'

'No Mike, you do not. You can go about your duties as normal but we own you. Do not forget that.'

'So what does this mean?'

'It means Mike that in about two hours a car will pull up outside your mother's house in Cleveland, Russell County, Virginia. There will be a knock on the door and she will be given notification that Shelly Michael Hall, along with his crew, was lost in action. And that is it my friend: you no longer exist until after the war.'

'What if I do not accept that?'

'Ok, there's a squad of guys waiting outside – a firing squad. It's your choice.'

And so that is why I am now just listening to the sound of the trees being swept by the breeze and the birds singing, just thinking of my mother and father, brothers and sisters. Standing in a field, at the end of the runway at Seething, waiting for my orders to carry on in this fucked up war that should not even be. To be told that I must go on secret missions now as well as ordinary flights is really getting to me. I could end it right here now but what the fuck – must be rid of this guilt and be proud of who I am and my family. My country is really giving me a bum rap on this one. A secret organisation that works alongside the rank and file of this country, what this unit does I have yet to find out.

Chapter Twenty-Eight
Montgomery – War Cabinet – January 1944

What if there was an idea of a special unit set up within the mainstream rank and file of the Eighth Army USAAF and the Royal Air Force Bomber Command for the sole purpose of one objective in the lead up to D-Day? We, the ultimate power within the Allied movement, only know of this objective and the proposal of the D-Day assault and the European advance through the Low Countries and on into the heart of Germany. We, the Allied supreme commanders, know of this assault – us and the politicians of this great country and America. The Russians know we have something scheming, it is true, but they do not have an inkling of what is in store. They have their own way of dealing with things, yes, they have many many bad generals and fierce soldiers such as the Cossacks who when fired up do not take any prisoners whatsoever. They, as I said, have made their own plans and God help the German people in their paths because they have awoken a sleeping giant there that will not rest until it has its revenge, that I am sure. That is their party – now this is ours.

I intend to put forward a plan gentlemen and I have as you say, put the wheels in motion. There has been planning for this. This is what I propose. We send in three teams of specialised personnel that by the records now do not exist. They have been chosen well. This is a plan within a plan my friends. It is a strike at the very heart of Germany to rid us of its leader the Fuhrer, and if we are very lucky, to strike a further blow – snuff as many candles out in one go as we can.

You ask how is this possible? It is a master plan my friends. At any point we will destroy the planes that will carry these personnel if, and only if, plans go away from our control. This has been planned for a considerable time. We have had agents getting close to the hierarchy of the Third Reich. We anticipate casualties – this we know – but we have two plans gentlemen. Plan One – to snuff out in covert action with trained snipers, the top dog and his top generals in a flash. Plan Two is the D-Day landings with the Allied forces going for the liberty of Europe at the expense of many lives my friends, but Plan One will cost the lives of only a few and American to boot. This is a plan that even Ike has put a stamp on: he has said his pilots and crew would take it as an honour to do such a great deed for the free people of this land. We have our boys in this as well but their risk is minimal compared to the Yanks, their task is to knock out third-rate generals that are easy targets, no problem. And gentlemen, we also have an ace up our sleeves: the planes that go over will be ours in livery but will in fact be B-17 Flying Fortresses. Ike has promised me this, he is all for it and there is also great enthusiasm from his generals – they like the look of the plan. Let us hope with good speed gentlemen we bring this matter to a close with the loss of life at a minimum. My beloved Desert Rats will be at the head of the pack into Hitler's lair and will fish him out if Plan Two goes ahead. We shall see.

I speak to you, the War Cabinet, knowing that what I do say does not go beyond these walls. Churchill is a good leader. The rank and file look up to him as does would you believe the Royal Family? He is only the figurehead, he is not the controller by any means and neither are we. There are powers-that-be that control the way we are and they are best left alone, the wheels of power are very strong and should be given utmost respect.

The full concept of what is going on in high government does not ring true in the paths and roads of mere mortals, as the man in the street's concept of life is trivial to say the least – the full picture does not come into sight whatsoever. We are born, we are then brought up in the arms of our parents or relatives; we go to school, we educate ourselves to a degree where we survive in this society. We gather our own family and the cycle starts again, we then fade into the depths of old age and die. Is that all it is? Has all this been created so we just survive for a short while then die?

For some it is written that they will be used like cattle being taken to slaughter. In the times we live in it is so – you only have to look at history to realise that. But there are those who are above all that – above law as we know it, above all we stand for because they have set the rules. Your very existence is the bedrock, for all that exist throw away the rule book. You are but a number from the day you are born until the day you die, and depending on where you were born and to whom, this decrees the blueprint for your existence. Takes some believing doesn't it? That is because you have been manipulated in the same way. Just go about your daily business, do what is expected of you and you will be rewarded with self-knowledge and the one thing that really controls all of us – money.

No matter what you think, war is started for just one reason – power. Power over one another: greed for others in power and the biggest stash of loot in the bank. One is played off against another, depending on where you were born signifies the position you play in the game; if you are born of low calibre stock then you are put to the sword very easily, if you survive to fight another day then so be it there are plenty to take your place. Money is generated to control the masses on each continent. Control: when one power gets greedy then they wish to be rid of a said country or continent and take what is theirs, the spoils of war. It does not matter. Of man, woman and child, if we get in the way then no matter for there are always others that will come forward to fight for a cause they are told to be true for that depends where you are born and to whatever culture. We are but slaves to the system, how can you fight against it? You cannot – it is law.

Now we go to the next stage. Those that dictate the laws do not write the laws, they only take orders and wield the big stick. These are middle government figures – the statesmen of individual countries who are the figureheads and who the people of the world look up to for they know no different. If these government figures were to say 'jump' then jump you must because it is the letter of the law and you as an individual must be good and lawful.

When brought into a war situation and you are drafted into the armed services you have no choice – that freedom has been taken away from you – so much for living in a democratic community where your freedom is of the prime order. There are those in this world who do not have any choice in life whatsoever, their control is of the highest degree – some for good, some for bad – it depends on what side of the fence you are. The controllers – the next step in the ladder, they know who they are, they are the feeders of war and contempt that put a shadow over all the living beings on this planet. The control at this level is total, again it depends entirely on where you are born on this planet. Religion does not come into this level of power, we are above all that.

Religion is but man-made for the control of the masses. Religion is the spark that lights the fire, for whichever religion we are born into dictates a lot of our thinking. So it is controlled in a way to educate those of different faiths. Go back in time and you will find the Head of State is not saying, 'We shall go to war', but the Head of State is first asking his bishop or man of the cloth in High Council for their views and then saying, 'We shall fight for the cause and the fact that God is behind us in every way means we cannot lose.' Religion has had its heart ripped out for the true beginnings of real faith have been manipulated to suit whoever was in power. When you have control you can give power away and quite easily return it.

So, throughout many many years you get to a point where the power lies with those that have no faces, the ones that control by a mere lifting of one finger and can set a ball rolling that will gather speed and crush all in its path, and if you or I are in its way then so be it.

I am but a pawn in a very big chess game. You play to win. The outcome is the same – whoever is the richest at the end of the day, and the people who act out all this are me and you. Who sacrifices their lives? Me and you not them; they sit it out in high places and observe the slaughter. How many die is insignificant – theirs is not the worry, your families are there to pick up the pieces and get on with their lives until it happens again, when others will be there to take their place, and so it goes on.

I do not like to make decisions that effectively end someone's life but that is the evil that war is, so the decision has been made. I have the power to end somebody's life, but that is not *my* power – it has been given to me to carry out. Now that is the power in its purest sense, God help those who go to their grave because of my decision. I know I will get the blame because those individuals will look at me as a person who calls the shots, if that were only true.

In my time here now it is very emotional for me for I have the best intentions for all concerned; the well-being of my men is of prime importance to me as a Field Marshal and the very thought of human lives being lost for nothing is unforgivable but I have to make decisions that ultimately will affect lives, and the loss or the maiming of them. I am but an instrument of war, the middleman, the man that the guy in the street who has to die for his country or be maimed for the liberty of one's way of life has to have as someone to blame: that person is me. The person or persons who originally made that decision are non-people – they do not exist. In the street, the man, woman and child no matter where, are pawns in a chess game that the ordinary consciousness of the mere mortal does not have any conception about. They cannot comprehend the magnitude of the game.

To them it is one country against another and one belief against another's – that is what you are led to believe. I tell you this, throw away the rule book of life as you know it, to see what is truly going on you must dig deeper the information that is allowed, and the information that is the disinformation that is circulated – the conspiracy factor. There are multitudes of these and they will proceed to multiply for the real truth behind all Top Secret information is so bizarre that the structure of human life will deflate or implode on itself. You as a man or woman in the street, going about your daily tasks and thinking this must be the way of life as it should be; you work to get money to feed and clothe your family, to put a roof over your head and raise a family, to do exactly the same thing over and over again. You are controlled.

There are kings and queens, dukes, lords, barons and now politicians, to govern what we say, do – everything. Even to the point of ordering you to sacrifice your very existence and for what? So where you live remains rosy? But those who you are fighting on the streets are exactly like you in every way. They are human. They breathe the same air. They are you but they live in another country under another flag. They are controlled just as you are and at a set time and date they are sent against people like you. You ask why? Who exactly starts a war? Some disagreement with a politician and maybe an argument gets out of hand – that was the one that the set off World War I, just one man dying from an argument in Sarajevo that is all and look at the mass destruction that developed into mass slaughter – for what? Control at the end of the day.

You might not realise it but that is what it is. You and your country are the victors, ok, but you go back to your job and try and bring some sanity into your life and you get on with it, all those that perish are gone. End of it as far as the authorities are concerned, it has brought the population down, it has allowed one unit to expand and gain power where it had not before and so carry on. You have been used. You have survived but there is always a next time

Free-thinking populations of great mass are not tolerated; small groups are put into slots in a very good way and not to cause great concern. Those that amass a great amount of followers are dealt with very effectively. Whether that be negative or positive depends on what side of the fence you are on. In this present time we are bound by country and flag and that is the way it has been for many hundreds of years. The one who has to lay down his life is the person in the street. I have power in the sense that someone has given that power to me; I have no power of my own, I am but a man in the street also that has been told to go ahead and do these things. I know I have been trained for this very purpose but don't you think it is funny that I and the politicians around me at this point should suddenly appear at this precise moment in time? We have been put in place to act out this game because that is what it is – a game – and you must play by the rules set out in that game. Look at those that have power over the populations of the globe, they themselves do not sacrifice their own lives – they leave that to you and me.

So be it as it may, the decision I have come to I haven't taken lightly; it is for the good of all that some are sacrificed – that is the way it should be at this time. For all that I do now I ask for forgiveness because I do not want bloodshed, especially for those that are on my side, but my hands are tied at this precise moment. It is true this idea was put forward by the higher authorities and labelled as an opportunity to be looked at along with other ideas. The powers that govern on a higher scale are not pleased with certain individuals and their behaviour. It must come to an end, there must be no more bloodshed in this way for the suffering of the mass execution of one race is not tolerated in this fashion. The perpetrator of this must come to justice and the main centre of this power is the Fuhrer himself. He must be eliminated at all costs.

It has been brought forward to the Council of War that this idea should be looked at more closely. The prime players in this are the Americans, they have the gung-ho approach in everything they do and the authorities in that area have the players at hand. We have in this neck of the woods the same players as it were, but they have the wrong approach. The likes of the M16 and so forth – the spy network – they are too valuable to us and the war effort, there are bigger fish to catch than Hitler, believe me. He is only the bandleader, we want those that make the music and play it well, with more vigour than the normal run-of-the-mill musician. A funny way of putting it across, but that is the way it is. The Americans have, as I say, a way about them – they will get the job done.

The job: three teams working independently of each other; one main team who do not exist – a specialist team that are ready at any time, the other two are to be put together with the talents of the individuals, namely shooters. They are snipers of the highest calibre, they will hunt their prey in packs. Two packs will go for Target One, the other pack will go for Target Two. That is all I will say at this time; they have the green light now, we have the option to make that red at any time if circumstances change.

The end is in sight gentleman, of this attrition – at this time give reverence for that alone. We live in troubled times. The overall view must be taken. The will of the masses overrules the good of the individual. Let us send our best wishes to the men and women of the Eighth Air Force of the Allies and hope and pray that they deliver the golden bullet to the head of the lone wolf in his lair. That is our goal gentleman – let us not waiver in our judgment. Now thank you for your time; may God go with you.'

Interlude 3
by Dave Kelly

Pausing for a bit after those terse and guarded words of Field Marshall Montgomery addressing the High Council of War, I feel it's perhaps important at this point to describe exactly and precisely how Michael Hall, the main narrator, began communicating this story to and through me.

I have already said earlier that I heard the name Michael Hall in my head in February 2001. More precisely, the events of that important month happened as follows. On February 18th I had my first ever 'out-of-body' experience. Such things have become more common in recent years for many people and are now sometimes abbreviated and referred to as OBEs. Different people have reported them happening in circumstances varying from grave illness or serious medical operations or as part of work in the psychic realm. In my case, I was in bed at home and I think I was just on the point of falling asleep when I became aware of an energy above and around me which was in fact slowly coming towards me and growing ever more powerful. I was aware of a glowing face in front of me and just feeling apprehensive, but I was also quite excited.

It was in fact a glowing female face – she was quite beautiful with long flowing hair. Looking at her was a bit like looking at somebody's face through water and I felt safe within her presence and almost immediately felt she was my guardian. I felt a pulling towards levitation – a floating feeling as I tried unsuccessfully to wake my wife who was in a deep sleep beside me. As I rose above everything else in the room I touched the ceiling and bobbed up and down like a balloon – that's the only way I can describe it. Then suddenly I was away like a rocket – through the walls – I had a feeling around my wrist and my hands as if I was being pulled along at great speed by this protective female.

Then I was aware of being on what seemed like a factory floor in a building: there was lots of noise going on and a step ladder going up to another level. My next impression was that I was really in an engine room – something like the lower decks of a sea-going ship at sea. The lady was walking in front of me and we eventually entered a small room with a table – she sat one side of the table and I sat opposite. She looked at me with the eyes of a teacher and I proceeded to tell her that this for me was an experience that I had always wished for and dreamed of after listening to other people and through reading books and accounts of similar experiences. It was now seemingly my turn. I can assure you that this felt totally real – this was most definitely not a dream!

I was also aware of another person to my left who was very angry and I felt his anger, he did not speak but just looked at both of us. I looked at him once and felt the hatred burning in him, I didn't look again. About two or three years later on I found out that this person was in fact me – in the aspect of being part of me.

I proceeded to tell the lady that I had only been 'opened' to Spirit for a matter of months since attending a healing workshop with my wife Pauline the previous October. During the following five months I had studied Reiki healing and taken courses to Mastery level, and I had also been experimenting with Spirit. This 'out-of-body' experience I sensed was just like opening a new chapter for me.

As we sat at the table I asked the lady where I would be going and what would my pathway be? She asked me, and I am quoting now from my diary, "What did you do in 1944?"

I replied that I was born in 1955 and did not relate to her question at all. "This is 1944." *she said.*

This surprised me and in some ways shocked me as well; she continued by saying that I had died in 1944! I was still in shock with this but carried on, saying that I really wanted to develop even more with her; I was simply sitting looking at her, not really fully understanding what she was saying about 1944.

She then said: "Look around you – it is 1944." *but she still didn't say exactly where we were. There was a lot of heavy gunfire outside – lots of sounds of a war situation, I looked around and was aware that I had a cigarette in the corner of my mouth and I could feel myself slowly going down to my right side – at this point I became panicky. I am not a smoker – I had stopped many years before. I began sliding sideways and then became aware I was back in my bed. I was fully awake and went downstairs to write the detailed notes which I have partially reproduced here. All of this happened at approximately two o'clock in the morning.'*

A few general points about the 'out-of-body' experience perhaps need to be made clearer here. Although you know you are out of your body it is still a physical thing. You know that you are not dreaming just as you do when living your normal life every day. There was nothing 'angelic' about the experience, I felt protected by the lady in a situation that was full of hostility and the noises of war in a very generalised sense. The only way I can describe it is that I have a strong inner certainty that this indeed did happen. In some ways it is a bit like being a child and being given a really exciting present such as a bicycle or a little car of your own that you can drive around the house, or getting a brand new exciting car of your own as an adult.

To flesh out the experience fully, four days later I was relaxing in bed after waking early on the morning of Thursday, 22nd February 2001. I was not in a dream state. A name quite clearly came to me straight out of the blue – the name 'Michael Hall'. I didn't think much about this at all at the time but throughout the same day this name kept coming into my head and I wrote it down. In the following day, along with 'Michael Hall' again, I was getting more names coming into my head, one that came very strongly was the name Claire Louise and I later was given to understand in the same way that this was the name of Michael's daughter who had been born from his marriage to a local Norfolk girl.

I was also seeing pictures in my head of a Second World War plane in flight, along with symbols – dollar signs – either side of these pictures. I saw a man in a dress uniform and someone in front of a plane which I thought was a P-51 – a Mustang – I felt this person was an American and that 'Spirit' wanted me to connect with someone on the other side. I felt the reason for the contact was that this person wanted to connect with their daughter and I might help them as a medium – this happened well before I went to the American library in Norwich and did my first bit of research.

Wondering how best I could proceed, I then got in touch with one of my friends who had knowledge of American servicemen dying in the Second World War in East Anglia who either wished to 'move on' or to make contact with their bereaved families through mediums. In a matter of days after this the next name to come through was 'Buck' – Charlie Quinlan. I began to go on a bit of a quest at this point and started in earnest to do some research which included working with other mediums.

Before long the energies were coming in so strong on this story among several different people in the Norfolk and Suffolk area that we all felt moved to connect more. Different groups of friends and colleagues received confirmatory information, and much of what I had already received through my head was substantiated in this way.

To cut a long story short, a week or so later on Thursday, 1 March 2001, I continued to feel that the information coming through was solely for me to help an American serviceman to contact his living daughter. On several occasions I had direct exchanges with an entity who said he was Michael Hall, about his daughter Claire Louise and her mother, from whom the crash had tragically separated him. Then it was on the evening of Thursday, 1st March that quite unmistakably the indication was given to me that I was to write a book about Michael Hall and his experiences and I was even given the title very clearly.

It was at this point that I realised without any shadow of a doubt that I was to be used as a channel. Strangely enough, I even felt angry with myself that I hadn't realised before what I was meant to do. I found myself thanking them for supporting me in this. To quote my diary written that evening, I simply concluded by saying, 'I have to write a book about all this – and I have to call it 'The Pathway Back'.

Having said all that, let's move on again to the fateful final day of this story in a wet and wintry wartime Norfolk on 10th February 1944. The tense crews have assembled for the mission at Seething Airfield although they will not know exactly what it is until they open sealed envelopes given to them just before take-off. At their own request it seems, they are about to be addressed by their chaplain who described himself simply as 'The Preacher' when he came through to me to join his experience to this bigger story. He did not otherwise offer a name, saying only that he was 'a player in the game'

PART FOUR

THE TOP SECRET MISSION

Chapter Twenty-Nine
The preacher – a player in the game

My story in all of this is may be a ripple and a very small ripple in an ocean, but it must be recognised even more so than if it were a wave. My name...do I have to put a name to this story? All that you know and learn is governed by the statutory: 'Name? Status? Date of birth? Location? Right, we're ready to start.' Then, and only then can you begin your story.

I am a person – a living human being – that is good enough. I live very comfortably it is said in these troubled times; I am but an observer in this period of time. How can this be, you must be under a flag of a nation no matter where you live on this earth, you must have identity. I have a place of birth – it is Earth. That is good enough, I belong to the Earth; I belong not to one nation's code of conduct.

I belong to Earth – the ancestors of these nations now at war. It grieves me and them for they do not wish this happening now. The hate that starts with one then multiplies a hundredfold until it consumes all and you are then swimming along with the flow of the ever-increasing water until it flows into the sea and immerses everybody that comes into contact with it. Only the innocent suffer in conflicts of war. To envelop a nation that is on your borders and feels like easy prey; a beautiful land that thrives with life, people enjoying life and taking what is given from the earth. You, standing on its borders, wanting and yearning for what they have in abundance and the only way to have that is to take it – by force if necessary. The end justifies the means as they say. Perhaps that is true, but all those that have to be sacrificed in order to attain that goal, all those that stand in your way: old, middle-aged, young and the very young; women, men, children, the animals of that land, the birds that fly in the sky – they all have a right to be there just as you do so why must they perish so you can stand in their place? What gives you the right to do this?

Life is precious – your consciousness enables you to experience just once in your Earth Walk – just one time. There are many Earth Walks you have been on and there will be many more so to rid a being of that one precious gift at this time is wrong – to snuff out a life as if it were a candle is wrong. The power of certain governments is too much. To govern all is powerful, how to maintain that power is another story. If you have the love of the people it can move mountains. Why not love all the people and animals, why do you have to love just one race or culture? The Bible says many things but what it does say time after time, is love your neighbour like a brother or sister. Somewhere along the line we have got our wires mixed up, the work of the Scriptures speaks a lot of truths but you must read into them the true meaning of what they really are – messages to be taken and looked at, and not to be used as a weapon against others. Love is the key. Learn to love and not look at wealth and the power of money as the false god to pray to.

If we listen to ourselves and not others that want to be all-powerful then we have a chance, just maybe. All those that die in this conflict at this time will have given up their one life. Whether it be for the good or not so good, it depends which side of the fence you are standing on. I live on this Earth in a lovely place and I as an individual must make a choice. Do I walk with God or walk down to the recruiting station and sign up? Now there's a dilemma. Do I walk on this Earth a free man and do as my intuition wants me to, or do I go to Uncle Sam's calling? I know what choice I want but fate has taken hold. You must forgive me – I cry because I cannot do God's work as I would wish. It grieves me so in a way that consumes my very faith. How can the Lord forsake me in this way?

I have given my life for the Beloved One since I was young enough to read the Scriptures. My grandmother would tell me stories from the Great Book and I would be consumed in its greatness. Every page would be a new adventure for me; I would be there in mind, body and spirit. My family actively encouraged me to read from the Bible at every opportunity, even upstaging the local clergy at the sermon every Sunday. It was a joy to see my mother and father, grandmother, brothers, sisters and cousins looking at me with tears in their eyes as I read with a passion so strong even I was amazed at what I was saying and how; it felt at the time that somebody took my very voice from my lips and said these words in such a way as to actually make them sing. It was then that I truly felt the hand of Jesus on my shoulder; I knew I should follow Him and his teachings and so I went into the clergy with such a love that it overtook my very consciousness. At one point to give of myself was all that I had and nothing more. This was and still is my life but now everything around me has changed – my surroundings, my family, are no longer with me.

I feel alone. For once in my life I feel alone. Has Jesus abandoned me? Have I awoken from a dream and found myself in a nightmare? If that were only true – I have awoken that is true, but to a nightmare that is living every day and consuming all the love in this place and turning it into a living hell for me and countless others. I have my faith, very slim at this time, but the roots of my beliefs are strong and it will take a lot of hurricane winds to bring my trees down to ground level. It is the level of hate and destruction around me that gives me cause for concern. Why must this be? It goes over and over in my head like a record player that never goes off the needle, always getting continually stuck at some point and scratching at the same tune.

Life is sacred but why are we killing people and why are they killing us? The pain we are all suffering can't be a small part to the innocent in all of this – we are just caught up in a mess that has got out of hand. Because of my background as a preacher (that is what I am called 'preacher'), I have been swept along on a sea of conflict and purpose for the good of the nation. I am here it is said, under duress. I wish no harm to anybody, it is written in my mother's diary: 'This boy only wishes good, he is a beloved son and God is with him.'

So why am I here in a wet-sodden jacket on a dreary winter's day on a made-up airfield in the middle of the Norfolk countryside, standing and giving a sermon and prayers to a bunch of guys that insist I do this? Ok, people know I was once a preacher but these guys have insisted I do this out of the way of everybody. It looks like three crews; they look at me – every one of them looking to see if I alone can call in the Divine and whisk them away to their families back home, every one of them looking for a saviour in me. The rain is now pouring down, they do not move and for me to move would be not in my interests – there are two lots of government figures either side of me, they mean business. This is no ordinary mission, this is something very special. I do not want to know my only concern is that these guys come home safe and that whatever they do it will cause minimum bloodshed and death to those that are on the end of those bombs.

'God speed, you boys,' I say with tears rolling down my face; in this weather you cannot see the tears. I know they are crying... even the officers are, as I close I see all of them look up towards me and look knowing that they may not see this land again. They walk into the night one by one and disappear into the darkness. God bless.

Let us pray together here this day. For we as a nation of God folk who live by the law of He who gave his life, should recognise the good and bad in all of humanity. We must question who and what we are doing to one another at this time. We live in a terrible time – a time of change not only for us but for all those that live on this Earth. I thank the Lord each day as I rise to the sun that I am alive and living as I am, for there are innocent ones – young and old who are suffering at the hands of those who give nothing for life. I thank the Lord that I have been put into this body here and now not in the body of a preacher, a man of God, in a foreign country that is bordering the Germanic world: the wolf's lair.

Does it make me any less of a man that I wish not to be a man of God in those places? What about the man who is there, what of his feelings towards all that is going on? To have a family – to love a family: to be part of a oneness that cannot be separated even though these certain individuals may try their utmost to do so. Separation in the physical can be traumatic – to think of one's wife, husband or child being tortured or maimed, even dying, but dying is a release from the horrible things these lowlifes will do to extract what they call 'information' against the one power that is controlling them. They are also swept away with the emotion, mentally too for it is that which is manipulating them as well. They are not to blame initially for given certain powers they and their personality will take it into another realm. Their ego will run riot with the situation; you may have one Fuhrer in power overall but really what you have is many thousands of Fuhrers who have just been switched on. As their innermost hates and problems come to the surface you have many thousands of people who control their mini-worlds and the energy they create is a hell for those caught up in that area. Give certain individuals power and you escalate the power further for one gives it to another.

It is like an airborne disease. One cannot see it but it is there nevertheless. It is greed. It is the control over the weak. It is bullying. It starts in the playground. To take control of one part of the ball park and then grow it is in everything we do, we even laugh about it not knowing what the real essence of it is. We accept it because it is there. It is what we feel so accept it. How wrong we can all be.

I love what I do, the clergy, to serve the Lord. It is what I have lived for from an early age. The true meaning of the love of Christ is blessed for He gives you the power to love and He also gives you the power to hate. It is you – *you* must live your life, *you* have that choice – no one can take that away from you, that is your birthright. I love the Lord so at an age when I can, I go and find out the best course of action to take that would take me into the world of more greed, more power than I ever imagined – the world of the Church and the world of religion. It is a maze, it is a sea in which one must swim to the nearest island and survive there until a new strength can take you to another land mass on which to survive.

There are more corrupt people in the Church than there are in the political arena. The Church is all powerful, it controls the masses.

The true meaning of the love of Christ is but a small light now in relation to its true meaning. The man who gave His life for us – what would He think of the Church now? What would His reaction be to the death and destruction that has been caused in His name, for the cross of Jesus has been a banner for many years and there have been many deaths at the hands of those who stand for Jesus and the will of God, as if it justifies them actually doing it in the first place. What right do they have to do this? What right do we have to stand and say 'In the name of the Lord God I now take what is yours and now it is mine'? This has been going on for years and what does the individual man, woman and child think? Who cares? They do not matter – it is what the community thinks: get the strong behind you in the community and you manipulate the weak.

It fascinates me being here in the Norfolk and Suffolk area of Great Britain that there are houses obviously, but there are slum areas, impoverished areas that should not hold human life, yet in every village and town there is a Church built to the glory of God. These houses of the Lord are sacred but at what price the lives of the locals who gave of their time to build such monuments? And in the cities it is of even more sacrifice, the cathedrals and monuments all built by the man in the street, what power controls that? Faith, certainly faith, but why build these in the first place? They are but a symbol on the landscape to say: 'We are here. We take your money. Ok, come and worship.' Do you know who you are actually worshipping? 'Ok, come into this fine house you built, but you must pay for that privilege. Come with us, and pillage new lands and those not of this faith. We shall teach and if they will not learn then they shall die because we ordain it to be.'

So who is right and who is wrong? All the faiths have one Lord at the helm – Jesus, we celebrate his birth at Christmas. Even that is manipulated to a point to mask the truth; it is true he was born of that time, but it was not a Christmas celebration as we have been taught to entertain. We must celebrate His life also but that is put to one side, His true birthday is not even known; it has been turned and switched around to give credence to whoever is in power. Strong words but they are my own – nobody else's, they are not doctored or censored they are my true feelings and I have the right to say those words just as any free man in this world has.

Being in the military you have to pick and choose what words to say. I say 'military' for even we are conscripted into this situation, never wanting to go to another country and wage war against other humans. It is against all that I live for but it must be said that when a power is so evil and corrupt as this German power is, it takes another power of good to counteract the status quo. There are corrupt and double standards in all societies and the society I live and work in is no exception. There are things that go on even I must question, and I do – I question with my own conscience and it hurts to the extreme that my own faith comes into question.

I have given a sermon to three crews in the dead of night to give God's blessing so they must die or let others die in the cause of freedom. I have given them blessing. Standing on a box above them, I have said 'The Lord is with you at this time'. I have said that. These guys look at me and believe that, if they die and God is not with them who is to blame? Me. It is a lot to stand at an altar and give a sermon, a talk on a bright, sunny day to the brethren of a local community. In the Church the talk is of really mundane day-to-day stuff that can be talked about with ease but this is something else. The eyes of every flyer are looking at me, for these few moments I am the anointed one – the Messiah. The guys look at me, their eyes see sanctuary and peace and in the deepest depths of my heart I know I am not telling the whole truth – I have been manipulated to say things and go about the teaching of the Gospels as they, the powerful ones wish me to do so; that is not what I believe in my heart. That is why they call me the preacher – they know of my past and that is fixed to me like a number plate on a car. I am more than that, I have seen the light but not in the way they think: to look and see with new glasses and a lot clearer understanding is the new light.

As I disappear into the depths of the lists of names that someday all will look at sometime: the long lists of names that disappear into the consciousness like a never-ending train clicking on the tracks as it winds itself into the horizon, you might just glance at one individual name, it might bounce out at you – I am that name. It doesn't matter which one or what regiment, whether it is the Air Force, Navy or Army it will be me for I speak for many who will give their life for their country. As a man of God I ask, why they should give up their lives? What does it all mean? I shall die – I know I shall not survive. You have a feeling – your intuition, your gut feeling. You must sacrifice your life, I only ask why? That is all.

Chapter Thirty
My name is of no consequence, my nationality is British

The teams that make up this trio are very brave indeed and it has to be said that whatever happens in the next twenty-four hours will either be put into the history books as the one thing, the one step that made a difference and a positive end to this war without more bloodshed or it will be wiped clean from all records. No one and I mean no one will survive right down to ground crew, and their very families are in danger also. This goes beyond any Top Secret documents – this is national security at its highest level. If any of this got into the newspapers or to the general public at large then we would be the laughing stock of the Western world if not the whole planet.

These individuals will systematically wipe out the High Command of the Third Reich in one fell swoop. They have been trained and will execute the mission, once they do so they will go their own way. They will assume new identities so for them there is no coming back. If only one gets through they must succeed where the others would have carried on, that is why there are two planes for Germany and one for the islands off France – Jersey and Guernsey. At this point my colleagues and myself are in danger of even saying these words, there has been talk of secret missions before but even the Top Secret organizations – and believe me, they exist – even they cannot stop people from talking, that is human nature. We must know all around us (even if on occasion we are given a load of bullshit we believe), and sometimes the truth comes forward, in dribs and drabs.

I owe a great deal to the American guys. They saved my life on one occasion and I must tell my story. My name is of no consequence for it only fills a space, nothing more – what you truly are is without names. I work for the British government in its vault of secrecy that all governments have. Like all states you have to sign a piece of paper to say you will never give information to another party, so signing a piece of paper changes your life. You no longer behave rationally; you are constantly looking over your shoulder at people in the street. There are many secret societies within all governments – it's like a rabbit warren when you first start up the ladder but as you learn more and more you find it's like a beehive closer to the top, the one Queen Bee needs to be served constantly by its workers and its army of soldiers. Look at the insect communities through a microscope and study them. We are the same, the only difference is that we are on a very large scale, much more sophisticated and adapted to the terrain. They are obviously smaller and also adaptable to their terrain but the structure – the very core of existence – runs parallel in so many ways. The people know fuck all – not a drop in the ocean. The individual means nothing in the collective hive. As soon as one is eliminated then one takes its place – all that matters is the existence of the Queen, the one ruler. In our existence, our meaningless existence, we are used purely to feed the Queen that is all, nothing more nothing less. What we do in pleasure time is for our own development – to keep us happy, that is all.

We are all controlled by a greater force let's not forget that. I work for an organisation so cloak and dagger that it doesn't exist beyond the highest government walls of red tape. It was constructed by Oliver Cromwell initially during the Civil War for the reason of surveillance of the King's men in France and Spain. He brought together a band of men in the highest orders and their families, and swore them to secrecy. He even kept the younger ones and the wives of these lords in a state of confusion, he said he would put their families to the sword if they gave away the secret codes and the very will of this society if this they did. They gave their very souls the third degree, they went into this new venture with such vigour that Oliver Cromwell had to denounce them in Parliament. When a very loud backbencher shouted at him asking why did his army know every turn the Royalist army knew, in his reply Cromwell stated, 'My army is very good at what it does, I can say no more.'

This group of 'brothers' (for amongst them they called each other this only, for secrecy) disappeared into the countryside posing as the enemy, not to be armed but purely for surveillance. To observe and nothing more, to extract as much information as they could about a source and to relay it to small groups back to the hive where the information would be collated and used, some for good some for bad. This group had no say in what they did; they served and that was their purpose – nothing else. They worked in small groups of men and women posing as families, some poor some rich, all gathering information, no confrontation whatsoever. If there was any leak or any kind of interest from the enemy they would disappear into the night.

They were given special consideration by Oliver Cromwell himself – he alone would take the information given; only his most loyal guards knew of this group. When Oliver Cromwell died as Lord Protector of England and the Royal household came back to power his group was disbanded, but the idea and motive behind it was always smouldering in the fire. So the new Oliver Cromwell took its smoky embers and brought it to a flame for he was the people's champion – he had the hearts and minds of the people of this fair land. His name: Winston Churchill, a man amongst men, a leader, a born leader. A person that would take you the last two hundred yards after a twenty-five mile run with your lungs left ten miles behind – his one word of inspiration would lift you to sprint those last two hundred yards with the feet of your very weary legs not even touching the ground.

Mr Churchill knew of this disbanded group. Through the corridors of power swing many doors, and doors that are left open too long give many whispers ears to listen. So he knew that they existed and was intrigued by this and in the situation he now encountered he thought it was a timely entrance for this once proud unit. Not even bringing it to the ears and eyes of the backbenchers because he knew that there would be opposition to his plans – to let even government officials know about this would take away the very essence of the true gift of this unit.

Not even Oliver Cromwell knew of the daily routine of this group – if he knew half of what they got up to he would have looked at it again with new eyes. They were dangerous, very dangerous; they surveyed everything leaving nothing in their path even to the point of spying on their own troops for spies within the units. If you were caught with the fact of being a spy or conversing with the enemy you were brought to bear with no shame whatsoever. First all information was extracted from you, and when there was nothing left then you would be disposed of by all manners, but not by the group. They had given their word to Oliver Cromwell himself and that mattered, there was one line that they did not cross and that was that.

I can tell you of one group member who excelled at his job with such force and determination that he was given primary status within the group and had the full backing of the Protector. His name was Matthew Hopkins he later became synonymous with being the Lord Protector's Witch-Finder General after the war. He was a very nasty bit of work indeed. He did not, it is said, put a mark on anyone, he let others do his work. He manipulated the weaker ones with his very presence, and it has to be said a very clever man in his own right, he knew how to control situations in that time. He would not be allowed to use and ridicule individuals today in that way, we would look back at it as very barbaric. The group today in this time of war is very different but the core of its existence is the same, we look and listen then dispatch what we know. The technology has obviously moved forward since the 1600s so we use radio and other forms of communication that are advanced even for these times.

So now for my story of how the Americans saved my life. I was taken into France by our very own Lancaster bomber one night eighteen months ago now. Parachuted into southern France my objective was to find out information on POWs – their camps, where they were. In my time there I was given one area to work, other operatives were given areas but I was given a route to go round and acclimatize myself in such a way that all suspicion would cease. My papers were of the highest calibre – my background was of German aristocracy. I would mingle with the high society.

Being in this group is as I said special and you have to shall I say, own some special power yourself. Mine it is said is to be 'The Face', that is my group name – you and nobody else will ever know my real name. I have many identities – that is how I survive, I become this person for so long and then disappear. No one has caught me yet and they never will, I become the night and when the sun comes up I become the day – that is all. I become for this particular journey into the abyss a prince of Germanic blood that is so Arian Hitler himself would shake me by the hand and put me in charge of the Hitler Youth with a snap of his fingers. The German race at this time is so fucked up they do not know their arse from their elbow. With such nobility in its ranks you can walk freely. As I said, this group can walk into anywhere – that is the power game in high office. Do not underestimate its tentacles – they stretch far and wide and will devour anything in their path.

My mission at this time was to locate a prison within a forest which was closed to the outside world. It housed all the officers of all nationalities within the Alliance – American, British, Polish, Australian, Russian – all the opposition, only the officers. I have pinpointed only a few but within the Alliance there are many countries represented here, some you are not aware of, that is all I am allowed to say about that.

With great difficulty I located the site. I again am not allowed to say the location of the site – I am out on a limb giving this information. My objective was to give its map reference to the local freedom fighters who would systematically blow its outer pathways up leaving it helpless – no one would be able to get in or out. The objective of this was to extract two personnel that are vital to the High Command, my mission was to find this place and to inform the hive – it was the turn of another elite group to breach the camp and extract these two guys. My task complete, my mission now was to gather information on the way home across occupied France. I had been given a contact name and hopefully a ride home – it sounds easy but believe me it was far from that. My task was easy, the difficult bit now was to get home for all the Hitlers come out of the woodwork at this time, they in their own way are trying to get their own little empire going. The local policeman, the local gentry, all looking for someone out of the ordinary that is why I blend in. I will take someone's identity from them – life has no meaning for me.

In this line of work you have no hidden agenda – nothing, only survival, that is my key to the next day. If I am good then all the better, only survival gives of the best nothing else – if you are no good you are dead. If these animals, and that is what they are, if these beasts come out of the forest looking for food then you must defend yourself at all times through deception and through violence. I will tear their heads off to escape at all costs, they mean me harm and if these animals from the zoo of the SS and the Gestapo catch up with you then you must fight to survive – mentally, emotionally and physically.

First they will tempt you in and once they have you in their clutches they will manipulate you; I know, I have been in their clutches many times. I have walked through their doors many times and survived, that is why they call me 'The Face' – nobody knows my true identity, nobody knows – that is how I like it. To be somebody for an hour or twenty-four hours or one year – it does not matter to me, I will kill for survival. I have killed many, some I regret some I do not.

I have even got next to the Fuhrer – it was a bonus I must admit. I was on a mission with top clearance from the hive to eliminate an elite soldier within the ranks of the newly-formed National Socialist (Nazi) Party. I was not in the group I am now, but then we were given clearance to kill any obstructions in our path be it members of the public or government officials.

This particular individual was felt to be the true backbone of the National Socialist Party. As in all power struggles you do not at first look at its leader, you look at the puppeteer rather than the puppet and this man was sending all the right signals. His name is not important, I eliminated the problem but in the process I got close to this person and I got close to the inner circle in meetings. All the strategies of this newly-formed party were at its highest strength, it had scope; it had a new meaning to the German people. The actual workings of these blueprints were to be acted out at a later date but the foundations had to be laid, and at one meeting I was introduced to the one they elected as their leader, later to become the Reichstadt Fuhrer. It was an honour to shake the hand of the great dictator. His eyes looked through you like fire from the depths of a volcano, the burning light ready to explode, not knowing when that moment would be. There seemed no compassion at all – nothing, just a blinkered look at the main objective which was total annihilation of all that stood in his and his Party's way.

He spoke to me and asked me about my family and what the new Germany would be like for them. I gave him a load of bullshit of course, wished him well for the future and gave the salute without saying anything. He smiled, patted me on the shoulder and carried on to the next person – for what I know now I could have saved a lot of lives that day. But could I, at the expense of my own? Could another have taken over, someone who could have been ten times worse? You forget the seeds were already sown; the man himself is but only a puppet – the figurehead, someone to take the blame. The real leaders, those that make the real decisions – those that do not have faces – they are the ones who are dangerous. The secret societies of hundreds of years survive for one purpose, power, and they are not to be taken lightly; they exist but not as you see them. I will say no more of them for the term 'walls have ears' is not just propaganda, it is as it says – walls have ears. This may sound as if I am completely out of my mind but this is as it is.

My survival is dependant on my knowledge of incidents and I know things. If the real truth came out of what is really going on then the people of this Earth would look upon it very differently and would evolve far better in peace. But there are powers out there that do not want this, they want total power and they will sacrifice life and limb to keep that power. I am working for one such power as is all that exists. It is our place within this structure that dictates what we as individuals are prepared to put in. Who do we play for? Who has the better team on the day? Life has no meaning; only to the individual, nobody else, that is how it is, and in situations like this it manifests itself to its full and ugly self.

You might think you are on the right side but we all have our dungeons. It is how well-camouflaged these dungeons are that shows who will win the vote of the collective. How we go about our meaningless lives is up to us. You have to maintain justice, yes, but you set that up and give laws to live by then the collective will ultimately look after itself. I work for an organisation that does not exist, I have no identity and that makes me angry. I know I should not talk of this but it means so much to me as an individual in all this crap of a war.

I had accomplished my mission, I must return to the hive via whatever route it took me. At this particular time I was dependent on markers. I knew the RAF would be the obvious markers for my return but the Americans had been in the ball park a good time now and I knew that they frequently let us say, carried out secret missions especially along the French coast. I must make my way to the safe house. I had not far to go to get there. Living rough in the forest is to be expected, catching a few rabbits to eat, lighting a fire and moving on, only sleeping in the deep undergrowth. No chance of being found – no chance whatsoever, that will not happen. I would not allow myself to fall into the enemy's clutches – I would die first.

It took me three to four days to find the safe house run by a couple, middle-aged, very good Resistance workers. It can be said that if they were in trouble and got caught, the whole combined forces would unite just to find these two people. That is how highly regarded they are, it is not my place to name them for to give their names would take their magic away from them, they mean so much to us. A lot of airmen and

POWs who escaped have passed through this house and believe me it is well-guarded – the Resistance holds this like we would hold Buckingham Palace. I spent a day and a night with my friends, drinking and laughing, they did not obviously know who 'The Face' really was, just the one I allowed them to recognize.

They told me of a rendezvous I must make if I wanted to return to England soon. There was a personality – that is all I knew, he was returning to England. He has friends in high places, it is said he would return and he would be safe – no chance of the enemy around. This indeed sounded strange but as long as I returned no matter. I said my goodbyes and left, I did not have long to go, the 'kick' as they call it was at 1300hrs. It all seemed very out in the open, so very lapsed; this 'personality' as the couple called him was obviously a Yank. Maybe with the brashness of it he would fly his own plane back, maybe a Mustang, their equivalent to our Spit...no on the other hand, maybe not. I was even driven to the drop by the local policeman – he was obviously in the Resistance and what a brilliant cover it was! I said my thank you's and hid away until the time.

My endeavour to hide away was somewhat taken as a massive joke: 'Come on sport. It's not all cloak and dagger with you Brits is it?' said this guy coming out of the shadows, I knew this man's face but the name eluded me.

'Hi, how are you? Nice to meet you.'

'Just getting a few of the guys to light up for our boys to taxi in, huh? Ever seen one of those beauties come in from the yonder, hey?'

'No I haven't.'

'Great to have you on board, you they call 'The Face', yeah? I could get you a job back home after your little exercise is done here.'

'Where would that be – what you call 'back home'?'

'Why Hollywood, California, LA. You would be a sensation – you know that.'

'So you are this personality then.'

'Well, I suppose I am.'

'I am sorry but I do not recognize you – you are familiar but I have lost the name.'

'My name? I like teasing people, how about I keep you in the dark for a while cowboy and you will find out sooner or later?'

With that a flare went up and in a matter of seconds not minutes this massive B-17 came out of the darkness. These guys meant business – they brought this monster down on the field like it was a toy. They sprang round, doors opened and the personality said, 'These guys don't hang about. We'd better jump aboard.' I walked on and found a corner to fall in.

'Alright buddy?' a real Yankee voice shouted from above.

'Yeah, I'm all right.'

'Where can I drop you – The Hall or Buck House?' With this everybody laughed – these guys are great, through all this fucking shit they have time for a sense of humour. The guy they picked up was giving out the booze and cigars now, what a war. That guy – I just couldn't get his name.

So my return to England on that mission was a grateful one and opened my eyes to the Americans. My gratitude to them is immense and my pride to work alongside them in this bloody war. They will certainly win us the day against the Germans that is true, but at what cost? They have lost many men and so have we but their resolve is magnificent – to have a sense of humour while you lose brothers and sisters in this conflict says something about the bravery of those individuals that fly the planes and those guys in the infantry also.

So that is my little memory of the Yanks. As I disappear now into another mission my hopes are of survival and victory – for all of us.

Chapter Thirty-One
Members of the American Elite Forces

'It seems a good time to look at the real and potential difficulties we have with this situation. Gentlemen, I am not happy, not by a long way. In this explosive – and believe me when I say this *highly explosive* situation, if the American people as a nation get to hear about any of this then the shit will hit the fan big time. You have no idea what we are dealing with. I have three crews of dedicated officers ready to give their lives, that is not in question, what is in question is how they give their lives. I am not going to allow the governing bodies to overrule a command and have those boys blown out of the sky for the simple reason they have trained for this one moment. If they succeed it will be a bitter blow to the Reichstadt and they will not give up, I know that, but at the same time they will have to regroup and the sting will go out of the scorpion's tail, this I know. Please gentlemen, I implore you on your decision.'

'The overall picture looks good for us. We believe we have the stamina to hold together for a few more months. The D-Day proposal is on the table and at this time is in fact in the stages of going ahead but this situation we have now could – and I say could in brackets – save a lot of lives and needless bloodshed. It is right that we should lead an airborne land-sea offensive against the German forces in one almighty sweep, that is in place. But this act we are lodging forward today is a breakthrough of such magnitude that even if it fails it would go into the history books to be looked at and played over again and again for its utter genius or utter stupidity – it's that fine a point, the devil or the deep blue sea, my friends. To eat or be eaten, that is the question. We have to act this out but what we are dealing with is a 'go'. If this is a 'go' then it stays that way. We ride the storm. Let it go into motion – not to remain in two minds about it. But if we go and change our minds or a greater excuse comes into the equation, then what are the alternatives? In this time we can erase many things, it is a case of just moving one little box into another bigger or smaller box. That is how I see it.'

'Thank you sir for that little sentence; how trivial you come across. As I know your name that is not important, what is important though is your total disregard for life. Just in that one sentence I can tell that you couldn't give a rat's arse about human life, and friends that is precisely what we are here for. Not whether one political or military leader holds a flag and salutes in a foreign country, it's about you and me – about human life on this planet. How we live our lives with one another, not only that, what effect has this on the environment. The animals that live with us on this rock – what effect has this on them? They have their own world, they couldn't care less about our little squabbles but they are being blown up just the same. I know some of you will be wondering what the fuck is he on about but they have a right to be on this rock as do you or I – don't forget that. So, gentlemen, I will not vote to sacrifice my fellow countrymen to be blown away and I will give my foremost attention to the full well-being of my fellow Americans in this European theatre.'

'It is true we have been unavoidably catapulted into this conflict by the Imperial Government of Japan and consequently Germany and Italy. And not forgetting that my country is made up of a lot of the said countries' ex-patriots who have given their allegiance to the Stars and Stripes:- the very people you are now talking about, their roots are in this country. Italy, Germany, Russia, and the Low Countries – their ancestors came from the very place they are now being told to bomb. If they thought long and hard about that they would question it but they are not allowed to do that because they would be put up against the wall and be shot and that would be the end of the matter as far as they were concerned this has to be said.'

'There are only a few of us in this bunker under the Houses of Parliament. Gentlemen, we have been put here by the people – let us at least represent them with some dignity. I am a politician from the Senate, not used to the political arena of this magnitude – the history alone blows you away. But I am here to defend my country and my countrymen at all costs. I am not giving up my life: I can now walk along the River Thames with the rain on my face, breathe the air. Nobody can take that away from me and you ask me to take somebody's life away as if it is like swatting a fly. I hold too much respect and honour for my fellow countrymen than to listen to a lot of fat, winded hypocrites like yourselves – no, and I mean NO to this. My prayers go with my fellow comrades. God be with them.'

'As I said, my name is of no consequence, names mean nothing, only to the individual, but what does matter is the feelings – the pain and the pleasure we encounter in this lifetime. We on a conscious level are led to believe we are here only once and to make good use of that life. I have deep religious beliefs taught to me growing up in the deep south of America, a country that is within me. Not just a place to live but to enjoy life, not to have bitter squabbles among those that wish harm against you. We must learn to live with each other. I have my own beliefs, they are personal to me. I do not burden my beliefs on others – that is wrong. Those that do that are looking for personal power over others and will persevere until they bring those individuals into the fold – into the collective.'

'It is true you can be taught at a younger age about the religious beliefs of your parents or guardians but ultimately it is you that has to make that decision, to forward your beliefs in such a way as to change your life and probably change other lives. Religion is there for the people. It should not be rammed down your throat. Coming from the south, we have many evangelists doing the circuits, going from town to town spreading the word. Some are good, some are bad – as in life, beware a wolf in sheep's clothing. I must as a politician be given the chance to support and give credence to my fellow countrymen at this terrible time: I must support what they say and what they feel. I will disappear into the night like all individuals that take part in this particular time and eventual history and I will become just a sound in the orchestra – so it is. The free people of the future I hope will look at the individual and what he gave up for freedom – his one life.'

Chapter Thirty-Two
Michael Hall – Mission Flight 10 February 1944

Time is ticking away slowly, it matters not to me. I have said my prayers. I have done everything I can, gone over my equipment many times. Once I start reflecting on certain situations I must question why we, or more specifically, why I am on this plane going on a secret mission that might be terminated. When I say that – terminated – the fact is I know too much about this mission to outlive it. I will survive hopefully, but not actively in war.

How can I explain it? I must disappear from the records. Ok, sure, my name will be there but not the truth. The truth is too condemning, it will not appear. My name will be put as *Missing in Action* or as a POW; that is for my family's sake nothing more. I am married to a beautiful girl from this country, the pain of leaving her behind really gets to me but I have no choice. My family is around me – these guys are my family: I must not let them down. They are in more danger than I ever will be they are going into the Devil's Den to accomplish this mission, I am there to get them in and get them out. When I say return it is in a neutral country that we will land, wait, and then return and rescue these guys. We might be in a position to return to this country, I very much doubt that. The powers-that-be have made it plain that this is very important. We will be marked men – the whole might of the enemy and some of the Allies will be upon us make no mistake. The Allies are all not sweetness and light. There are many within the rooms of power that are not all steering for us but that is not my problem, my problem is to survive the next few hours. Hopefully we shall redeem ourselves and go forward into the light, maybe. We are all jolly and morale is not low, we look forward and may God go with us.

The plane – our lovely *Betsy* - is standing by herself as if gleaming, smiling and saying: *'Come on! Let's get on with it!'* with the security these great planes give us. The name was given to her by my pilot Buck.

I do not know where Betsy is or if Betsy really exists (that is his story to unfold not mine), but in giving this majestic figure a name he chose well – let us hope it gives us luck. I say a prayer to all new planes. They hold many memories and thoughts of those who flew in them before us, so it is only right that we should bless them with our energies beforehand. A lot of the guys do not believe in such, but I have experienced many things back home and while being stationed at different locations in and around Norfolk and Suffolk.

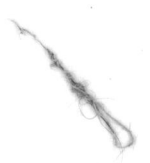

Chapter Thirty-Three
Al Permando – Mission Flight 10 February 1944

It is at this time that I feel very emotional for my family are far away over the water and the bond I have with them is all too clear now. At one point in my life it was not so but with growing up in an environment that is so violent you look at things in different ways. With the eyes of a young one you are very adaptable and can be very influenced by the younger and older members of your family. I am American one hundred per cent but I am also Italian and that part of me cries tradition, it is the old country that calls. I know the Italians have sided with the Germans and that is that, but I am American. All the white people that settled in America came from European stock at one point that I know.

Growing up in New York is a cultural extravaganza of such magnitude that you must take it all in and not avoid it at any costs. My family are steeped in tradition it is true but I walk a hundred yards down the street and I will meet a German family that is the same, an Irish family or a Russian family – it goes on. We are all brought together for a purpose. All of us love our mother countries through family but we are Americans and we must fight their cause and not waiver at any point. If I am captured by the Germans or the Italians for that matter, then I am dead – no questions there, I die – for what? Because I am an American and I am fighting against what they believe in, and I have Italian blood in me; it is much worse for the German-American, believe me.

I am proud of this moment. It fills me with pride at the thought that I might give my life for a cause so just as this. I know my family would approve of this. The whole idea of what might come of this mission gives me goose bumps. I have had so many upsets in my life, so much heartache, and to be given such an honour is something that gives me great joy.

We embark on this journey into the unknown with open eyes for we are now one with the aeroplane. We as a crew will survive I am sure. We are family with this mission. We are now somebody's, not deadbeats that should be shown the door at any cost. We are not thrown into the skies at a certain time to do our duty as cannon fodder for those that sit behind their little desks; the only danger they come across is when they might have to take a dump in the toilet and the siren goes off – big deal! There is much anger amongst airmen now as they are not treated very well it is not the way it should be. We all want to get home that is why we grab at as many missions as we can to get to that magic twenty-five so we can rejoin our loved ones back home. Logically this will not happen but that is all that spurs us on, that is the one thing that drives us on – not killing the enemy, not blasting the fuck out of the Germans. It is a job to do – get in and get out – nothing more, nothing less.

My contribution to this mission is simple: do what I have to do and return home. They have dangled the carrot and I intend to take a fucking great big bite out of it before they pull it away from me again. I have seen a lot of blood shed in this war, a lot of lives lost and for what...I know – peace! But it comes with a price – human sacrifice. It goes on until you are the one who has to sacrifice pain or ultimately your life. For you to forfeit your life you must go through an initiation first, it can be swift it can also be very long-winded. What am I talking about? Death of course – before we rid ourselves of our physical selves we must endure physical pain. This comes in many forms and the human in us has brought forward many ways to kill each other.

To see someone's brains splattered all over the cockpit – someone who you were just talking to about the girl the night before in one instance. To see a mass of blood and guts and then be expected to control yourself emotionally and control a plane – the guys around you depend on you to get home. The guy at the back of the plane, his leg blown off by bullets from a 109 that sprayed his guns, nobody dare tell him that his arm is so severely shot that it will obviously have to be taken off if we survive – at this point he would be better to just slide to the door and fall to his death.

You see there are many ways. A living death also, but who wants to live in a shell of a body? It's bad enough to grow old and have to have someone wipe your arse but what about that at age 19, 20, 21, 22, or 23 – what about that? Your life, nobody else's, has been taken away and by who? Some flea-bitten German in a 109, who has probably crapped himself in the confines of his cockpit and doesn't give a rat's arse about Hitler and the Third Reich! All he cares about is getting back home in one piece just like us. Ironic isn't it? We all of us don't want to be here doing this but we have no choice. That's taken away from us.

I have been with crews that are basically nutters. Because of the high turnover of crews you mix and match: in a very small percentage do you stay with the same crew. People die so you have to recruit. Others come in, others go and some just disappear into thin air. I know – I was with a crew for a short while and their rear gunner was injured, not much just enough to put him out of action for a few weeks. I was assigned with these guys and believe me they were all wacko; they were on some form of drug, some hallucinatory drug. I do not know its proper name – some guys called it the 'Red Dragon', this particular crew were stoned on it all the time. On this one mission which was deep into the German industrial north – a real deep one – we were given a target and in so much they said: 'When deployed make your way home, from where we don't give a fuck, just get that baby home to us so we can go up again.'

Well with that kind of attitude all our crew wanted was to get as much dope as we could and that was possible by doing the business and going over to Spain to pick up a load. Who gives a fuck where we drop the bombs as near as damn it. How we took off I will never know. The plane's name – *Dragon's Breath* – was a good one. The pilot was some guy from Michigan, his co-pilot a cowboy from a deadbeat town in Texas. To look into this guy's eyes was to look at death: he had no country this guy, if you met him back home he would shiver you for a dollar so why not take advantage and use him to kill the enemy? Now add the drug and you have a fatal weapon on your side but you must control because the bastard might bite the hands that feed.

These two guys – and I am not going to mention their names for good reason – would kill their grannies. Believe me, the rest of the guys were just as bad, it seems the authorities knew of them and they put all the bad apples in one basket. Even the plane's name which is given by the pilot was enough to tell you. The guy who drew the dragon was good – one of the best artists around, obviously did this for a living before being signed up. As in all lifetimes there are heroes – those that shine above all the rest, all through history they are there, they make their mark and they are gone. These are those guys. They choose what way to go. If they are blasted out of their heads on Red Dragon so be it – it is their choice. To fly a B-17 at one thousand feet and five hundred feet is something else. These guys do and do it well – I crapped myself looking out of that little window on the tail of the dragon shooting at anything.

Of course we had to go along the mainstream highway into Germany joining up with other wings to have the final kill. Once the payload was delivered from Uncle Sam it was playtime and we could run amok as it were, but before we got some refreshment time in Spain we'd give the Germans a kick in the ass. We had broken away from the main group; the two pilots knew where they were going. We went low over the treetops and headed for an airfield – lots of small aircraft, just run-arounds, nothing major. All the 109s and heavy stuff were probably after our buddies going back home, they were not expecting a B-17 to come out of the clouds with its undercarriage down as if to land.

Now I had not taken any form of drug – not even a drop of whisky. I knew where we were but did the rest of the crew? We landed – still running the engines – not even cooling down, just running. Lots of activity now, I could see guys running to the gun emplacements along the runway. Where was he taking us? Then suddenly, 'Come on guys. Unload all the hardware into that mother fucker over there as we go round. Our baby's going to be on just one wheel going round, so be good!' So we did into what looked like a very large bomber, nothing I had seen before matches what my eyes saw then, we unloaded a lot into that and we managed to get speed up and get the fuck out of there.

I could see the flames and the black diesel smoke pouring away from me, and a couple of explosions that were very small; I thought we risked our lives for that, but then at a reasonable height I saw from where we had been (which by now was a few miles away), a massive explosion, something that even put the clouds into a spinning wheel – I am sure I felt that force myself. Now this was big – our little baby had taken some flak, 'It's time for Spain guys, let's go.' We made it just over the border, our plane landed very well it has to be said.

We came to a stop. 'Siesta time guys – just have a good time. We have three days till Uncle Sam wants us again.'

I didn't need to be asked twice. I did have a good time. Now these guys knew what they were doing, the drugs just gave them that edge to go over the line in war, you need that. I was interrogated by our own people when I got home, a lot – four days I was kept in the cooler but the rest of the guys in the crew just went and carried on as if that was a normal mission for them, it probably was. The little talk with the authorities when I got back was purely for my point – nothing more. I was being groomed for a bigger party, that I know looking back on it. I was a little naïve then but not now, I know what I have to do and I will succeed in every way, no matter what.

My name if you wish for a name is Al Permando – Alphonse Luigi Permando – an Italian American from the sunny part of New York, here to make a mark on this war for Uncle Sam and take hopefully myself and my friends back home. To enjoy the rest of my days in my father's business of making good food for the good people of New York, to enjoy to look into my mother's and father's eyes to see their loving son cry with them. It is for them that I am here, for them, for the German family down the street, for the Irish family down the street and for the Russian family down the street, OUR STREET.

Chapter Thirty-Four
Buck Quinlan – Mission Flight 10 February 1944

The night draws in now like a shroud that suddenly covers you and takes the remaining light totally away. Sitting on the runway, waiting for the final push, going through all the spot checks over and over again; this is the most frightening time for me because any little mistake now will be a monster one when we are airborne – it doesn't do to daydream at a time like this. On the other missions I have been on you are looking forward to the bright sun coming up – the light that makes a difference. I often daydreamed then of home and what the smell of home is right now; to walk down my little part of town. The times I said it was the biggest shithole to get out of and how I looked forward to the day that I would do just that, and now at this time I am wishing in my heart that I was there, with all its faults.

Funny how life can put you in these situations; the sights I have seen since the start of this crazy war have opened my eyes. The thought that someday people will look back on this: just flick the pages until the interest is no more then return the book to its place neatly on the rack next to the other neatly stacked books of reference and we are no more until someone takes an interest again. Not really looking between the lines – to look there you will find out the real sacrifice.

What is it your self and I have in common? We breathe the same air: it hasn't changed over the years – it is the same air, just circulated. In this time – 1944 – I am breathing the same air you are now breathing, I am feeling the ground you are feeling, the surroundings are all the same. We live as you will live – living, breathing human beings. We are all the same.

Those that for countless missions I bombed the fuck out of were living, breathing, individuals as I am, ending their life because of my actions. My actions – nobody else's, I put those individuals to death. I am solely responsible for that. When you start to think about what you are doing and the responsibility for those actions, then you start to question the real reason you are doing what you are doing. Is it because I get a kick out of this? No. Is it because we are told what to do by a greater power and we have to do it or we lose our dignity? The answer is yes, for King and country or in my case, for country, the Stars and Stripes – old glory for the freedom of those that were once in slavery. How the values of our great country are split – here are we blowing up people in another country for the right of freedom and back home the black man cannot even sit in a public place and have a cup of coffee without being ridiculed and spat upon by his fellow countrymen.

These things you look at more clearly when you are in a position of uncertainty, when your own life becomes so insignificant to the authorities that it almost becomes just as insignificant to you at a personal level, all your dignity stripped away until you become a shell of the person you once were. I know I am going to my death, I do not fear that in any way, what upsets me most is I would like a say in the way I would like to go. I have heard stories of guys going on missions looking out of the cockpit right and left at B-17s and B-24s that they know should not be there but they are, and the names on the planes all of them ghost planes. It puts a shockwave through you like nothing else to see these guys waving at you then tailing away out of formation up into the sun, and disappearing before your eyes. It is not for the faint-hearted.

There was one particular mission I went on with P-45s out of a Suffolk airfield – I am not allowed to say which one because of security reasons. We were to meet up with a mass of B-17s and B-24s coming over from everywhere – the sky filled up with these things. We were on escort-only to the French-German border – unfortunately our tanks could not go any further. We escorted these guys no trouble, we were then told to go back to base, refill and escort back again. On the way back all should have been quiet but on this one day I was flying no problems, then in the corner of my eye I saw a group of spots.

Calling to my group leader to see if he could see what I could he replied, 'Hey Buck. You need some sleep guy.' I looked again – these spots were coming straight for us. We were now over the Channel, I could not go anywhere I had to stay in formation; we only had enough fuel to return to base. I was not going to be foolhardy and follow these spots – they seemed to be following me. The guys in formation could not see them at this point and I did think that ok I need some rest but no, I stuck with it. They came in formation, six B-17s, straight as an arrow, no sound, just flying to my left. I now shouted to my wingman, did he see anything? 'No,' was his reply. Now I was getting goose bumps all over starting at my neck, it was a feeling that someone was walking over your grave. Should I look? Are they there? What now? What if they are? Should I look?

My neck now being turned by another power outside my body; a quick turn there they were in all their glory – one at point, three below two above, flying like one plane. Now the names on these B-17s – get closer – should I now go out of formation? My wingman was going to go ballistic if I did – at what cost my sanity? Back at base this sort of thing goes around like wildfire and the fact is that I am a B-17 pilot and was only there for basic training for special operations because P-45 pilots are not B-17 pilots, and vice versa: big truck drivers don't get into small racing cars – get my drift? There is a code, a gentleman's code, amongst the fliers, we give each other the respect for our respective planes and that is it. I was only there because of special assignment, cloak and dagger and all that – we say nothing, just get on with it. The guys back at base would give me a right going over – take the piss big time if I said what I had just seen, but how could I not ignore this? Must now get info on these guys, count the numbers. LYMOD *Flying Dutchman* on point, LJFID *Dandy Joe* next to me, LSAFD *The Hooch* above. Those three I could see, the other guys were flying in such a way that they were not in a position to look at – they were too far away and in formation.

I scanned the nearest plane to me as my leader shouted, 'We are now over land guys, we are back home.' That shook me – his voice. I scanned the B-17 for life: I saw bodies just standing by the gun turrets to the cockpit and a pilot talking to his buddy. I looked intently, his face was not visible; my eyes now straining, nearly popping out of their sockets. The pilot's head slowly turned in my direction, his eyes not blinking once (this plane was that close to us). He looked as though he now saw a light, he looked at me, smiled and saluted and with that they were off to my left – away into the sun and out of sight.

How do I explain that to the guys? You must keep that sort of thing to yourself; do not at any time risk talking about that sort of thing it is frowned upon. Ok, so rumours fly about but where do those rumours come from? Nobody knows. Once back at base I debrief not letting on about anything, but the information I get from looking at records of these planes. I have some time owing to me and I know some contacts: see what they can find out for me without causing suspicion within the unit. I get a message to Lenny, one of my old pals back at Seething, see what he can drag up. Just go on as if nothing happened, that's the best I can do. It takes a couple of days but the info is mind-blowing. Six planes, the three logos I gave to Lenny plus three more, all from Thorpe Abbotts, went down together in suspicious ways. All men lost. They just vanished on one mission, no POWs – nothing. Lenny did tell me that the authorities were interested in what he wanted to know, his excuse was "just looking up old buddies" – they were not amused.

So these guys went down in a sea of confusion. There was a pack of B-17s out of Thorpe Abbotts this particular day and a pack out of Seething meeting up with packs from other Suffolk and Norfolk bases. One big push, six months previous, something to do with U-boat Pens being located and destroyed. These six B-17s were in formation together, apparently no problems, and went in for the strike. The pack met with very big flak on the target and in the next few hours these planes just vanished. No sign of explosions seen by other crews because, believe it or not, we do look out for one another – just willing you out of the plane is enough. Not a sign. So these guys I take it are now going around the loop as it were, in another dimension looking for a way home – it's enough to make you not want to fly again. Well, time for daydreaming is over, my mission now is to get these guys safely to their objective and to get me safely home again, tucked up in bed. Fat chance I suppose but I will try my best. They are my responsibility now, nobody else's, not even Uncle Sam; he has provided the hardware, it is now my turn. Not a cloud in the sky as we taxi to the end of the runway, may God go with us and show us the way on this cold February night in 1944. It is as if you could pluck the stars out of the sky with your hand.

Chapter Thirty-Five
Michael Hall – Mission Flight 10 February 1944

'Just before we depart this little bit of England that we have come to love as our own, it gives me great pleasure as a member of your illustrious crew to warn you of the impending danger we are embarking on at this time.'

There has to be a joker amongst the pack and we have ours in Steve Lursquom. His jokey ways are a great support at this time, he makes the statement quoted above solemnly and deadpan over his intercom as we begin to taxi for take-off. We have all been through a lot of ups and downs of different sorts whether they be personal or to do with this job. It's hard to turn off from this because we live and breathe this war. It's not like back home – the nine to five job, turn off and go out with the guys down the pool hall or go drink down the bars, chill out. No chance. Even going out from the base is an exercise – you have to be on your best behaviour. It's not all plain sailing, believe me. I have a wife and child – the child is not yet of this earth but to me she is here, with me. This I know. Funny thing to say but I know in my heart that my wife is carrying a child and her sex is female. How do I know this? Not even my wife is aware that it is a girl, but I know, she has come to me in my dreams, I know her name – Clare Louise. That is what I will call her.

Unfortunately with this job I do I have to make a sort of will-cum-suicide note for the authorities, it lets them off the hook as such, makes them look good in front of the public back home to see that everything is tied up you might say. It doesn't work out in lots of cases, I have known it when crews not coming back left all their gear and notes laid out as rituals against other crews – a sort of dare if you like to give a bit of gamesmanship to the order of the day. You come across this everywhere: leave the gear, personal gear, laid out on your bed and wait. If you are lucky you come back, if you don't it's a dare who will take your gear. Up until this particular occasion nobody touches anything – it is an unwritten law amongst all crews that you will not touch or go near their bunks until they return, to do so would be bad luck to your crew or yourself; it is something you would have to live with.

On this occasion a crew went on a very bad checkout – a raid that they knew would be very, very important but highly risky. So they left their possessions neatly on the beds and the final bit of papers, all neatly folded in the brilliant white envelope respectfully provided by the authorities, with the name of your spouse or guardian or parent; to be opened only by them and no other. These crew members went about their business into deepest Germany – an ammunitions factory deep in the Ruhr Valley. Their ship was *The Lightning Strikes* – very apt. They struck their target – their tenth mission as a crew, a very good success rate keeping together as a crew for that amount of time. They did the job and according to reports were making their way back home when disaster struck: a rogue wolf pack of ME-109s came across a bunch of our guys. No cover from the Mustangs, they were torn to shreds; it was lambs to the slaughter – no one survived.

How do we know this? Only by reports – there are always reports, sightings. These people who make the reports suddenly disappear into the mist. Well, these reports come back to base on the initial day; when ships do not return we wait – it doesn't matter how long. In some circumstances ships on deep missions go to ground, safe havens, there are many in certain areas – some neutral countries, some not involved with this conflict. So as I said, we wait. On this occasion a certain individual (I shall not even mention his name) along with a couple of other non-individuals, took it upon themselves to take from the crew of *The Lightning Strikes* their personal effects. This did not go down well with us, the guys in the front line. To think that someone who is a part of us should stoop to take personal effects is unforgivable. We were distressed and the authorities also took a dim view of it, they wanted to deal with this.

We took it away from them. We dealt with it in our own way. These particular individuals would not be doing that again in a hurry. There are ways within our groups to deal with such matters, within a family unit you deal with it in-house, within family. There are many, many things wrong with set-ups like this. Within a war situation there are those that abide by the rules, there are those that toe the line; there are those that take advantage – they are fighting a personal war, a war of gain, not for their country but for themselves – this is a fact, do not be blinkered into thinking otherwise. In life dog eats dog. No matter where you are there are those that take advantage especially here within these small camps away from prying eyes. Things go on but through it all you have to have rules – Gentleman's Agreements. Without justice in the playground people will just step over one another and you will lose all discipline.

Do not let me digress from my story. I have a note wrapped along with a toy for my daughter with her name on it. If I do not return from this mission then I leave my legacy for my wife and child and hope and pray that they will both survive this madness and live their lives to the full, this I would like very much. Nobody touches my gear, it is bad luck. I will watch over it. These guys are my family – here the bond is of family, and with that as we taxi to the end of the runway, my thoughts are with my wife and child.

Just to keep the record straight, my name is Michael Hall. I am a proud American serving my country, and with all the wishes of my fellow countrymen serving here in this far away place, a haven I miss is my family and Cleveland, Russell County, Virginia: back home. I think these thoughts before every mission, this is no exception believe me, none whatsoever. All my fears are running through my head at this time.

My love to my wife and child. May we go forward and complete this mission in the prospect that it will be a turning point in this struggle, and the loss of life that has been experienced will come to an end on both sides and all the innocent ones caught up in all of this on both sides be at peace now. May we have God's blessings in what we are about to do and that it is swift in its execution.

Chapter Thirty-Six
Rupert Kovloski – Mission Flight 10 February 1944

Before all this started I was just a simple kid going about his business just like any other kid in the neighbourhood. Growing up in the area of my birth is not everybody's cup of tea and especially at this time, it is very difficult looking back on my childhood. As I sit gazing out of this giant bat in the night waiting to lift off into the stillness, looking at the stars it seems as if they look down on us giving judgement: they see so many things. They look and see – no more, just that – until the next time we see them and they come into our conscious state, probably in the twelve hours previous they have been judging others on the other side of the globe. All these things pass through your mind when you are put into a situation such as this, the minutes count down in this metal-winged object, you are confined into a space you would find hard to have a crap in and be comfortable. For maybe five to six hours we have to endure this – except for this one mission.

We are individuals going about the battle. We know what the task is – we have been given the orders from on high. Those great leaders have come to a decision not to dirty their own hands, that would not do – let us give the task of ridding this world of maybe its greatest tyrant to a bunch of lowlifes that can be easily replaced by other such lowlifes. They are expendable – there are so many of them they are replaceable, is that not so? We such individuals have a gift – a gift given to use for a purpose. How we use that gift is up to us, so we think, but those that wield the great power have other ideas.

It is so that we have been given a gift, a gift to hunt maybe, and to hunt you have to bear the tool of a sword, or bow and arrow, or stick, or mallet, or gun, or rifle. Our gift is the gift of sight: to see as a deer sees its predator, to move with grace away from danger; the stealth of the fox to hide, to see others before they see you, to stalk one's prey for days – to have that hunger for the kill.

Not to have any hate or guilt but to be as one has to be to live, nothing more, nothing less, nothing to prove, nothing to gain; to be as the wind, to gather as one then be still until hungry again. These are the true gifts we have been given but in this world situation at this one time we are put into a bloodbath we have no control over. The authorities in their own judgement have given us a window – an opportunity to show our talents off to the full extent. Ok, sure, we have had our little trial runs, our walks in the park, but this is World Series time. We are in the Master Leagues now; this is the one big hit into the stands with the Big Joe hitting it with all his might at the big game at the Yankee Stadium. We have come of age.

Throughout the ages – it matters not when, fifty years ago, five hundred, five thousand, we are all individual human beings with minds and bodies that feel all emotions – hate, love – we all feel emotions of pain, not only physical but mental as well. We are here for a purpose, to look at yourself – not as others look at you but as you see yourself – the real you. How you are as a person – your personality. You influence others as they influence others, you have kids and they carry it on – the chain reaction. Look at yourself and see the real you – then and only then will you gather your own power within and go on and be *not* like everybody else. Do not run with the pack, be a lone wolf.

That is what we are: we are a bunch of guys brought together – all lone wolves, all with one talent that can be exploited at this time. Forgive these words they are what I think at this time maybe hours before my physical death maybe, maybe not. Perhaps I will successfully complete my twenty-fifth mission and return back home to the States, back home to Mum and Dad and sanity. I am allowed to think that, at least they cannot infiltrate that part of my being. The powers-that-be do influence the lesser-willed individuals that make up this grand land, sea and air armed force, there are many that wish to voice their opinion on how they are manipulated not of their own free will.

Ok, sure, there are those that go about this sorry state of affairs with the vigour of the free will to give as much pain to lesser more devout peoples of this world. The playground bully: give him a loaded gun he will cause mayhem, give him a cause and he will win you a war. Not everybody in the boat wants to row – get my drift? You need persuasion of a different kind. Mind drugs, manipulating drugs that will give the individual a purpose – a purpose to kill and like it. Ok, go about your daily business but in the heat of war it needs other gifts. The days of mutiny will diminish. The guys in the last war – the ones that saw the light – they were easily extinguished not only by firing squad but by other means. You get the mood of the people behind you and the world is your oyster, you can do anything. The deserter in the First World War was a lone wolf. You do not in the day-to-day life of one's self understand what is going on. You are seeing the world and what goes on in that world by manipulation – pure and simple. There were many deserters in the Great War even to the point of being a colony of them in the trenches – dug in, not moving, not being scared but saying individually with one voice: enough is enough, why should we lay our one life down to be shot like animals to the slaughter? Why? Will anybody hear our cries? We have a right to live.

Not in that situation and at that time – that was to be the straw that broke the camel's back, deserters or free thinkers were then silenced by the papers of the time. Ok, everybody has to know what's going on but the press that has been put in place is regulated, not a free press – they are only just tolerated or given a ceremonial burial after a short while, but the press we have is not for the free thinker, no way. The deserter would be thrown to the wolves, believe me.

Forgive my thoughts, for they are as I think and I know through experience – seeing. You see a lot in this job, you also have to keep quiet as well – doesn't stop you thinking. I love my country make no mistake I will give my life this is not in question. What is in question though is those chosen individuals that have been voted in by my fellow countrymen – my mother, father, brothers, sisters. Those men in office – do they...do they give a fuck about me and thousands like me? That is the question – they are not at the gun barrel's end are they? One shot, one perfect shot to a point on the body and I am no more – gone in a flash. How do I know it is my gift to be of the arrow, to be the blade of the cutting sword, to be the point of the bullet? Just one bullet – that's all it takes, nothing more, nothing less.

Rupert Kovloski has this gift and nobody will take that away from me. I will survive no matter what, I am sure. Sitting in this bucket gives you time – time to think and reflect on one's mortality. Please our Lord, give me the strength to go forward and do what is right by my own forgivings. Please keep my family safe as I go forward into the darkness.

With that the sudden movement: slowly along the runway, slowly gathering speed as we have done many, many times before, but this time the feeling is very different. We are all thinking as one on this trip, will we survive? Who can say? I have come to terms with it, not without a fight I might say. My last words are written for my dear mother, left on top of my private belongings in case we do not return. The letter I wrote when I went on my first mission was used many times, not opened, just thrown in the back of the locker until next time. But I ripped that up this time and wrote out a whole new letter a few pages long – a very long confession to my mother who means everything to me. This one mission has that sort of edge to it, something we all feel. As I say my farewells, especially to my mother, our love will never die – they cannot take that away from me.

Chapter Thirty-Seven
Steve Lursquom – Mission Flight 10 February 1944

It's the long walk to this rust bucket we call home for a few hours in this cold night air. We are not very good at night flights, especially covert ones in deepest secrecy. To see the sun on the horizon as we brief for the up and coming mission is on a different level to this. Really want to get on with this: I have a bad feeling about this mission. It does not smell right for one thing, if there is one lesson I have learned working and living in this environment: watch your back at all times. These British are a funny breed, they look after their own; they might talk about each other behind their backs but they do look after their own in wartime. I do not trust these people. It is true we are fighting on the same side but the people in power are very different to our top brass. How do I know? Just to say it is a feeling I have.

To say I have a chequered past is an understatement, this is a walk in the park compared to what I have seen and experienced in peace time and war time. Do not think I am some Yankee kid who knows everything and is gobby as well: I had killed before this war began – my first kill was before the war working for an organisation that doesn't officially exist.

Sitting and waiting for Buck to kick the start button on this mission brings me to think of the mission I was given just before war broke out, as I said, working for a non-organisation. Being so young you get into arenas and official places a lot easier, the authorities know this and they take notice of it.

I can fire a gun or a rifle at any given object and I do not miss – this has been my legacy since I was very young. My father taught me to extend my gift in gun clubs. The eyes of the authorities are everywhere. I was approached to do a hit, the choice I thought was mine. What the fuck do they want a fourteen year old kid to do a hit for? Where are the morals of this country? Gone to the dogs? Two guys turned up at my door and talked to my father for two hours. A lot of shouting and then he calls me.

'Look, these guys are from Internal Affairs – social workers. They say that you will be put into care and I will be put into prison for using illegal weapons and allowing a minor to fire and use and carry weapons without authority.' Ok. We had not done anything – what's the deal? First they asked my father to leave. I sat down.

'Ok my friend, this is the deal. We know how good you are with the rifle, we've been looking.'

Is there no privacy in this country, I thought? 'Fuck it – who are you guys?'

They looked at each other and laughed. 'Like we are going to tell you kid.'

'Yeah, we are just the delivery boys. We are here to take you to somebody that will explain more. Is it a deal?'

What choice did I have? As I went to leave, my father looked surprised and worried, 'Where are you going son?'

'No need to worry Pa, they will not harm you or me. I have to go see my head teacher at school.'

'Alright son, don't be long.'

'I won't be. I'll make sure of that.' I replied as I closed the door.

In all this confusion it gives me much pain to think of what might have happened to my father in all of this, a proud man he was, I say was for now on reflection at this time, he has passed on in a way that was not his time. The very thought of anything happening to me and he would be there comforting me as a very small child. He was my guiding light, someone to look up to. All fathers are supposed to be like that I know and all mothers are in their way supportive, but I thought this man to be invincible and the uppermost thought in my mind was his best welfare also.

I was given a letter by my superior officer when first coming over here. I felt a kind of jolt – a current of electricity if you will that went straight up my arm, the letter falling to the floor like a leaf falling from a tree, struggling not to hit the ground. The writing I knew instantly was my mother's on the address, my name bouncing up into my eyes like a rude awakening from the past. Should I open it? Should I just put it with the rest of my personal stuff and get on with my life? Use it as a guiding light to read every night and hope on keeping it to my twenty-fifth mission then open it? What if I would not return one day and all my possessions were returned to my mother with the letter not opened? What would she think of me as a son? All these things trigger off memories and reflections on how you should act.

As I picked up the letter I carefully tore it open to find the smell of my mother's perfume wafting from the pages within, the smell consuming me with joy of her yet crying inside knowing I am far from her. Inside the carefully folded pieces of paper, a photograph of my father and me at the age of ten taken where we would always go in the desert alongside his truck. We stood with guns held like two outlaws, the camera held by my older brother who was pig sick at the time of not being in the picture. Someone had to take it and he lost the toss. My father was obviously proud of both of us but he shone a light on me I have to say, probably because of my being the youngest. My mother disapproved of going into the desert. She used to go with my father when they were first engaged but something spooked her when they were there late on one night and since then she would not venture out there even during the day. She had grave doubts about the young ones going out there but my father was adamant about it: he was a forceful character and he won through.

I remember his jokes about my mother going out there that night. He said 'I cannot remember a thing about it! She says there were lights coming over the horizon at such a rate that at one point she thought they were meteors. Nothing we know of then and now could fly at that rate. The lights got much brighter and then pure light all around, then pure darkness.'

My father even admitted they were late getting back because my grandfather was just about to set off and search for my father and mother. They had lost two hours and could not explain to my grandfather who was very upset his one and only daughter, who he cherished, was in the desert of all places late at night. So since then my mother had not ventured out there. My father in his way laughed it off but what I heard was my grandfather threatened his life: he put the barrel of a gun to his head and said, 'Once more and I will not hesitate to shoot your head off if any harm comes to my daughter.'

With that I think when the children came along he put all his love into us and left mother to her own little world. I think what made it worse was the lights in all the county went off for two hours that night, no explanation. The local authorities said that a very bad storm in the hills had built up, and gathered and struck several power cables down and a freak happening made it strike out all of the county.

'Ok, what should we think? Their explanation was credible and we got on with our lives,' said my father, but he knew deep down something happened that night to change my mother like that. Perhaps he could have been hypnotised along with my mother but it would have been too stressful for her and she was against anything like that. She wasn't even aware of any kind of counselling that would be of benefit to her. She was quite happy to just get on with her life.

In the letter her grief was very much apparent. Every character was jumping out of the page in pain at the loss of someone who had been her life for so long and was now taken from her. She was devastated, and the fact that little old me was a few miles away from home didn't go down too well either. My father was special to me but now I have to be focused on what the moment has for me – I should now let him rest in peace and show what I am made of. This mission is the one that shines above all that has come before – to be recognised by your own Government at long last and not be used by Government non-organisations that pop up or disappear at the turn of a hat.

Chapter Thirty-Eight
Buck Quinlan – Mission Flight 10 February 1944

Sitting on this chair in this rumbling mountain of metal just waiting for the go from Ops, you can't help from reflecting on your fortunes and misfortunes in being here at this moment in time and hoping you are going to survive maybe the next few moments or the next few hours. Who can tell? You are at a knife's edge all the time. I know nothing of this mission. The boys who are connected with the little brown envelope that can only be opened when we are on our way will not let the cat out of the bag. The less I know as a pilot the better it will be for my survival. Sounds good – they will only give you a heading on this one. I know it's a drop not a bomb run, that puts me still at a loss but I am here to do a job and get on with it. It still doesn't take the nerves away – my left leg will not stay still. I try holding it down but it gets worse.

This sudden hold-up also gets to the mental state as well. Don't know what's going on. If it was a bomb run I would understand but we are sitting here all on our ownsome waiting, I know it's only minutes but it seems like hours. I feel like nodding off – not used to night flights, against all my training this. But we are only the guys that do the dirty work; those that make the decisions are tucked up with their cups of tea.

We are all jittery at this time and it doesn't hurt to have a memory you can reflect on at times like these. I come from New York. It has a European feel to the place more than the guys over in California would think – they can't get over the culture shock and the weather. Living in New York we are used to cold winters, far colder than here, and the locals are nice – they make coming home the best for me. I am a long way from my family, these people I regard as my substitute family.

It is true I have an ability to get on with people. I talk. Perhaps not to everyone's taste that is true, but on the whole I generally make a good impression especially with the local girls. I wish I could go further afield to try my talents on picking up girls. I went to London – didn't do too bad there. The added incentive is that tomorrow you could be dead meat in the morgue or splattered over your buddy's window. That really gets to you – I have seen it. You cannot walk away from incidents like your best buddy lying there in a pool of blood and the night before you were drinking and having a laugh – the two just don't go together. In a thought you have to turn off and focus on something else to get you over it and to survive your next mission ok. Not everybody admits to cracking up.

There are an abundance of B-17s in this country but there are not that many good pilots and their survival is paramount to the cause, so if you are feeling the effects of tomato soup all over your jacket and pants then it's all over for you. The powers-that-be have no time for crybabies. They want you to go out there and fight, not break down, crawl in the corner and wait till it's dark to come out. Their objective is to win at all costs – to individually look good. If my CO gets the job done he is in line for promotion and he will step on your face to get that stripe or star. When you get a few of these guys wanting recognition it gets to be a flood, so you get this second skin. Ok, you have been given this target of twenty-five missions and you are a free man to go home – a living hero to the American people. A long shot maybe, who will reach the twenty-five? Some lucky bastards will, maybe me, maybe not but someone will – it's that mentality. You might be the lucky one but until then you are an unlucky bastard, in which case that puts you smack in line for a good screw with the nearest good-looking bird or if it's late in the day, the nearest-looking bird, who cares what she looks like? And on top of that, let's get pissed out of our heads and crack a few skulls with the locals, there's none of them around here can look after themselves anyway. You might get the odd local who's home on leave but he's probably searching for his old lady – she's being shagged by a Yank somewhere. We are all the same – if the Brits were over in our country and we were off fighting somewhere they would do just the same, so we are here, let's get on with it. We are all here to fight the same enemy. If those jackbooted bastards were marching up Pall Mall, who would be shagging the locals then?

And they would probably shoot them in the head after they finished with them.

I have no fear or illusions about this enemy, they could not give a frig about my life or my country and what I believe in so why should I give a toss about them? If I am shot down I will try to regain my composure and God willing return to these shores. But if not I will take on and kill as many of the enemy as I can before putting the gun to my mouth and pulling the trigger. There is no way I am being taken by the Gestapo or SS; I have heard stories about prisoners being taken and all manner of things done to extract information. No way! Clean and simple: a bang to the head; a little messy to other people, but clean and simple to me.

So you can see the mentality of some of the guys in the way they go about their lives. I only hope when this war ends that some of these loony tunes don't end up on the streets of the big cities back home – let loose on the general public. No doubt some of the local mafia or gang areas will welcome them in with open arms, the only trouble is they don't know what they are dealing with; the cuckoo clock has chimed a fair bit for some of these guys. Some of them would love to be caught – then they would do some killing. The pain inflicted on them would be trick or treat compared to what would be in store for the local Gestapo.

I did hear a good story, maybe it was true maybe not, but the local jungle drums had it relayed around the camps at a fair old rate of knots. The story goes that some high flier in the authorities at the Pentagon came along with an idea that if they got a squad of inmates from separate secure units from New York to San Francisco – a ten man unit that in essence would be the worst, most evil gang members, murderers or rapists this country had ever put behind bars – this gang could be unleashed upon the German war machine. This person who has no name also knew that if these guys were put into a proper unit they would put the risk of death on other guys in the rank and file. This was not good, and also, these guys would do a runner that is for sure. So the sweetener was parole, full pardon and a heap of money on their return if they returned home, one mission that is all. No chance of keeping tigers in a cage the size of Great Britain, they would cause mayhem and also, it would not be in the best interests of the American and British governments if the press found out that American prisoners and Category 'A' ones at that, all lifers, death row, 'dead man-walking' candidates, were roaming the streets of old London Town. You thought Jack the Ripper was bad, this would be a hundred times worse.

So, the solution – these guys get dropped behind enemy lines, one objective, the Fuhrer. If you are going for the big fry let's have a big one – a bit bold. They would have their orders, his location and whereabouts from local informants, then, unleash the hounds. That was six months ago, no sound of them since; God knows what happened to them. No squad leader would go with them – let's face it you would be signing your own death certificate. The idea went the whole way, touchdown for the man with no name. Somebody somewhere knows the truth. Perhaps it was a load of bullshit, perhaps not, who knows? Makes good storytelling. Who in their right mind would put a scheme like that together? Someone who didn't give a rat's arse about his own fellow patriots and countrymen I'll be blowed.

Still, not to worry – nothing like that for us, we just bomb people from a great height. I feel sorry for our guys on the ground, it's not good day in day out, constantly going forward no break. At least we have a break from this; those poor bastards endure all manners of crap and on top of that the thought of being captured would frighten the fuck out of anybody. Sit tight, get on with the job, tomorrow is another day – I will be drinking at the local or saying hello to Jesus.

Chapter Thirty-Nine
Mike Preston – Mission Flight 10 February 1944

These last few days leading up to this mission have been the most stressful I can remember. I know I have a good pilot in Buck but I have had the jitters about this one, not because of the secrecy surrounding it but the whole mission is not as it seems – the emotions of everybody and the feelings I get are not right. I have been on secret missions before but this one is clouded in mystery as well as everything else. For a start we are not told (that is, the pilot and myself) we are not told anything only to head for a co-ordinate on the map, unload the cargo and return to base. That is the mission for us but this one is not running right. Ok, we have unloaded cargo before for the British as in covert ops where operatives from organisations within the government are shipped out to destinations unknown. How they make their way back is up to them, the less we are told the better – if we were to crash and survive we would be interrogated by the SS or Gestapo and who knows what we would let out of the bag as it were.

As Buck is doing the checks on this one, I reflect on what might have been in the case of myself being a pilot. I wanted so much to work for the government but my father and the war had other ideas – my family thought it right to go into the air rather than the artillery.

Waiting is the worst, let's get on with it. The rain now starting to form on the windows – not a great sign at the best of times but at night it's not good. I try to stay focused on my instruments, the constant checklist over and over again, but it's for the best. If something was to happen – our engines fail or something rather than anti-tank or shrapnel damage, we would question our pre-flight checks.

These overwhelming negative feelings I have are still with me. I must reflect on what was rather than what is now. I am at my best when the thoughts of my family and friends are with me, it seems as if they reach out and somehow touch my physical self and they comfort me so much.

Living in such a beautiful place as Mundo in California, it needs a pinch in the side to think I am here rather than there. I should be there with my family but I chose to be here, fighting for the very existence of where I belong. Fighting for a freedom that should be everybody's right on this planet, not for a dictator or governing body to take or try to take away. But on reflection our very own country has had its very bad moments in time: the hurt and the suffering of the Native Americans, the Civil War uprising – these things take time to heal but in some quarters they do not heal whatsoever. The personal tragedies are the worst. The government of the time only look at figures that suppress the enemy victory at all costs and the ultimate cost is human life. Their argument is we have victory so you that are left and your loved ones can now live in peace. But what of the personal sacrifice? No thought of that in the collective. No chance. You are given a military funeral ok, but the ultimate sacrifice is not what we want, we want to survive this war and live the rest of our lives with our families around us. We do this because we have to but if our lives are in vain and do not have the proper respect then that is a different matter.

How can I put this so you can understand? Say you were now in my position, positive in the ultimate goal of victory and wanting to end this conflict, you die in the course of your duty and the government – the actual structure of what you are fighting for – suddenly discards you: you are no longer a soldier, sailor, or airman of the USA or of anywhere; you are slung on the scrap heap along with countless others. In certain thinking and belief systems who gives a fuck you're dead – so what? But if you had a chance to come back, how would you feel? Hate? Remorse that you and countless others have sacrificed their lives, not even a simple 'thank you'? A recognition of any sort is not there – how would you feel? You would not rest until such a time as something should reconcile that.

Look back in time: the Civil War. How many innocent people – men, women and children – gave up their lives through no fault of their own? Suddenly this involvement many miles away; something completely out of their control is sweeping the country. You have to bear arms against your fellow man – your brother, your father – because of different thinking and values. You are confronted with the smell of death around you. You as an individual are suddenly thrown into this world where values are no longer there. Your wife, your children, your mother, your father – all are vulnerable to the goings on many miles away, so to uphold any kind of dignity you sign up. What for? Because all the other guys are!

All those that sign are looked upon as true to the cause, either to the blue or the grey. You must now fight for your very existence; to kill if need be for you and your family to somehow get over this. If the cause is just and the feeling is right then so be it, but if you are just cannon fodder for the slaughter how would you feel? Not good. To see mass slaughter in battle is for some a relief – this is what they want. Their life up to now has been a shit ride, 'So what if I kill a hundred or a thousand soldiers – this is what I want.' But for the guy thrown in and told to get on with it, it's a different way of life and in the long run they do not survive, so your way of thinking has to change for survival. You are a very family man not wishing any harm to anybody. Suddenly your family are ripped apart by war, your wife beaten and raped, your children put to the sword. What are your values then? You cannot dismiss this action – you are thrown into a turmoil of indifference; you cannot return to your lifestyle as before you must survive in this time and place.

And with that comes another sacrifice – that of one's self. Discard the old robes and put on this new cloak, return and fight but this time with a new companion – he calls himself 'Hate'. This warrior called Hate will kill anything and everything in his path, so you are consumed and transformed into this creature that now wants revenge and anybody that holds up any type of armament or colour that represented this campaign against you is ripped apart. Your own survival does not matter because a part of you has died with your family. The Indian wars are the same but with one difference – there has been no declaration of war between two nations. Greed is the warrior there and that consumes everything in its path with no survivors whatsoever. And what is left? Only what has been gained, only waiting for others to come forward and claim the prize.

Now little old me, sitting in this iron box, is waiting for a signal to go on a mission. A secret mission probably to my death – a bit melodramatic but that is what I feel at this moment in time. I have had a reflection on my country's past. It gives me not the greatest of positive outlooks I must say, but that is all I have. I pray but to whom do I pray? Will He help me to survive? Will He help me if I die? Big dilemma: should I just get up, walk away back to the barrack room and try to get back home? Of course not! I cannot even allow myself to think like that. For one thing I would be court-martialled or even shot as a deserter, but that doesn't mean I should try to squash these feelings of remorse. 'Go with the gut feelings' Buck always says. If that were true I would not go on this mission, no matter what they threw at me.

'Come on Mike, snap to it, we are 'Go' for lift-off – I thought you were unconscious for a minute!' I wish I was.

Chapter Forty
Michael Hall, rear gunner –
Mission Flight 10 February 1944

This is the moment we have all been waiting for, this one minute in time captured for us here. We shall never experience this again. What happens in the next twenty-four hours will put us in history, captured forever in a time-capsule to be displayed whenever and whatever the occasion perhaps, or maybe we will disappear into the darkness never to return. Let us not dwell on such things, we are here to do a job let us focus on that. We are ready to go, we have the thumbs up; we gather speed, she lifts for a moment – then away – we are airborne, gliding through the darkness. We are glad we are now in flight, no obstacles left. We know what to do, everything is ok.

We fly from Seething, low-level for us; we have been told this – it is not our normal practice it is said but in this situation we are told it is normal. We always receive our flight plan with distaste anyway; usually the high fliers from the other bases get the high fly at point and above. In this mission we are basically alone; we do not want to cause alarm so we are needed to avoid our own radar, for what reason I still cannot fathom out. We fly for Norwich and bank right then head out east, this again is a weird flight plan, we are flying near the radar station itself – a more or less piss take we laugh! Perhaps these Limeys might wake up if we buzz them? Not tonight guys – of all things, not tonight.

We are blacked out ourselves – we are not in the best position it is said. Let's get past this radar station and then climb. With this very notion going through our minds it is clear that our position is not good. We are suddenly and without provocation fired upon with all barrels of such might that it throws us to one side with such impact that we are frozen in time – what is this? We are on our own patch and we are fired upon?

There is no let up. We cannot climb, our engines on the left side have taken the thrust of the cannon, we must now ditch. All these plans are now at the mercy of whoever pulled the trigger. We cannot say anything – we are still in shock. We spin out of control – our pilot is hanging on. It is not even possible for us to bail out, to end it here.

All my greatest fears have now come in front of me as if watching a film unfold, its storyline slowly coming to the end...and what of the end? It still goes on. We are still hanging in there. From my position I see the sky in front of me – its stars twinkling, ever shining and then, the bang of the earth. The jolt sends me spinning, hitting every part of this Flying Fortress – her belly busted around me. I smell fuel – its vapour going inside me. I feel around in the darkness, I shout to my friends – I hear cries, nothing more – the engines still churning. What has happened here? I crawl through the belly of the plane – what is left of her – on the ground. I walk as if not harmed – I dare not look at my limbs: my death would come sooner if I saw my arm or some part of me lying on the ground. I look – it's not a pretty sight; I am a mass of blood. I still feel fine though – it seems strange. I cannot see the other guys.

Suddenly my legs disappear from me. I crumple to the ground. The shock is going through me at a tremendous rate. Now my blood I feel for the first time, oozing from my legs like small waterfalls – I look at them and say to myself, is this really me? And in this confusion I see clearly in the distance six figures walking towards me – the light around them blinds me for a moment – these figures, slowly walking towards me and I blink just once and they are gone into the night.

It is now I hear screams from people running around. These two hands caress my head, 'Don't worry my friend, you are with us now. We will take care of you.' I look up and this young girl looks at me with water in her eyes slowly running down her cheeks.

'What's your name fella?'

I say, 'Mike.'

'Well Mike, you are the only one left alive, your mates have all died tragically.'

I say at this point, 'I wish I was with them.'

The pain is getting worse, I am losing consciousness now. She is drifting away slowly, her voice an echo, I try and grasp hold of her hand but the strength has gone at this point. I am by her side, looking at her and looking at me – strange. A hand comes from the darkness.

'Mike! Welcome – you've made it!' It's Buck and the rest of the guys.

Now my story really starts. Where do I as a person begin? Is this really happening to me? Is this a crazy dream and will I wake up in my bed with the noise of shouting and laughter and know that this I am experiencing now is and was a nightmare of a dream? My friend alongside of me looks at me and smiles.

'This is no dream Mike – we have now gone to heaven or hell, whatever label you want to put on it.'

My mother was religious and talked about things like this. I for one didn't take a lot in and thought if you are dead, you're dead, so this experience is out there – this is not what I expected. It's a funny feeling. I am of body. I feel all my limbs – my physical shape is the same – I have not sprouted wings or anything like that. It's as if we are waiting to be briefed after a mission, that's what it feels like – just waiting. The guys that smoke are just doing that. It's as is if we are surrounded by an inner peace, just feeling calm. A release if you will – that's what I am feeling – and when a person says something it's as if I hear that voice in my head.

Buck has a lot of anger you can see. For me, the pain I was in – I am glad I do not have that. The issue not of why we are here but the reason of how we are here – who murdered us? Because that is what it is murder, nothing more nothing less. Perhaps now we will find out what is really going on here. Am I experiencing this? It's a lot to take in, in one go. So perhaps in the time I have before we know I can recollect my thoughts and feelings at this time, a time for reflection and the realisation of one's being.

There is a time for reflection, it is so, but with all the might I possess I cannot help the anger around me gaining strength and taking as well as giving power from within to the many concepts of what is happening to me and to those around me. We are being met by other comrades-in-arms who have been talked to in briefings but the thing that gets me is we are not talking. We are communicating but not through speech – through thought. This is really bizarre. Some of my crew still believe this is a dream and we must interact with it, but I must confess that in all the dreams I have had I certainly did not interact within them and we cannot all be having the same dream, can we? Or can we?

As soon as that thought came to me, a light – quicker than anything I have ever seen – shot before me. Its appearance was a glowing white ember; its form now took shape – a wise man like an old medicine man from back home. He told me: 'This is no dream. You must now evaluate your entire existence and ponder your thoughts. Time has no relevance here so to begin to go forward you must relive and think of yourself in your duties – not only to yourself but to your neighbour, your fellow being.' And with that he went – like turning a light off. And while I was talking to him, his self commanded all around me – it is as if all my friends suddenly disappeared. Now they are back.

I must now see some sense in all of this. Am I dead? Yes, that is the first hurdle I must conquer before anything else – the Afterlife. My family obviously had their beliefs and were a God-loving family that went to church every Sunday, and from a very early age I was told to pray. We all went through that, to be baptised at birth or just after was accepted because that is what everybody else did. You did not dare question this, it is written in the Big Book that sits on top of the family piano in the corner of the room. All that is sacred is in that book, all that we adhere to and you must accept, and those that fall by the wayside are taken away it is said, to hell. There is only heaven and hell, no middle ground, just black and white. Am I in hell then or heaven?

What is all this having to think about one's own thoughts and rules in life? All the praying for forgiveness has done me no good whatsoever. The person or energy that is me standing here, the Michael Hall that has spent this very short time on the earth, am I now having to relive all my life again like replaying something back, like an old newsreel from the picture house – is that what is in front of me? And time, this guy says, time has no meaning here – I tell you if this is a dream it's a beauty, no mistake.

Right, let's get together with the other guys. I look down at my legs – they are still bleeding a lot. I touch – I feel pain only when I touch, I look forward and the pain goes. It's as if consciously I am aware it becomes reality again. There are no mirrors here so I must ask my friends how I look – they are about somewhere. I turn around and I am in a green field low on the bank, the smell of the grass knocks me over. It's the height of summer, the small river behind me crawls along at its own pace, you could stand here forever – that is the feeling I am getting. It is as if you *are* the field, the river, the trees, the air – everything. You are not a separate entity – you are everything.

I walk forward. There are families playing in the field, the love from these people is overwhelming. They are not aware of me. I walk among them. They were a good distance from me but just bringing them to thought brings them to me or I to them. A family, a very young family, comes into view – a young woman and young man with a baby, not very old, only months. The couple look in my direction but do not see me, but the baby points in my direction and I talk with him in thought. He looks at me with those big eyes and stares as if fixed to me.

'I love you Michael,' he says to me.

'You know me little one? How do you know me?'

'I am you Michael. This is your beginning – your birth. I am speaking to you before I am entrusted into the ways of the speech and the material. I am you – you are me. Learn about me and you. You must do this before you can go on.'

'So these are my parents then?'

'Yes they are. Obviously you do not recognise them as yet for at this time you were still of Spirit. It is only when you grow up that you distinguish who is your mother and father and close family by looking. You feel at this age by instinct and touch, I know they are my mother and father but not in your sense. You will understand, do not worry – all will make sense in your awakening to the Spirit. I must go now, love always Michael.'

And with that I was back in the place I started, with all these things running around now in my head. Hang on a minute, have I still got a head? Should I feel for my head? Will it be there? Will I be disappointed if it isn't? Go for it. Should I do it quickly or build up to it? Just do it – touch. I feel wet...I bring my hands down – blood and lots of it. Here we go again. I have consciously thought and touched myself and so bring back the pain, and the pain is coming back. Look forward again, the pain goes. Well that's one thing I have learned – not to be worried if I am physically here. If I am dead then how can all these things be? I must now learn to look at myself as a baby and to talk to myself as a baby. Takes some believing but that's what it is all about – learning who I have become and who I was before I was Michael on Earth or in body. Now I am in Spirit.

What has become of me? How am I to deal with this? My own conscious state is in place for me to even comprehend what I am saying. It certainly opens the floodgates to one's imagination. I had imagination on the Earth plane, dreams if you will, but I only have to remember a place, a time, and I am there; I don't suppose they call it imagination here – so much to learn. I am being called and I am there, my friends call me. We need to go to a Justice Spirit – a sort of judge if you will, we have all been called to him for something. I know my friends are angry at their passing as I am, but we shall see. I know one thing – we cannot go back that is for sure, what is done is done unless of course these guys change things around a bit. Doesn't seem like heaven this – I can't describe it; the colours are so vibrant and everlasting.

Within the glimpse of an eye, the flash of a light, we are there with countless others all in uniform, all from different countries, many thousands all around as far as I can see with my eyes. Wait a minute – have I got eyes? Spirit eyes now. What am I? A body, energy or what? Perhaps this man can throw a little light on the subject or maybe a lot of light.

All these things I am feeling – all the emotions and pain from my death, should I be feeling this way? The religious pathways we were given in life didn't say anything about holding on to pain and those that do perceive you must go to hell or somewhere to repent in some way. If that is so then why are so many of my fellow countrymen here, and I see also men of the cloth around me so it seems that the religious teachings in the physical are a load of old tosh to say the least. Certainly we are some form of energy, I hold my hands up to that, but in what form are we Spirit and aware? Spirit; I am whole it seems, I look at others around me and know we are here – this is not a dream. I felt the pain of my physical passing and end up here. I can try and pinch myself – I look down again and the pain is too much, I see my injuries and it is too much to bear. I quickly look up and the pain goes. This is definitely not a dream.

I now look forward to some explanation for this. We are walking towards a glass monument – at least it looks like glass, its crystal and full of light. We talk. The lines of people are talking but not speaking. I know they are talking but there is no movement of the mouth. Weird sensation! I know what everybody is saying but I feel no pressure as everybody talking at once would overload normally but it seems this is not the case. We are now in the Forum, I say 'Forum' because that's the word that comes forward, we all stand with many thousands of others. A man is speaking down in the depths of the people it looks like, but I can hear every word he says without straining. I must admit he looks like Jesus from a distance – a large white robe that covers all of him with a hood held up around his head in such a way as to describe the features of his face but look as though his hood is up.

'Welcome friends. I bid you welcome. Please do not be afraid of what is around you. It is true you have passed to Spirit and in this – your adjustment time – you must access your latest trip as it were and accumulate your feelings and emotions to evaluate yourselves on your pathway to enlightenment. Time is irrelevant unless you have issues that need pursuing in the natural time in the physical realms. So my friends, it is a lot to take in, please be patient. You must understand certain things before you press to go on further. There are many of you here now and many more to follow. You must look at things now for yourself initially please.'

'I am speaking to all of you now but it comes across to the individual Spirit as if I am speaking one-on-one and this must be so for you to continue on to a higher self. Your journey – the physical life you have all just encountered – is just one part of that which is all of you. You have developed senses in which you feel sorrow, pain, yet joy and laughter also. It is a two-fold thing. You have encountered the physical many times in your physical selves, unless you are a seer – a prophet, then you would only have insight to certain things. The person who lives his life and encounters hardships that he cannot explain is there for a reason, just as you are friends. The conflicts of humans are no different to the animals that roam the Earth. The only difference is we have the ability to manipulate each other with power; the animal has power but works on instinct. Also, unfortunately, the human is willing to sacrifice all for power and manipulate others in the process.'

'And so those that cause death and destruction do not lift a finger, it is only the weak that sacrifice each other for the sake of glory. And that is, gentlemen and ladies, why you are here. There are those that enter a higher state or realm without really trying. That is their pathway in that lifetime. They will enter the realm and go forward to recognise the higher self. They may wish to enter another life to sample an awakening, it may be for a quick sample of breath on the physical plane, it may be for a certain imprint on another being to develop further. There are many developments and higher energies wishing to embark on the traumas of physical life to transform the awareness of the individual – to incorporate hardship as well as forgiveness and pleasure. You must look at yourself now not as a physical entity but as a spiritual body. You are solid if it is your wish, you may be liquid if you wish. It is your choice – nobody else's. The hardships and pleasures you have encountered in this life now must be resolved; the issues that were in a previous life have been resolved. Only this matters for your Spirit to develop and return to the higher realms where it belongs.'

'This may not seem like that now for you have anger, sorrow, emotional pain as well as physical pain. In some ways the emotional and mental pain is heavier to bear than the release of physical hardships. Enough of me speaking, it is time for you to enter your first phase if you will, of learning. Some may find it difficult at first but time has no meaning here so take your time, and be patient with yourself. We bless you.'

His speaking voice goes right to the heart, this you feel as if you are on the right road, and be patient.

It is a lot to take in all of this, but I am realising now the inevitable. My friends agree also. We must go forward in this. The concept of death has gone. We must find our true selves. In the course of time who can tell? First of all, I must discard this pain. Who must I see about that? And in the blink of an eye I am with a young girl, very serene in her appearance.

'You wish to discard your pain, is that so?'

'Yes I do. It troubles me that I am holding on to this.'

'You and your friends have this pain and will continue to hold on to it as long as there is guilt and sorrow, and most of all anger within yourselves.

Your passing was traumatic it is so, but first you must recognise this issue and face it before you can carry on into that which is chosen for you by your greater good. Am I making myself clear by this?'

'No.' I say, with still the pain slowly getting stronger.

'Look at the issue of your ending. Was it right or wrong? Who or if anybody was to blame, who was it? Your love of life has brought you and your friends to this point. You must trace what is the problem. You are my problem now. I must assist you in your quest for it is a great issue you must accomplish to find your greater self. Be patient. Time as you know it does not matter here. If you want to we can go back in your time and look, and also we can go forward in time to see the outcome. Do not forget this needs your attention for you to move on in your Ascension. This is vital to you and your friends, but I will give warnings also. There are those that wish to keep you here – stagnant, not moving. The more you hold onto that pain then you will suffer. That is all I am allowed to tell you.'

With that she is gone. We look at each other. 'What do we do now guys?'

'You address the situation, good friend. I am your guide, your friend who has been with you since conception. I am glad now to meet you and talk with you. I have done so in your dream state when you were on the Earth plane, but like many you were not aware of my presence. But now you know of me.'

I look at this man talking to me. He is an old Egyptian worker, I know him, his life, how he toiled working on the Great Sphinx, his face – rugged with age and dark, but not darkness. I know him like a father. But all these things are coming to me now – if only I was aware of this man when I was alive what a difference to things that would be.

'It was meant to be, young one,' he says, 'it was meant to be. All things are put into place and made to adjust their pattern in different ways. Unfortunately you do not see it that way yet but in the fullness of learning you will develop and see things clear again. I had a full life on the Earth plane in my last blessing for that is what it is, a blessing. There are many Spirits that wish to be fulfilled by gaining a body on the Earth plane, for a brief moment they can experience many pleasures that the Earth plane can give. But many do not get that chance and those that do sometimes do not fulfil all their deeds. The personality of the body has at some stage to come to terms with Ascension. This is not easy. A sleep state is all that must be developed in order to ease the pain and look forward to new beginnings. Do you understand?'

'Yes, I am beginning to see the light as it were.'

'I can tell you about my life. I was born many years ago to a poor, poor family. This was my beginnings, my choice as Spirit to enter these people's lives and experience their pain and joy in their company as their son. To be loved by these people and enjoy that before all the discomfort of what may follow. I decided on this family at conception, the choice was made then by me, it was my choice. The elders were guiding me it is fair to say, but for me to Ascend I must go on the Earth plane just one more time and so I did. As a boy I grew up in the shadow of pestilence and sorrow. I lost my Spirit voice at three years, I spoke to Spirit elders up until that time and that was lost to me. I grew up with the love of my mother and father, and two brothers who looked after me as I was the youngest. They were builders for the Anointed One, as was my father. My father was well-respected in many ways, the priests and priestess liked my father. He built many great statues. He was in charge of many skilled men who carved many great things for the Beloved One on the gold throne, so it was meant to be that I should follow in his and my brothers' footsteps.

My job from 16 years of age to 47 years of age was the Great Lion, this was a great feat for my family to be involved in and my mother was proud. The Great Pyramid that stands behind the Great Lion I finished my life on through hard work. All my family were buried with honour by the Lion for those ancient ones that were here before us, many, many years previous, this is what they wanted laid down in papyrus, and only the priests, the high priests of Horemakhet knew of the sacred writings. A great statue to the ancients, and those writings were buried well into the lion for future generations if they so wish. And so that was my life, my last life on the Earth plane and on my Ascension and learning. I am a guide to you Michael. I have looked over you from your birth. Your higher self wished to have that time on Earth for your development and now you must adjust and go forward, and combine with your higher self. I wish you well. My work is done, my blessings to you.'

With that he was gone. Wow, a lot to take in. What is around the next corner for me?

'So, what have we learned so far?' comes a voice, but from where? Behind me, in front, to my left, to my right...in fact, from all around.

'Should I be learning?' I replied.

'Oh yes!' comes the answer straight back, with a shrillness to the voice. 'You should be gathering all knowledge given to you to go forward and find the real you, nothing more nothing less, and,' with a pause, 'you will be surprised at the final result.'

'Interesting,' I reply, 'at this very moment time hasn't any meaning whatsoever, *here* is my situation regarding my own well being.'

The voice returns, snarling now. 'What do you mean?'

'Well, I am standing *here*. I do not know where I am. Am I dead or alive? The injuries sustained in the crash are still with me – in fact I should be dead the amount of blood I have lost and that is without the pain of it but, I have to say, only when I look down at my body. So what do you make of that?'

The voice returns with assurance. 'You must realise where you are. Once you have established that then all the pain you experience at this time will cease. You must go forward now – release yourself of pain, physical pain; the trauma of emotional pain and mental pain are to follow. It is up to you my friend, nobody else.'

And with that, silence. Only myself. The feeling of emptiness now overwhelms me to the point of crying uncontrollably, my hatred towards those that brought about the demise of myself and my friends fills me with pain in itself. There is one way, to wait for retribution in some way – to bide for time. It will happen, I and others will make it happen – manipulation to get back at those that did this. They are not going to get away with this.

As I am saying this I feel great power building up in me – perhaps it is rage. I have much to learn and my friends gather close by. I do not see them but sense them, then they come into view. If this is a dream it is the mother of all dreams. My friends are all in agreement. We gather strength among us for this long journey. There will be retribution and settlement for us and others that have given of themselves in conflict. Now we go in search for one or many that will tell our story in truth and light so we may continue our journey into the Great Beyond.

Love and light, now and always.

EPILOGUE – Our death is not the end
by Dave Kelly

In that closing paragraph by Michael Hall, he said: *'Now we go in search for one or many who will tell our story in truth and light.'* Well, it turned out that I was to become the first 'one' and some others including my wife Pauline and our like-minded friends, and Jayne Thomas who has taken on the re-reading and editing.

However, I think it might be appropriate for me to say at this point that although I took down the first fifty pages of the book over a period of several weeks, the idea during that time of being responsible for such a story was at first very overwhelming. I felt increasingly apprehensive as the days passed and then suddenly felt it was all too much for me.

At that point, in fact, I took the first fifty pages I had written out into the garden one night and burned them on a small bonfire because I was afraid of what I might be getting into. Those fifty pages which are now lost in detail, included information about Michael's first involvements with the Norfolk and Norwich area after his arrival from America. They describe how he met his girlfriend Trish who later became his wife after a wedding ceremony on his camp. I destroyed those pages deliberately because my apprehension was mainly fuelled by a general unease about not knowing what I was getting into. But in addition to that, there was also from the very beginning, a tangible sense of threat from what I will simply describe as 'the negative part' of the spiritual plane. That 'negative part' really does exist and doesn't want the contents of this book to become public knowledge. In fact, throughout the five and a half years or so I was taking down the story, there has intermittently been a sense of continuing 'opposition' and hostility from that negative area which I have gradually learned to overcome.

In all truthfulness, I should say that at the outset the very idea of becoming a medium frightened the life out of me! Only with the help of my wife Pauline and friends and family around me who encouraged me at every step did I learn to put these apprehensions aside, and also learn the professional ways that exist to actively protect myself against negative and hostile influences which are widely known to exist by people who do this sort of work.

Anyway, I stuck to the task of writing it all down over this five year period and thought I had really finished it all finally by the end of January 2006. However, I later found that what I had written up to that point was not entirely the end of the story. Since I stopped writing and began the process of seeking help with publishing the book, two other important communications from sources other than Michael Hall and his six fellow crewmen have come through.

I am going to present them in detail here because they have turned out to be very significant 'independent' confirmation of the most important part of the story – that tragic final plane crash of 10th February 1944.

I am writing this in late June with some practical assistance from an experienced earthly writer. Only a few days ago on 15 June a new message arrived, channelled via my wife Pauline. It came from an entity who said he was an English wireless operator named 'Bert' who gave his age as thirty-four, and said he had been working in February 1944 at the Seething USAAF Air Base. The way Bert's communication itself came through was unusual in that Pauline, whilst meditating that evening, repeatedly heard what she described as 'tapping and pinging noises' in her left ear. She ignored them for a while but they became persistent so she tuned in to the source and was told that she was hearing Morse Code, the radio communication method built around long and short sounds equating to dots and dashes. After she had 'tuned in' as she likes to put it, Bert explained to her that he had played a vital but unwilling part in the shooting down of Michael Hall's aircraft on that fateful night because he was the wireless operator at Seething and he had been forced to send in Morse Code the orders to shoot down the plane. The message went to a gun battery at Stoke Holy Cross close to the radar station.

There is still a communications station there today with two very high metal communication pylons – at least one of them owned and serviced by British Telecom – carrying dishes and antennae for all sorts of civilian telephone, radio and television transmission needs.

The tone of Bert's communication to Pauline showed that even after all these years, he was still extremely angry and distressed that he had been the instrument of sending the order, in fact his account was strewn with very strong swear words which I am going to tone down here. But all I will say is his communication became verbally very animated because, as he put it, he was an unwilling participant in what was 'an atrocious plan'.

In fact he said very vividly that he had to transmit the order with a gun held to his head. What follows is a verbatim account of what Bert conveyed to Pauline and later to myself, jotted down by me soon afterwards:

'The deed is done now and whatever happens to us is not up for debate. The matter is a bad thing, it was done with the intention of giving away life for no reason. I was told to do this. And orders are orders, and I carried this out with a gun at my temple. The signal had to be sent out at a pre-determined set time irrespective of my views. I have lived and died with this on my conscience. It is not right that this was done in such a way. I am not American and I felt for them then and have met them all since. And they stand along with those that have respect on this side and I applaud them. They shake my hand with grace and tell me not to worry about what happened. But I still do....'

'The bastards who literally put a gun to my head have no respect for life. They are no-nonsense pieces of s*** that reside in a place especially for scum like that. But that's another story. They appeared suddenly that night and told me to send the message. When I did, the response from the Gun Battery at Stoke Holy Cross was silence for a good few minutes. Those standing behind me continued to threaten me and told me to repeat the request which I did using my usual Morse Code. There was

still no response. Then back came an answer telling me again to repeat the request which I did three times. There was still no response.

'Then another message came back again: "Please Re-Affirm Target". Those on the other end of the line were obviously very wary of this type of command. The 'Jokers' behind me then said: "Re-Align Black Rod Target".

'With the gun still held against my head, I carried out their order, not once but twice. As they were about to leave they said: "Repeat anything of this and you no longer exist!" Then they disappeared. They left me shaking with a sense of relief for myself at the time, though I prayed for those poor souls that had been sacrificed.'

The starkness of Bert's brief statement adds a significant extra dimension to the end of the story told by Michael Hall and his friends in the final chapter of his account. Yet it was not the only 'independent' corroboration of the story to arrive after I thought I had completed the book. Another similarly powerful piece of evidence had arrived at the end of March 2006, again from seemingly 'independent' sources some two months after I had handed over my 'completed' hand-written manuscript to be typed up.

This information that came in March I received after I had a kind of vision if you like while I was sitting quietly at home one evening. Or you could also say I received a message in picture form. Three, what I will neutrally call 'energies', appeared in this picture. They were like balls or orbs of light and they indicated they were communicating with me from a smallholding which is about five miles from Norwich. They indicated that they wished to move on from there but the Second World War experiences they had been through when alive were still preventing this. Effectively they indicated that they were 'stuck' in that area.

At first I did not think there was any connection between those 'energies' and this book because a considerable part of the work I now do regularly with the Spirit plane involves assisting such energies or entities who are stuck to be released and move on. To do this the energies must first find a willing physical vehicle among the living population to help them to reach a state of peace and a way forward. I have studied and trained myself to do this so that I can effectively become such a vehicle for those who need it and help move them out of their 'stuck' situation towards their destination.

Once I was fully in contact with the three entities at this smallholding I was given to understand that they did indeed have some new information concerning this book. To my great surprise they revealed that they were American servicemen who had been blown up themselves locally in the later stages of the Second World War, partly they said, through their own fault although this part of their story had no direct connection with this book. They explained that they had been specialist personnel trained to clear the wreckage of crashed aircraft in Norfolk and Suffolk and all three of their USAAF crash clearance trucks had in the end been blown up on a mission, killing them. Because of this they subsequently had not been able to move on.

They went on to reveal that their special unit had been called to the scene of Michael Hall's plane crash at Stoke Holy Cross on the night of 10th February 1944 under conditions of great secrecy. Because of this and what they had been ordered to do they said they also still felt very angry and were therefore strongly motivated to add the following confirmation to Michael's story.

All three, without giving any names, said they were members of a Logistics and Clean-up Unit for the USAAF between 1941-1945. One of the energies acted as a spokesman for all three and presented the information they had very formally in a statement in the following words:

'This is a statement given by three individuals who were a team that in essence cleaned crash sites. They were cleaners and very good ones. Any crashes within the boundaries of their base region were eagerly seized upon. This particular job was a rush one. No prior notice was given and

why so soon we asked ourselves? In fact it seemed to those that took part in this that it was pre-conceived. That cannot be, though the thought that it might have been contrived in this way remains. But that aside, the deed is done and the statement must be given...'

'We were just settling down in our billet near Pulham Market (a small town about fifteen miles south of Norwich) and we were with other Sections. Our Commanding Officer was a bit nervous during the day, it was noticed. Why, we didn't know. We were all in a fairly stressed state anyway, working with the British and our own forces in this work. We use the British units like ourselves for UXB – unexploded bombs! We always send them in first!'

'It was around 12.45 am. Suddenly all hell was let loose, people running everywhere, mass panic! Our Section Commander rushed in shouting; "Come on guys, this job is for you. I don't know what all the noise is about – this has your names on it. Sorry."'

'The briefing was brief in the extreme. There were explosions and lots of gunfire, mostly battery fire over the radar base at Stoke Holy Cross, we were told. It was all very close to major bases. Big panic...Highly secret...We were told to operate under Code Blue – that was very, very unusual. They only ever gave 'Code Blue' to an absolutely complete clean up – nothing at all, not a scrap of anything must be left behind.'

'We gather our gear together. We are good at our job. We are in turn in charge of our cleaners. They are told what to do – robots if you will. We, or others, tell them what to do. They have no significance in this or any other mission.'

'Three trucks...all lights out...a good job it's a full moon in those dark Norfolk lanes. We even had to observe total secrecy getting to the place. Where there are no roads we go through anyway – across fields, anything. When we are only a few miles away we can see fire and smoke. This is a bad one. We circle the field – there are a few locals around...maybe five or six. They could be from the farm close by. We *cannot understand this. It looks like one of ours – although all signs on the fuselage, nose and wings have been blacked out for some reason.'*

'We get to work, first and foremost on the bodies. Whatever is left must be put aside – any ID must be put with them and left for autopsy crews. They will come in quick. We don't know from where. Devastation – we see one poor chap bleeding from the head and legs. He has got out but not survived. I am afraid his friends look like they were fried good and proper. These are our guys – the uniforms. Fuck, who did this?'

'It takes us right through till morning to clear – nothing left. We return the bulk of the plane, what is left, to Thorpe Abbotts. We burn it completely. They are our orders. The farmer is told to re-plough the field. There will be another Section come in and counsel the locals. See and hear and find out what the reaction is – probably put down some information that might distract the truth a little.'

The account ended abruptly there and the powerful and graphic statement is conveyed here verbatim from the notes I made immediately after hearing it at my home. Before that, in my own car, I had physically driven to the place from where the 'energies' had first made themselves known and these three energies had all asked to physically travel back to my home with me. It was there that I took down their statement on the understanding that I would then later take them on to where their wartime base had been at Pulham Market. Although this may sound very strange to anyone not familiar with this kind of work, the next day I drove my car with the energies accompanying me inside it to Pulham Market. There I stopped the car by The Green where they 'got out' of the car, said their farewells to me and disappeared towards a spot not far from the village pub where they said their original base had been and where they said their mates were waiting for them. By giving this statement to me in support of Michael Hall and the other crew members they said they had effectively released themselves from their 'stuck' situation and were able to move on within the spiritual plane.

As a footnote to this, I should add that 'Bert' the English wireless operator who was forced to send the shoot-down orders to the gun battery also said he had been forced to hasten the clearing up of the crash site by sending a Morse Code message to the clean-up crews and that's why they were able to arrive so quickly with the right equipment and lorries to take everything away. He said these crews left the orders to plough the field at first light and that nothing was to be left to indicate there had been an American plane shot down there.

When doing some building work in the area of Stoke Holy Cross a while back, I spoke to a local man who would have been a child at the time of the crash and he said he was told it had been a British plane that had crashed near the village but he did not remember ever seeing any wreckage.

The involvement with the 'energies' was not the only occasion when I had such an experience. Something similar happened in connection with Madingley Cemetery, near Cambridge. Pauline and I were suddenly asked if we could pay a visit to Madingley on a certain day in the winter of 2003. We weren't clear as to why this was necessary but Michael Hall came through very insistently asking if we could drive there on a certain day and allow him and the other six crew members to 'travel with us in our car'. This we did and on arrival at Madingley we saw that there were several coach loads of largely grey-haired former American USAAF servicemen visiting the cemetery. They were walking among the graves and when we stopped the car and opened its doors the 'energies' of Michael Hall and the others disembarked and went over immediately to mingle among the graves with the visiting Americans. Pauline, who has the ability to see such entities very clearly, said she watched in amazement as the seven former Seething crew members mingled with the real live American visitors among the graves they were inspecting. Then to our further amazement, when the visiting Americans got back into their buses, Pauline watched the energies of Michael and his six man crew also climb aboard the buses. The doors closed and the buses drove away carrying the visiting Americans who did not know that seven invisible additional 'entities' had joined them for some specific reason best known to themselves. Seemingly it was in general terms to enjoy their companionship in some way en route to their next destination. Whether they had any other agenda, I don't know.

That, along with the three 'orbs of light', was one of the more extraordinary experiences that this whole project has thrown up. Yet it has involved me in so many things that would have seemed totally beyond belief for me ten years ago. In fact as I conclude this *Epilogue,* it seems a very long time now since 22nd February 2001 when I received that very clear indication that a book was be written, and was given its title, the name of its author, and an outline of what they wanted the book to achieve.

Dave Kelly
Norwich, England

Postscript

While this book was being edited and prepared for publication it was decided to seek clarification of some of the details of the story by putting questions to its main author in the spiritual dimension, Michael Hall. To facilitate this, Pauline Kelly agreed on 20th April 2006 to trance channel responses to questions. Dave Kelly attended to support his wife but otherwise took no active part in the question and answer session. The session was tape recorded and what follows are edited verbatim extracts taken from a transcription of the conversation.

1. Why was your B-17 deliberately shot down?

Question: What we would like to know is how and why did your crew get the wrong envelope? Was it a mistake?

Michael: Just a mistake.

Question: Do we know by whom?

Michael: It was just events, the activity all around. People running; it was a man that ran up and gave us our envelope.

Question: Just took it to the wrong plane?

Michael: Yes, he took it to wrong plane.

Question: Was he British? American?

Michael: American.

Question: And the whole mission was aborted because of that?

Michael: We didn't matter. Bods would have got into trouble. People higher up than us would be in trouble.

Question: So the other two planes didn't take-off at all?

Michael: One took off and came back.

Question:	And did they survive?
Michael:	Yes
Question:	The crew lived?
Michael:	Died another time.
Question:	Accidentally or in the course of their duties?
Michael:	In course of duty.
Question:	So what about the third plane. Which one took off – the one going to Hitler?
Michael:	Yes.
Question:	And did it get there?
Michael:	No, it came back.
Question:	Was it turned back?
Michael:	Yes.
Question:	So that part was aborted too? Did they have the right orders?
Michael:	Yes.
Question:	Why was it aborted?
Michael:	Because they couldn't be shot down. There was nowhere they could be shot down. They were over buildings – over main places where they could not be hidden if they were shot down.
Question:	So was it just bad luck that you were over fields near open ground?
Michael:	Yes.
Question:	What about the plane that was going to Jersey. Did it simply not go – so its crew survived?

Michael: Yes,

Question: So to sum up, all the members of the other two crews who were involved in this very secret operation, they all lived, did they?

Michael: Yes.

Question: One crew lived until later when they died in an operation, yes? And what about the Jersey-bound crew, did they all survive?

Michael: They all survived it but they knew nothing of the mission. All they knew was it was just an aborted mission.

Question: So the crews of the other two planes that were safe did not know that your third plane was shot down deliberately?

Michael: No. We were just a statistic – 'Engine trouble.'

Question: How come after taking off your plane flew so low near the radar station? What instructions was it following?

Michael: The instructions given.

Question: In an envelope or through the radio?

Michael: On the front of the envelope....

Question: The one that remained sealed?

Michael: Yes.

Question: Do you know what was in that envelope?

Michael: No.

Question: So can we imagine that you were going to do the deed and kill Hitler?

Michael: We were going to do whatever was in that envelope.

Question: Were you ever told that you were going to kill Hitler?

Michael: No.

Question: So how do you know that that was the mission?

Michael: We speak in the Spirit World.

Question: So all your training was done without having any knowledge at all that you were going to try to kill Hitler?

Michael: Our training was to kill in the war. This was just another mission.

Question: But while you were still alive, you didn't have any details? You got some inkling of it in the Spirit World.

Michael: Yes, talking to others in the Spirit World.

Question: So you pieced this story together on the other side in the Spirit World and now you want this story to be told?

Michael: We want our story to be told so that we know that we did not die just for another's mistake.

Question: Is it a fact that your further progress in the Spirit World is prevented by your anger and your unhappiness at all this?

Michael: We do not have anger or unhappiness here. We have thoughts that others should acknowledge.

Question: Will acknowledgement of those thoughts help you move on? We are guessing that this may be the case – are we right?

Michael: Yes. We are trapped by others who caused our passing.

Question: You use the word 'retribution' in one of the final chapters. You said that you would like to have retribution. Can you elaborate what you mean by that?

Michael: To be acknowledged on a wall, on a grave, in people's thoughts... so that we did not just disappear.

Question: You had been prepared to do something very dangerous for the best possible motives, is that right?

Michael: Yes, we were prepared to give our lives for a cause – but not to lose them for a mistake.

Question: It seems awful that that one mistake of giving your plane the wrong envelope aborted a mission that could have changed the history of World War II.

Michael: Things are meant to be. Things are in place long before we do things. Who can say what one action will change one action by another person? We have the chance now to change. Change the thoughts and actions of others. Just as many soldiers now change the thoughts and actions of others. History has been written…we were just one part of that page in history.

Question: Do you feel a sense of injustice?

Michael: Not for the cause but, yes, for the mistake. I missed my daughter being born. Others missed their life plans. Their thoughts were destroyed by someone's mistake. But isn't that how war is? A mistake? No one seems to learn the lessons.

Question: Would you like this book to help bring war to an end? Would that be part of your ideal?

Michael: War can never end while there are others who are greedy for things that are not theirs. There will always be war. My story is just a part of the whole.

2. Allegations about the existence of secret world governments

Question: You make quite a few references in the text of this book to 'secret governments' which were said to stand above the known governments of the world at that time. Can you give any more information about who these people were and how you allege Germans, Americans and British met socially in secret while the fighting was still going on?

Michael: Look at the war in the Middle East. They have all colluded there. It is the same in every war, people offering this or that to other countries for something in return. It is the same all the world over – there is bribery and corruption in every war.

Question: Can we not change that? We would like to think we can change that and bring peace to the world.

Michael: Peace will come when others change their vibrations. We are just one of many who have changed our vibration of the past to affect the future.

Question: Will the correction of this mistake you outline in the book and its secrecy help in some small way to contribute in the end to peace?

Michael: To peace in mind as well as body. Peace in thoughts as this little lady* often says – 'Where thought goes, energy flows.' Everything can make a difference. *[*A reference to Pauline Kelly – Editor]*

Question: Was there and is there a secret government which exists globally, with members drawn from among very rich and powerful families? Is that the truth?

Michael: Yes.

3. The true fate of Glenn Miller?

Question: Glenn Miller is mentioned in the writings you've given us and they indicate that he was murdered. Why was he murdered?

Michael: Because of who he was. He had access to more than the ordinary soldier, the ordinary airman. People listened to him because of who he was and that included people high up. His passing left a legacy of his music.

Question: He was unhappy it seems going to Germany and playing in an Officer's Mess and spying – did they feel he might reveal that and that is why they killed him?

Michael: Yes. His music was being used for the wrong energy.

Question: You are saying THEY killed him – are we talking about the American government?

Michael: I don't know. He was killed because he went across enemy lines – lines of countries – because it was easy through his music.

Question: But this final flight he took seemed to be a set-up?

Michael: Yes, it was a set-up! Others died and were blinded by a mistake and a cause supported by others.

Question: So if it was a set-up, it would appear that it was men of his own kind, Americans or British who set him up?

Michael: Yes, in collusion with others.

Question: Intelligence personnel?

Michael: Yes.

Question: Military intelligence?

Michael: Yes.

4. Why does Monty appear prominently in your book?

Question: Field Marshal Montgomery comes through dramatically in your writings. He too seems to be very dissatisfied with higher authorities, is that right?

Michael: He was very dissatisfied. He could see his own men dying and things happening that were not what he wanted. His thoughts were being shot down by people above him. A man undermined. A man made to look different in the public eye.

Question: Was he very concerned that his soldiers were dying?

Michael: He was concerned that there was not enough back up. Everything was bitty. He couldn't do anything to change that. He couldn't help others.

Question: Was it his idea to kill Hitler?

Michael: He would have killed Hitler with his bare hands.

Question: But the mission that you were prepared to carry out – was he part of the planning and thinking?

Michael: Yes.

5. The role of a Hollywood film star

Question: There are references to a Hollywood film star in your writings. Is there any particular significance for this? Was he popular? Or disliked? Was he perhaps a spy?

Michael: He was a spy. And he used women to get information.

Question: German women?

Michael: All kinds.

Question: Did he go into Germany?

Michael:	Yes.
Question:	As a celebrated Hollywood movie star?
Michael:	Yes.
Question:	And did he meet German officers?
Michael:	Yes.
Question:	And Hitler too perhaps?
Michael:	He may have done. He got into places that others could not via women.
Question:	On the strength of his fame as a film star?
Michael:	Yes, his fame as a film star – and as a lover.
Question:	Did he find valuable information?
Michael:	Yes.
Question:	And was he liked or disliked because of this?
Michael:	Disliked on both sides.
Question:	Why?
Michael:	Americans disliked having to use someone like him to get women to give information. He was just a pawn, like all of us. Germany used him, the British used him.
Question:	This enquiry is going to sound strange even in my own ear, but do you have any communication with Hitler and the World War II German High Command in the Spirit World?
Michael:	No, they are elsewhere. They have not condemned their acts. They are kept from us.
Question:	Are they suffering?
Michael:	Suffering is the wrong word. They are kept in a different area as are people like Mussolini of Italy and Ceausescu of

	Romania – as well as all those who have hurt others. They are like...in another country.
Question:	Is it like a prison or a penal colony there?
Michael:	No, we have no bars and no cells. We have no prisons here. Each of us has to learn something. Each of us must make a new journey.
Question:	Have Hitler and Mussolini and others like them learned from their errors?
Michael:	No. They still believe they are the 'one and onlys', and even now they send their energies to others.
Question:	They send help, do you mean to continue strife and warfare on Earth?
Michael:	In many different ways.
Question:	How can that be resolved? How could we change that?
Michael:	Each of us has the power to change. We can each of us change the vibrations of many through our own pathways. We are just one of millions who are doing this. The Earth is more spiritual now, more understanding, more changing.
Question:	Will this book help this process?
Michael:	It will put another tick on the form of retribution.

After Thoughts

Perhaps it is inevitable that questions will be asked and subsequently cannot be avoided about the subject of the two remaining planes in this story, and so we shall begin the saga of the exploits of the first of the ghost planes. The personnel that comprise this particular war plane do not exist in the sense of your world. Ah ha, here we go, you say, talking from another dimension or the so-called 'Spirit World' – what shall we call it? Never mind we must focus on the question to hand.

To aspire in the world we know you have to have identity: a name, a number...whatever; a line, a cross, something to call yourself in the life we all love. But there are times when certain individuals lack identity. Yes there are given names but they are in perpetual turmoil as to who they are, why they exist, and who gives a shit anyway?

The powers-that-be now give these individuals purpose in the fragment of space we call 'now', and the now is 1944. A simple mission to eradicate the head of the black rain that now envelops the world, these individuals now have purpose. Please do not feel pity for them, they will overcome the element of surprise they have individually been picked to shadow the dark one and his generals. They will fly a conventional B-17, they are Baker Team. They will parachute separately at intervals along a set route, the last one flying the bird will put her into a dive and then bail out leaving the B-17 to crash and burn. If the authorities in the locality of the crash pursue a clean-up of the area they would find nothing to evaluate a link with an assassination or any individual. All would have perished in the dust.

What must go through the minds of individuals who in essence are above others in sequence? Those that believe must face the consequence of such actions. It is appalling to think that the human race is capable of such things. Thus we have spoken in true light and shall be heard above noise that is but a shower of rain in spring, but there upon the Earth we must walk and in truth abide by the rules set in stone. Who makes these rules? Who puts pen to paper? Scholars from years passed who had knowledge whereby the mere serf or layman had known.

And so knowledge is power...power over what? People? Places? Everything we see? In many ways, yes, and so we have knowledge and power: manipulation and who to manipulate. The power of the word, and with the power of the word we can accomplish a multitude of things, to manipulate the truth, or to manipulate the untruth or lie and make it what – another lie or the truth? We live in a world of manipulation: there are those that thrive on it, there are those that despise it, and there are those cannot live with it. Those that thrive on it and exist for it are the power. They, by one word spoken at exactly the right time, can influence one person or millions it does not matter how many; the deed is done, finish it, move on to the next one. That is how this Earth is run. It will always be that way, it is how we are.

Many years have passed since man has known this power and passed knowledge on through writings and word of mouth. Where am I going with this? Anger, a word that describes what? Rage...frustration...pity? All negative words, but put these words in another context with an emotion attached then you have something with real power-plus, couple that with loss of life then you have an essence that will not go away until another word is put in place: Justice.

It is inevitable that who pushes this pen will be looked at and scrutinised in this story of stories. He asks where these words come from? I say, they come from those that have passed on. Passed on to where? The Spirit World. What is the Spirit World? So many questions! Where one story starts a Pandora's Box suddenly opens and we are torn apart with questions that can be answered but are they truthful? Can they be scrutinised, dissected, and come back with 100% truth? The truth is up to the individual. What is your life? Has it consistency? Do you believe in yourself? Do others believe in you? Does that matter to you? Do you love and do you expect to be loved in return? Questions, questions, we answer, but again, is it the truth? Make your own mind up, that is the key. Live your own life as you want it. Do not let others scribe your life for you, they will try but be strong, for those that run a parallel line live how their fathers lived and do likewise. Very good, but what if time and space and your place in it dictates your pattern of existence for a short while? Then, changes exist and so spiral on and the domino effect is put in place: cause and effect. Your very existence is no coincidence. It will affect time and space and all that is in it.

1944, a very good year for some, a very bad year for others. Seven very different personalities put into a position of trust just like the others in these squads, the difference with these characters is they in truth do not exist along with their original records they only exist to God, no one else cares if they live or die. A bit strong in evidence don't you think, but the truth nevertheless. They do not care themselves so why should anybody else.

The powers-that-be – let's call them the collective – brought together a plan, at first just a blueprint. Others in the Allied forces had put together subsequent plans for the termination of the wolf, some had substance some were just discarded as mere fantasy. But the collective had three options rather than just one and if there was another way, these three options were expendable and the individuals who had the misfortune of being roped in this loop were mere cannon fodder.

These in particular came from prisons across America, all with certain qualities in survival. This particular squad was sanctioned by Senate itself and put in place two to three years previous. Some bright spark in the collective, an idea at first, but with the right people to put pen to paper and the right doors to open, maybe it had substance. Right from the early days of the war the wolf was hated amongst those with power and they would have loved to bring an end, a very swift end, to this tyrannic bastard that brought out evil in men's hearts just by saying one specific word.

It would be a feather in one's cap...those that have power in the collective would be very pleased...wealth and prosperity shall be in abundance if put in place. And the price? Nothing, just 1...2...3...planes and those that flew them – what matter? Certainly not to the collective, everyone is expendable, everybody. Let's get these guys out of these institutions, give them something to live for; that is their lives – they know nothing more, and if they die...so what? We wash our hands of them.

And so the story starts, these survivors of the streets of America are now to be trained to kill the enemy. Who is the enemy? To these guys everyone is the enemy, so it takes one special person to manipulate these characters and mould them into shape and hopefully get some substance of a unit, and to be mighty Top Secret in its essence. They will not work together until the right signature is put in place. They will know what to do. They will work individually, independent, totally self-sufficient. If anything goes wrong they will disappear: no regrets there anyway, a win-win solution to the collective.

A name – even if it is false, on a plaque in some obscure public place, is a full-stop to letting the public know what's really going on. The one person that puts together this band of brothers is highly respected and has good pedigree within the military and political stage. His claim to fame is his granpappy – he was in charge of the President's men who trapped and killed John Wilkes Booth many years previous in the glory days of the Union, so he has the right credentials for this assignment.

Michael Shelly Hall

Additional channelled session – 8th May 2012 talking to Charles 'Buck' Quinlan – Pilot

(Instruction – Look around, what can you see?)

Question: I would like to speak to Buck.

(No answer.)

Question: I would like to speak to Michael.

(No answer. Silence for a little while.)

Buck: Who do you wish to speak to? Charles Quinlan – is that who you mean?

(Silence.)

Buck: What do you want? Go on then. (Mikey...he is alright).

Question: Where are you?

Buck: Just in a dark room, just the two of us here, myself and co-pilot Jimmy Jameson. Just waiting, just waiting for the last 20 minutes.

Question: What date is it?

Buck: 9th February 1944 in the morning, 7.30 am. Briefing for the mission. Just come off high ops, just being briefed. Just waiting for these bastards to come and show their faces; lots of red tape. Boys just waiting outside – they want to get some sleep. My co-pilot...I call him Jimmy, he is Bernie Jameson. Don't like the name Bernie.

Only a certain amount of people know me as Buck, they know me as Buck because of my background as I talk in my sleep; Charlie is another one I am called by.

Question: Do you recognise the men who come in?

Buck:	Man with three pips – top brass, and my CO; just talking at the top of the room to themselves, best not to hurry them just let them carry on.
	It's hard to breath in the room it's stuffy, Jimmy keeps kicking me as he wants to go outside for a cigarette, just got to carry on.
Question:	What do these men tell you about the next mission?
Buck:	Top Secret – not allowed outside. They just kicked my co-pilot out, it's just me inside. It's some godforsaken stuff to drop 3 to 4 boys across the Rhine. Not telling me too much, not until in flight – just to get them there. They do not want me to bail out not even in a safe country. If I get into trouble I must not let the plane get into enemy hands I must bring the plane back.
	Concerned about my co-pilot as he is not in on this. He must be told, not happy with this at all. Will tell my co-pilot.
Question:	Will you get into trouble telling Jimmy?
Buck:	Yes, the rest of the crew must not be allowed to know.
Question:	What time are you to leave the base?
Buck:	You mean Thorpe Abbotts? At 10.15pm (22.15).
Question:	Where are you going?
Buck:	Seething Airfield.
Question:	Have you flown from there before?
Buck:	No.

(Instruction – Taking you forward, it is the evening and you are on the concrete runway at Seething Airfield.)

Question: Tell me what you can see.

Buck: It is slight rain, approximately 10.45pm (22.45), clear moon and a slight wind.

Question: How many others are with you?

Buck: There are 7 and two other crews; lots of action going on, lots of stuff going on around us. It's a B24 station and we are B17 planes. We are allowed in as they are blacked out, totally blacked out, just the tail showing white, blue, red. Tail 'D' has been blacked out but you can just see it. We go at 11.05pm (23.05).

Question: Who is there to see you off?

Buck: Just a guy talking, I am not a religious man but they are just talking, even the top brass are listening, two of us have stepped to one side. The guy who is talking they call him the preacher – he is not a preacher, the guys like to talk to him, he is more evangelist. Not my cup of tea...what a funny thing to say! I am picking up things from the British; it's all Bourbon where I come from!

Time to board the plane with the crew, just waiting for the CO to give us the last bit of information – a brown envelope type thing, 4 x 10, just stuck down. I will open it when I get clearance to lift off the runway.

Question: When were you told to open the envelope?

Buck: When I am in flight. I have a heading to go to then when in flight, to open the envelope.

Question: Do you follow these orders?

Buck: Yes. *(then made an "Mmmmm" sound).*

Question: Is there radio contact after take-off?

Buck: No, not after take-off. I am aware of other flight patterns – their missions are nothing to do with me. I know some of the other guys and they have not been told either.

(Think he means the other plane crews).

I am the first out; their engines are running when I climb to go. My heading is due south. Due south, north and due east pinpoint Norwich then out to North Sea. Then I am told to open the envelope and then I would do the heading.

As I reach due south past Seething, climbing, I leave Jimmy to climb and I open the envelope, I am not going to wait, no way! My crewmen mean more to me than cannon fodder. I must find out what is going on, I have three characters and they do not know, and I must drop them somewhere. As I open the envelope inside with Top Secret on the top it states my heading due east to the Alps and Berchtesgaden, and see if it's ok to drop leaflets over Berchtesgaden. I know they are not leaflets, they are snipers.

Question: What are they to do?

Buck: Assassination at the Berchtesgaden. Going after Adolf Hitler that's all I can say, or a top general. It just says Assassination. I have three snipers and three spotters and I am the only one going to be left on the plane, one to fly the plane, six to be sacrificed. They will have to find own way back and they do not even know. There are six other envelopes as to their parts in the mission – it's their own part inside.

While I am reading this Jimmy is peering down to my left. He is in hell of a state! He is seeing what he calls firecrackers about a mile and half down, and we are flying and can't fly high over it. It's like we are being attacked by shrapnel – it hits the wing tips and I can't climb higher.

Have thrown the envelope to one side – we think it may be friendly fire; we cannot gain height. Left wing shattered and our rudders are shattered! Our engine is now being taken from us, our option is to bail out – we are not high enough to bail out, to go down is our only option!

(Instruction: Immediately take him out of situation and into the Spirit World. [Did not wish to make them recall their deaths.])

Question: Look around, what can you see?

Buck: Lots of people playing music all around us, playing music.

Question: Are you happy to continue to talk to me?

Buck: Why was we shot down? I am not happy with what they never told us, they knew I was reluctant the way it was being done. There is no way they would know I opened the envelope. Should have opened it over the North Sea with further headings to go on.

Still feel angry at them and what we have all been put through, we have all been incinerated. We are all here together. Not sure if I am doing this, the crew are around I am aware they are around me, but I cannot see them.

Question: Is there anything else you would like to say?

Buck: No. *(Silence).*

Must have some kind of justice, must be an end to all this. It's been a long time now.

Question: Would you be willing to come back?

Buck: Yes, will try to do better.

(David said he felt like there was some kind of pressure on the lower part of his jaw and similar to a crash helmet over his head and nose, like he had a bad face and head injury.)

Another channelled session with Dave, Steve Lursquom, Mike Preston and Buck Quinlan

Steve Lursquom

Question: Who is with you?

Steve: There are three with me.

Question: What date is it?

Steve: 10th February 1944. We have been training for a while and basically don't know what for, have an idea to target and eliminate target.

Question: Where are you?

Steve: Seething. Some others are talking and they seem agitated – nervous. Three planes, two B24s and a B17.

Question: Are they all Americans?

Steve: No, some mixed American races: Puerto Rican, Italian, Indian. The Brits keep clear of us.

Question: Are the crews all specially trained men?

Steve: Ordinary and specially trained. I know four or five of the guys and their training is basically what I have done. They are very hard characters; the military keep a tight lid on them.

They know what they want to do, troublesome guys from different parts of America. They do things like I have done in the past. They know how to use firearms and go behind enemy lines – covert missions. They live ordinary lives but are called upon to do missions. Saw some of the guys in Thetford Forest know how to take targets out, they knew all about firearms before they joined the forces.

I have an idea, but needs must – there are three of us initially going to do the same thing. I basically know where the target is and I know what to do. I must keep silent in myself, there are seven in the crew going out, even as ground crew we know what we are doing. I was put down as a side gunner but I am a sniper. I am parachuting out on the target, there is a spotter with me. Groups of two, and if one doesn't get the target the other will. In my own head I am thinking who is the target? Have not been told at the moment.

Standing outside the plane, Charlie is the pilot, slight rain, cloudy, can see a clear moon. Just slight rain – when we get further up above the clouds it will be more clearer.

As far as I know of Charlie he will do it. It's his baby. Don't know the mission yet. Charlie he is nervous, keeping quiet, by himself. We are going along with it to go along with this guy.

Ten minutes before take-off 'the preacher' is getting us all together. Not done this before – all the guys, jokers, bandits, the type of guys that would slit your throat.

We are now on the plane and there is a lot of noise from the front, Charlie is going through his talk as he always does. Bernie is smiling.

I am just going into myself, close myself down; I am midway on the plane. Close my eyes. Noise of the plane engine juddering drives me crazy; as soon as we are off the ground I am ok.

We are first to take-off as far as I know. Taxiing now, lights behind us, flashing lights switched off, all lights switched off; black back here – no lights. Can see the lights of the tower; just gathering speed now. Darkness all around us, look up at the sky; just looking at the clouds, always look for the moon. Hard right bank. Being told to hold positions till juddering gets out of the way and we get into better positions.

Charlie is chit-chatting to Bernie, Michael Hall is shouting from the back – don't know what he is shouting about; Michael Preston is further up the plane, he is navigator.

We are about a mile up, lots of banking to the right. Can't roughly say where we are, just above the clouds heading out to sea. See nothing behind us at all, see lights off somewhere down there, and see no lights behind us.

Question: Do you have your instructions?

Steve: Not at this moment, Buck has all the instructions. My instinct says to get it done, my belief – it is the Dictator. To get down there with my spotter and get out as quick as possible. Others know, I feel they know who the target is. There was another target at the same time, Martin Borman.

Want to get out a free man when it is over, not to England, to America. Have been told if I get back I can get out as a free man. I am not a free man.

Flames on the left side sparking at me completely out of the blue, shots from the left, bullet traces – don't know what is going on, wanting to bail out, all grouping together.

(Then went silent).

Mike Preston

Question: Where are you buried?

Mike:	We are not buried in America. We are not buried. All the crews' remains were put together and burned – classed as *Missing in Action*.
	Angry about our passing – all of us angry. The dog tags were burnt along with us – that memory we tried to keep to ourselves as every time we think about it brings us pain.
Question:	Would you like your names on a wall of remembrance?
Mike:	Will not happen. It will never happen. It is good that our story is told this way, but we do not all comply with Michael Hall's wishes.

Buck Quinlan

Buck:	We are not buried; we don't know, all put together. Not in America. There is no grave. We were spread over the land.
	We have a lot of unfinished business with the bastards who did this. This is why we came forward for our story to be told, we do not exist anywhere.
	We are angry that we cannot answer all the questions as we are being held back by those that do not want this to come out.
	The man who is writing this book needs to be taken care of as he may be in danger. When the book comes out there may be repercussions denying this happened, but there are people that know it is right and the truth will reveal itself one day.
	Take care.

Another channelled session with Dave talking to Michael Hall

Question: Where are you?

Michael: Got a cigarette.

Question: Where are you, Thorpe Abbotts?

Michael: 14th June 1943.

Question: What kind of day is it?

Michael: Hopefully nothing going on. Breathless for a fag – too much to drink.

Question: Where?

Michael: Local distillery, local pub, just across the road.

Question: Do they like you there?

Michael: No they put up with us.

Question: When do you see Trish?

Michael: Hopefully tomorrow. I'll answer questions if you wish.

Question: Where does Trish live in Norwich, any particular part?

Michael: I meet her in the city – we get a lift into Tombland.

Question: Is she English?

Michael: She is, but her parents are Polish, they had to come to England as...there is a name but I can't remember it for the love of me. *(I think he means refugees.)*

Question: What are her parents' first names?

Michael: I know her family name – Kovac...yes, Kovacs.

Question: Does Trish have a job?

Michael: She is a secretary to a solicitor in the city. I know where she works, Queen Street, meets me at dinner time only a short time. Trouble I get to get off this base for even 15 minutes.

Question: What do her parents think about you two getting married?

Michael: Asked her many times, she says yes, they say no. Who am I marrying, her or them? They do not want her to marry, she is 18 and a bit. She has a younger brother, Stephen, aged 7.

(Instruction: Go forward to January 1944.)

Question: Where are you?

Michael: At a children's party at the Thorpe Abbots Base. They are local children.

Question: Are you married now?

Michael: Clare Louise, 4 months to go. Just in case anything happens to me, trying to get married in the Registry Office, beginning of December, Theresa Hall...keep schtum. (Puts finger to mouth.)

Question: How is Trish's first name spelt?

Michael: Trish is my nickname for her. Her middle name is Jane (not pronounced as our 'Jane').

Question: How did you decide upon Clare Louise's name?

Michael: Louise is my mother's name back in Cleveland, Russell County, Virginia, a long way away. Clare was my grandmother's name.

Question: What do you drink in the local pub?

Michael: Bourbon – your equivalent. We go to Mikey's Maid's Head. Mickey Sturges plays poker there, he is the Jeep driver who we get our lift from.

Question: Have you been to Seething?

Michael: Seething? They fly B-24 Liberators from there.

Question: Not as good as the Flying Fortress?

Michael: No!

Question: Betsy the half-naked girl painted on the plane, is she based on a real person or one of the boy's girlfriends?

(No answer given, just a smile!)

ACKNOWLEDGEMENTS

From the very beginning of this book I have had some very special people with me on the journey and I would like to mention them here.

First of all to my wife, Pauline, who with her knowledge and guidance from the very start of my awakening has guided me to open up to what is truly there and thus enabled me to assist the energies that wished me to work with them.

To Jacque for her support in the early days and for her continuing support and friendship now; also to Glynis for designing the original front cover, Esther for the graphic design on this edition and Mike Page for the background image; to Mike, Rita, Jayne and others – you know who you are, thank you all so much.

Thanks are due to the 100th Bomb Group Memorial Museum at Thorpe Abbotts for the permission to reproduce the photographs and the illustration in the centre of this book.

It is and never has been my intention to harm any person or person's reputation. This book was written totally as Michael and others from the Spirit world wanted it to be. This is their truth and I thank them.

Finally, I would like to say that three of the seven crew of that fateful flight are listed as *Missing in Action*, the others we have not been able to confirm. There are similar names but we would not change them to just fit. The names are written precisely as they came through during the writing of this book.

Dave Kelly
September 2012